Signing Smart with Babies and Toddlers: A Parent's Strategy and Activity Guide

Signing Smart with Babies and Toddlers

A Parent's Strategy and Activity Guide

MICHELLE E. ANTHONY, M.A., PH.D.

and

REYNA LINDERT, PH.D.

ST. MARTIN'S GRIFFIN ❧ NEW YORK

www.stmartins.com

Book design and composition by Gretchen Achilles

Library of Congress Cataloging-in-Publication Data

Anthony, Michelle.
    Signing smart with babies and toddlers : a parent's strategy and activity guide /
Michelle Anthony and Reyna Lindert—1st St. Martin's Griffin ed.
      p. cm.
    Includes bibliographical references (p 216) and index (p 224).
    ISBN 0-312-33703-5
    EAN 978-0312-33703-2
    1. Nonverbal communication in infants. 2. Interpersonal communication in
infants. 3. Nonverbal communication in children. 4. Interpersonal communication in children. 5. Sign language. 6. Child rearing. I. Lindert, Reyna. II. Title.

BF720.C65A58 2005
155.42'2369—dc22   2004057819

649.122

FIRST EDITION: MAY 2005

10 9 8 7 6 5 4 3 2 1

To Natasha and Kylie, who helped us discover the magic of *Signing Smart*.
To Maya and Nadia, who inspired us to shape *Signing Smart* into
what it is today.

To Scott and Nick, whose love and guidance helped us turn the dream of
Signing Smart into a reality.

To all the Deaf families and ASL users who have shared their language
and culture with us, and trusted we would carry on its power
and meaning with integrity in our work.

CONTENTS

Acknowledgments   *ix*

A Note to Readers   *xiii*

Introduction   *xv*

CHAPTER 1: Get Ready, Get Set, Go . . . On Your Way!   1

PART I

Signing Smart Activities for Every Day
45

CHAPTER 2: Diaper and Dressing Activities   46

CHAPTER 3: Mealtime Activities   56

CHAPTER 4: Bathtime Activities   74

CHAPTER 5: Bedtime Activities   86

PART II

Signing Smart Activities for Play
101

CHAPTER 6: Floor-Time Play   102

CHAPTER 7: Active Play   134

CHAPTER 8: Pretend Play   154

CHAPTER 9: The Magic of *Signing Smart*— Encouraging Little Minds and Strengthening Young Families   174

APPENDIX 1: The *Signing Smart* Illustrated Dictionary   192

APPENDIX 2: Likely Child Versions of Each Sign   208

APPENDIX 3: Additional Resources for Parents and Baby Sign Language Instructors   216

APPENDIX 4: Frequently Asked Questions by Topic   220

Notes   223

Index   224

About the Authors   228

ACKNOWLEDGMENTS

THERE ARE SO MANY PEOPLE who made this endeavor possible. We extend our deepest thanks to all the families who have entrusted us with their babies, who have contributed to our research studies, and who have participated in (and given us feedback on) our *Signing Smart* programs and materials. Without your stories, your keen eyes, your willingness to work with your children in new ways, and your devotion to our vision, we would not know what we know today, nor would we be in a position to share it with so many others.

We are especially grateful to the families who have opened their homes and their classes to our video and digital cameras, and allowed us to share their *Signing Smart* children with the world: the Gershefski family, the Duff family, the Fontaine family, the Young family, the Hook family, the Amspoker family, the Fieseler family, the Hoechst-Weinstein family, the Cross family, the Reat family, the Betts-Piturro family, the Tobiga-Haldorsen family, the Goedert family, the Kreitzer family, the Massey family, the Orloff family, the Odejewski family, the Rasmussen family, the Ortiz family, the Lorman family, the Spence-Wallace family, the Anthony family, the Coury-Toups family, the Hinton family, the Odron family, the Hoyt family, the Mellberg family, the Williams family, the Dylan family, the Robinson family, the Chedester family, the Roth-Aguinis family, the Sigman family, the Elogbi family, the Mayer family, the Nicodemus family, the Childs family, and the families in the Denver and Portland play classes whose children appear in many of these photos. We are also grateful to our *Signing Smart* adults who posed for the dictionary at the back of this book: Serena, Michael, Rachel, Don, Anny, Rina, Scott, Louise, and T.R.

Thanks also to Ross Dylan (and his wife, Paula) for taking these photos and for their many consultations on graphic and photographic issues. We wish to express our great appreciation to Graland Country Day School for allowing us to continuously use their beautiful space for photo shoots. We also wish to thank Rina Coury, who took many of the class photos in this book.

We are greatly indebted to the Deaf families and ASL/NGT users around the world who have shared their language, their culture, and their ways of communicating and interacting with us. Our direct and indirect work with these signing families has informed many of our *Signing Smart* strategies and techniques, and has allowed us to share the wondrous aspects of ASL with hearing families. We continuously strive to remain true to the language and to humbly share the intricacies of its culture throughout all of our programs and materials, and it is with the deepest gratitude that we acknowledge the importance of the language and culture upon which *Signing Smart* is based.

In addition, our program would not be what it is and where it is without the wonderful *Signing Smart* instructors around the United States and abroad whom we have trained in our methods and who now offer *Signing Smart* play classes, workshops, and materials internationally. It is through all of you that so many more families are able to benefit from *Signing Smart*. Thanks to Michael Thompson, Beryt Nisenson, and Karin Leite for the influential roles they have played in this project. We appreciate the guidance, focus, and vision that Cate Wisneski and Angela Fieseler have brought to our *Signing Smart* endeavors. We wish to give a special thanks to our ASL consultant, Rebecca MacLean, who has shared with us her talent and her heart, and whose expertise and guidance has been an integral component of our program and this book. We wish to also thank our Denver and Portland instructors for their insights and enthusiasm.

We owe a great deal of thanks to Marian Lizzi, who found us and suggested creating this project together. Along similar lines we are extremely grateful to Sheila Curry Oakes, who stepped in for Marian as our editor and lent her skill, expertise, and observant eye to this work. We cannot fully express our appreciation for the extent to which she advocated for this project, and her instrumental role in bringing our vision of this guide to life. Thanks also to Julie Mente for her tireless efforts on our behalf. We would also like to thank Jennifer Weinberg for her patient support whenever we asked her "one more question" about the book-writing process.

Of course, we are deeply indebted to our extended families for their steadfast belief in our work. From Michelle's family: her parents, Bonnie and Robert Anthony, and Bruce and Barbara Rubin, who patiently listened to research result after research result and story after story of the how and why of *Signing Smart*; a double thanks to her mother for her tireless support of all aspects of *Signing Smart*; her sister Tricia (and husband, John), who gave us activity ideas, personal stories, and dedicated support; her brother Scott and his wife, Jo, who read through early manuscripts and have provided invaluable feedback, editorial support, and business guidance time and again; her brother Mike and his wife, Jess, who read every word of the newer manuscripts, lending novice-signers' eyes and new parents' perspectives to the process; her brother Peter (and David) who shared the ideas in *Signing Smart* with everyone who seemed interested; her grandfather Robert N. Anthony, Sr., for his steadfast support in all areas; Ardith and Doug Hunter, who agreed to watch Kylie and Maya for "just one more photo shoot"; Mark and Katherine Hunter, who took a leap of faith and introduced this "crazy idea" to their son and then spread the wonderful benefits to everyone they knew; Chloe-dog, for keeping Michelle company while writing, no matter what the hour; and to Michelle's devoted friends Helen Eaton, Emily Platt, and Marci Young for supporting every step of this endeavor. From Reyna's family: her parents, Roberta and Larry Proman, who always asked and never tired of hearing about the ways in which *Signing Smart* evolved over the years and who lent critical editorial eyes to earlier manuscripts; her grandmother Florence Stein, whose confidence in her and her work never wavers; Lin and Peter Lindert, Kathy Lindert and Eric Metee, and Alex Lindert and Noemi Dizon, who continue to show interest in and excitement for this project; and Elena Jeffries Nadgauda for her friendship through the years.

Michelle and Reyna also thank their ASL/NGT colleagues from UC Berkeley: Diane Anderson, Yael Biederman Galinson, Nini Hoiting, Lon Kuntze, Amy Lieberman, Jennie Pyers, Helen Thumann, and their adviser Dan I. Slobin. We especially thank Yael and Amy for their friendship across the miles.

We could never have accomplished this project without the love and support of our children and husbands. Both directly and indirectly, this book is a labor of love that began the moment we looked into our children's eyes and knew we wanted to give them the world. Instead, they gave it to us, and we are so very grateful and humbled. Natasha, Kylie, Maya, and Nadia, each in her own way, also showed unwavering patience during crunch times while we "finished one last chapter" or extended "one more phone call." And without Scott and Nick's loving encouragement and unfaltering belief in the importance of our work, neither of us could have begun—much less finished—this project, and *Signing Smart* would not be what it is today. "Thank you" is not nearly enough!

Lastly, we wish to thank each one of you—for opening your homes and hearts to *Signing Smart*.

THIS BOOK IS BASED ON Wide-Eyed Learning, LLC's *Signing Smart* programs—child development play classes, workshops, and materials that use American Sign Language (ASL) signs to facilitate early communication, foster intimacy, and promote long-term learning in young hearing children. Our research has shown that the use of ASL signs in combination with *Signing Smart* techniques allows communication, spoken language development, and conceptual understanding to happen earlier, more easily, and more prolifically in both typical and developmentally delayed children. Please know that children *participate more* in familiar games and activities. If your child seems to *observe* more than talk or sign at first, return to his favorites time and again.

Signing Smart is an international program with play classes and workshops offered by trained instructors around the United States and abroad. To find local programming in your area, please visit our Web site at www.signingsmart.com. You can also be trained to become a *Signing Smart* instructor and help introduce other families to the magic of *Signing Smart*. For additional resources for parents and instructors, see Appendix 3, page 216.

In the many case histories throughout the book, some names have been changed to protect our clients' privacy. In order to remain gender neutral, we alternate between using "he" and "she" in our examples. Additionally, although we often use the term "parent," all the *Signing Smart* strategies and activities are equally effective for child-care providers and preschool teachers.

Throughout the book, signs are indicated by capitalized words in boldface. To learn how to produce the signs suggested throughout this guide, please see the photographs and descriptions in the *Signing Smart* Illustrated Dictionary on page 192. To help hone your eye to what signs look like on infant and toddler hands, we have included numerous photos of children signing throughout the book. In addition, you will find descriptions of common child versions for the 130 ASL signs contained in this guide in Appendix 2, page 208.

In noting which ASL signs to use while you are speaking with your child, we follow English grammar and tense markings. For example, we write **HIDE**, **HIDING**, and **HID** to refer to the single ASL sign **HIDE**. ASL has its own grammar and means of marking tense. However, as *Signing Smart* is about layering individual signs onto English sentences, ASL tense markings are not often used in baby sign language interchanges with hearing children.

Some photos in the *Signing Smart* Illustrated Dictionary on page 192 depict the starting position of more than one concept. In these photos, the arrows refer to the first sign described in the caption.

Letting Children Tell Their Own Stories

MAX'S STORY: IS SIGNING "NONSENSE"?

Max's parents had heard of using American Sign Language (ASL) signs with hearing infants and toddlers but, in the words of his mother, Tricia, they had felt it was "ridiculous." Tricia remembers:

I wanted my child to talk, not sign. I just thought the whole thing was nonsense. That's what those flash-card-wielding moms did and I wanted no part of it. I invested my energy in having language-rich interactions with Max. But when he was eleven-and-a-half months old, my sister was visiting from out of town. Her thirteen-month-old daughter was signing and speaking up a storm. What really changed my mind was when I saw my niece sign AIRPLANE. My sister told her (with words and signs) that that was not an AIRPLANE, but the MOON. My niece signed AIRPLANE and said "no." She continued signing, "MOON. WHAT MOON?" I was floored. Max had three spo-ken words at that time but was nowhere near being able to ask me about the moon. Who wouldn't want their child to be able to do that?! I decided right then that signing was for me! Within weeks of getting involved with Signing Smart, Max had over thirty signs and ten spoken words, and we too were having the kinds of conversations I thought were months away. Although initially not a fan of signing, I have never looked back.

As Max's sign and word vocabulary grew, so did his parents' use of *Signing Smart* strategies. At sixteen months, Max had over sixty signs and twenty-five words. At two, Max was one of the most verbal children Tricia knew. As Tricia remembers, "Especially being a boy, he was light-years ahead of where I would have expected." Nevertheless, she still found that her *Signing Smart* strategies played an important role in her interactions with her son. As Tricia recalls:

I remember a time when I couldn't open the drawer Max's bath toys were in. I told him it was stuck. Distracted, I heard him getting more and more upset, repeating, "-uck Mommy. It's -uck." He became frantic and I knew a tantrum was coming. I turned to see him signing DUCK. I sat down and explained in words and signs that Mommy had said the toys were STUCK; I wasn't talking about his DUCKS. He calmed right down and I was able to fix the drawer and get him his floating ducks. I know that without the strategies, I would have kept reinforcing "stuck" when he had heard "duck." Talk about cannon fodder for a tantrum!

Signing Smart gave Max's family the gift of early communication and reduced frustration. Bringing his favorite "quack, quack" **DUCK** up to his face to get fifteen-month-old Will's attention, four-year-old Max now shares *Signing Smart* with his brother.

JADA'S STORY: FRUSTRATION AT EVERY TURN

Signing Smart also brought relief to Jada's family. At eighteen months, Jada pointed, grunted, and cried in her attempts to communicate. A few months earlier, Jada had been evaluated as having a speech/language delay. However, like Max's family, Jada's parents wanted her to talk, not sign. They worried that because signing would be "easier" for Jada than speaking, she might sign and never talk. Finally, on the advice of Jada's speech therapist, her family joined a local *Signing Smart* play class. Within hours of coming home from her first class, Jada began signing

back. Very quickly, her vocabulary grew to over forty signs, and her tantrums at home and her resistance to speech therapy disappeared. Jada's mom relates:

Aside from all the relief it brought, Signing Smart has helped me realize Jada has more words than I realized. Her pronunciation was so rough and incorrect, we didn't realize she was trying to talk, but the sounds were too garbled to recognize. Maybe if we had learned the Signing Smart techniques earlier, we could have helped correct her words sooner and prevented those incorrect sounds from becoming so ingrained. At least now we can all communicate, and we're on the road to better understanding and reinforcing her spoken words.

Although neither Jada's parents nor her therapist can predict when talking will become easier for her, they are relieved to recognize the many things Jada is trying to say, and to realize that she is able to communicate while clearer speech is developing.

ROSS'S STORY: CROSSING OVER THE THRESHOLD TO COMMUNICATION

Elizabeth watched her son's happy-go-lucky personality change when he became a toddler. Ross was sixteen months old and, like many typically developing toddlers, he was able to say only a handful of words. However, Ross understood many things around him and had a lot he wanted (and tried) to say. More and more, Ross's mom saw him communicating with her in the form of grunts, points, whines, cries, and tantrums.

Elizabeth recalls:

When I heard about signing with young children, I was immediately interested. But I wanted to use real ASL signs, not just random gestures, and I knew Ross would want to communicate about more than just **BED** *or* **MORE** *or* **PLEASE***, so I scouted out a Signing Smart play class. Within weeks, the Ross I knew and loved had returned. It's as if Signing Smart opened a door that Ross was*

Ross's mom uses *Signing Smart* strategies to enhance learning. Here, she helps seventeen-month-old Ross to distinguish the words "hair" and "hare" by signing **BUNNY** on Ross while reading.

ready to walk through, and within no time his signed and spoken vocabulary has taken off.

When asked if she continues to use signs with Ross—almost twenty months—his mother echoes sentiments we hear from many *Signing Smart* parents:

He doesn't "need" the signs anymore, but we continue to use the Signing Smart strategies to better understand his words, for storytelling and learning, and to help Ross with tough English vocabulary, like "bare" and "bear."

As we have seen with the toddlers in our programs, when their speaking skills advance and they begin to use more words, the usefulness of *Signing Smart* changes but does not diminish. It shifts from use for primary communication to supporting conceptual and spoken language development.

SIGNING SMART: FROM OUR HOMES TO YOURS

Our own journey with *Signing Smart* has been a personal one. Reyna relates:

> My husband, Nick, and I began signing with our first daughter, Natasha, when she was eleven months old. One month later, she had a small collection of signs, and her vocabulary grew quickly from there. By the time she was eighteen months old, she used nearly one hundred words and signs, and she was talking in minisentences.
>
> I can remember the joy I felt in being able to see the way her little mind worked from such a young age. One day, fourteen-month-old Natasha toddled over to the porch door and signed **BIRD**. To my surprise, there were none of the usual blue jays at the feeder. Natasha signed **BIRD EAT** with a questioning look—she was remembering the birds we liked to watch together. She was barely walking, and here we were talking about something important to her and present only in her memory!
>
> Looking back, I wish I had started signing with Natasha earlier. But I had felt so exhausted by the everyday tasks of mothering that using signs seemed like too much additional work—even though I was a fluent signer! When Michelle was pregnant with her first child, Kylie, we talked about how we might draw on our background and training in ASL and child development to make the incredible experience of signing easier and more enjoyable at earlier ages.

Michelle recollects:

> It was then that we began developing what would later become the Signing Smart program, and Kylie benefited immensely. My husband and I began signing with Kylie when she was six months old. At eight months, she began signing her version of **FAN**, and a whole new world of interaction opened up. At twelve months, Kylie had over seventy-five signs and we as parents were participants in the adventure of our lives!
>
> One memorable event occurred when Kylie was ten months old and was devastated by a terrible bout with a stomach bug. She was severely dehydrated and was on the verge of needing to be hospitalized because she couldn't keep anything down. While we were waiting for her stomach to settle, Kylie looked up at us and signed **MILK**. Surprised, I tried nursing her. To our delight, she was able to hold it down. After that, we waited for Kylie to tell us when her system could handle more milk, and to our relief, she continued to keep down all of the liquid she requested.

As in many homes, *Signing Smart* has been a family affair. Michelle's husband,

The techniques we developed for *Signing Smart* gave Kylie the tools to let us know what she needed and felt from a very young age. Here, fourteen-month-old Kylie lets Michelle know she is feeling **SICK**.

Scott, recounts a less dramatic but no less memorable story:

> *When Kylie was twelve months old, I was reading a new book to her: "Bunny jumps over blocks, and a train, and a ball." "BUNNY TRAIN WHAT" she signed. "The bunny JUMPED over the train," I explained. Not satisfied, Kylie again signed BUNNY WHAT, asking for more information about what the bunny did to the train. "It JUMPED over the train," I said and signed to her, lifting her up and jumping with her, both of us laughing with delight. I never thought reading would be such an interactive activity with my barely one year old!*

When Natasha and Kylie were babies, there were no signing programs near Berkeley (where we were getting our Ph.D.s), and very few around the country. Neither of us felt the available baby sign language books and materials gave parents—including ourselves—the tools we needed to easily integrate signing into our hectic and varied life with our babies (and we each had only one child!). Despite our backgrounds, we both faced the challenges and frustrations of signing without proper support or tools.

Building from our experiences as early childhood teachers, parent educators, Ph.D.s in developmental psychology, certified ASL users, and—most important—*mothers*, we developed the *Signing Smart* program. Our goal has been to do more than simply teach parents a handful of useful signs. Rather, we have sought to help *enrich what parents are already doing* with their babies, using signing as a medium. To do so, we have developed programs and materials that give parents the tools, strategies, resources, information, and understanding to be able to enjoy using signs to facilitate both early communication and long-term learning, beginning from their baby's earliest days.

As we have learned from our own children, there is a tremendous difference between a child who can sign **EAT** or **MORE**, and one who can interact with his parents and his world in new and wondrous ways. In short order, interest in our *Signing Smart* programs has spread around the country and abroad, and thousands of families are experiencing the benefits of our child-focused, family-friendly strategies and techniques.

And the magical journey continues. With both Natasha and Kylie—preschoolers at this point—we continue to use our *Signing Smart* strategies to facilitate their learning, conceptual development, and reading skills. Meanwhile, we have been blessed with new babies born only days apart, and we are again *Signing Smart* with our youngest daughters. The experience is no less magical the second time around. We have both seen the difference in using our fully developed *Signing Smart* techniques with Nadia and Maya. As Reyna relates:

> In contrast to Natasha, who did not see her first sign until she was eleven months old, Nick, Natasha, and I started signing with Nadia when she was not quite six months old. At seven months she had three signs and has continued to add signs steadily. From her earliest signing days, we loved that she could tell us from across the room that she wanted to play with her ball tower. By looking up at us and bouncing her hands toward each other, she influenced her world in a way that was incredibly powerful for her, especially because she was not yet crawling.

By the time Nadia arrived, she was able to benefit from our fully developed *Signing Smart* program. Here, seven-month-old Nadia asks Reyna to bring over her favorite **BALL** tower.

More and more we are seeing very young signers like Nadia within our programs—*Signing Smart* families with children younger than eight months old who are developing sizable vocabularies for these little babies. In fact, some babies who start *Signing Smart* from a very young age are able to begin signing before they are five months old. Such was the case with Maya. As Michelle recounts:

> We began going to our Signing Smart play classes when Maya was only three-and-a-half months old. At not quite four-and-a-half months, she produced her first sign: KYLIE—the name sign we used to talk about Maya's favorite "object"—her sister! At only eight months, she had over thirty signs and was able to string them together into four-sign sentences—something most nonsigning children cannot do with spoken words until they are upward of two-and-a-half years old!
>
> But even a single sign Maya uses can make a tremendous difference. On one memorable occasion, Maya was seven months old and particularly fussy. I was going down the list of "what might be wrong": was she in pain, hungry, wet, tired? When I tried nursing her, she turned away and signed BED, BED, BED. I began rocking her but when she started to cry again, I got up thinking, "maybe she needs teething gel." She started signing BED, BED, BED again, so I just continued to rock her as she fell asleep, in-

Some children are extremely early signers; such was the case with Maya. At not quite four-and-a-half months old, she produced her first sign; at eight months old she had more than thirty. Here, seven-month-old Maya signs **BED** to let Michelle and Scott know she is done posing and is ready to leave the party.

termittently awaking with a cry followed by **BED, BED, BED**. *So instead of giving her medicine or other things, she could tell me that she just wanted to fall asleep but was having trouble doing so.*

As a parent or caregiver of a very young child, there is no greater *relief* than knowing what your child needs, and no greater *delight* than knowing what he wants, what interests him, and what confuses him. And while you cannot read your child's mind (much as he may think you can!), you can indeed begin *Signing Smart* today, allowing *him* to tell you his thoughts for himself.

SIGNING SMART

In our research and work with thousands of typical and developmentally delayed children from our *Signing Smart* play classes and workshops, we have heard countless powerful and compelling stories that mimic our own. More and more parents are learning how ASL signs can change the lives of their hearing infants and toddlers. However, before experiencing *Signing Smart*, most families are not aware of the seamless success that our program affords. With a few simple tools, you will be able to take advantage of this powerful communicative and learning vehicle.

By drawing on the information and activities in *Signing Smart*, you will not only learn how to enrich the interactions that you naturally have with your child, but you will also learn how signing with your child can be transformed from something you have to work at to something you can treasure and (most important) enjoy. And, what's more, the *Signing Smart* techniques we have developed will allow you to become partners in your child's development and will make signing useful for more than a few months—you will learn ways to benefit from and enjoy *Signing Smart* for years to come.

Our research at the University of California at Berkeley Sign Language Acquisition Lab demonstrates that children use the picturelike quality of signs to more easily learn them. Here, Michelle and two-year-old Nicholas, diagnosed at eighteen months with apraxia of speech, combine pretend play and learning during their *Signing Smart* Intermediate Play Class, talking and signing about becoming **BUTTERFLIES** at the end of *The Very Hungry Caterpillar* by Eric Carle.

TRUE ASL SIGNS VERSUS INVENTED GESTURES OR "BABY-FRIENDLY ASL SIGNS"

Some people ask whether they should go to the "trouble" to learn true ASL signs as opposed to simply making up gestures or using "baby-friendly" modified signs with their child. *Signing Smart* uses true ASL signs, but that does not require you to learn the entire language. Rather, we use select ASL signs while speaking and interacting with young hearing children, to foster communication and learning. Our research at the Sign Language Acquisition Lab at the University of California at Berkeley has demonstrated that very young children use the iconic quality of true signs (their conceptually based, "picturelike" quality) to more easily learn and begin to utilize them.[1] Invented gestures and modified signs therefore deny children some of the powerful learning information that authentic ASL signs possess. There are many additional compelling reasons to use ASL signs:

- The first and primary one is our firm belief that language facilitates language. Because we use signs to foster language development, we strongly suggest using real language to do so.

- ASL signs are all done with the hands, allowing them to be easily adapted using *Signing Smart* techniques. Such adaptations allow young children to have access to the sign *and* the word as they *simultaneously* continue to explore their world. Our research demonstrates that the *Signing Smart* Adaptation Strategies (described throughout this book) make signing happen more quickly, at younger ages, and more prolifically.

- ∗ Some suggested invented gestures may be done with facial/lip movements alone. However, using facial gestures to represent a word is limiting because such gestures are often very subtle and require your child to stare you in the face to notice them.

- If children are looking at *you,* they most often cannot *also* be looking at the object of interest at the same time, and thus the learning cycle is broken.

- A parent cannot simultaneously be saying, for example, "fish" and producing lip movements to "sign" the word. This prevents the dual vocal/visual input that speeds acquisition of both signs and words.

· One Key to *Signing Smart* Success is *recognizing your child's version of any given sign.* We call the child's production an *approximation.* Knowing "how" and "why" children's signs (like their early words) differ from their parents' can make the difference between a successful signing experience and a frustrating one.

* Just as we would never invent sounds to take the place of "complex" words (e.g., calling alligators "ba-bas"), there is no need to invent gestures, simplify hand movements, or make up facial gestures for "complex" signs. Your child will produce both "easy" and "hard" signs equally well, producing her own version of *both* early on.

Despite the chaos of his first birthday party, Cameron is able to tell his mom and dad that he is **FINISHED** with his birthday cake.

* Make no mistake, *children will create their own versions of even "baby-friendly" signs.* Why waste your time (and energy) trying to invent what *you* may think are "simple" gestures, only to find you still need to decipher your child's versions anyway? Instead, your time is best spent learning the *Signing Smart* tools that will allow you to predict and recognize your child's versions of signs, as described on page 36.

* When parents use true ASL signs, they benefit from being able to learn what their child's version of any given sign is likely to be. They are then well equipped to recognize their child's earliest signs much more easily. For likely child versions of the signs contained in the *Signing Smart* Illustrated Dictionary, see Appendix 1, page 192.

• Because we developed these *Signing Smart* techniques to grow as your child grows, you can take advantage of all they have to offer for years to come—from the infant years through the time when young children are learning to read. For long-term learning, it is particularly advantageous to use signs from a real, conceptually based language like ASL.

Within six weeks of starting *Signing Smart*, nine-month-old Jacob had three signs. Here, his parents know just what he wants to say—he looks right at his father and signs **DADDY**.

GETTING STARTED WITH *SIGNING SMART*

With this information in hand, we welcome you to the world of *Signing Smart:* a collection of at-home activities (paired with strategies and developmental information) in which words, signs, and experiences are integrated into the hectic lives of young families. In this book you will find all the information you need to make *Signing Smart* with your child accessible, usable, and, most important, *enjoyable!*

Chapter 1, "Get Ready, Get Set, Go . . . On Your Way!" outlines all the information and *Signing Smart* strategies you need to get started, as well as those that will benefit you down the road. First, in helping you *get ready,* we will lay out the specifics of how *Signing Smart* can enhance your child's development. Next we make sure you are *set to start* by giving you information about the "how and why" of choosing your initial signs. We then describe the anticipated time frame for your child's own signing milestones and introduce you to the Four Keys to *Signing Smart* Success.

The seven chapters that follow "Get Ready, Get Set, Go . . . On Your Way!" contain songs, games, and activities we developed to make your family's journey to increased communication, intimacy, self-esteem, and learning as fun and easy as it will be memorable. We designed these new activities to allow parents and caregivers to incorporate signs easily and playfully into their everyday life with their infant, toddler, and even preschooler. We have interwoven our *Signing Smart* strategies, Developmental Details, and long-term learning techniques into the activities themselves.

As countless *Signing Smart* families have

told us time and again, knowing some signs and being motivated to use them is one thing. But what makes the difference in how easy and successful signing with your child feels is learning the *Signing Smart* strategies and techniques we have developed for our play class and workshop programs. In this guide we provide you with these *Signing Smart* tools in the context of activities we developed specifically for at-home interactions. From the time your baby is five to eight months old into the preschool years, you will find that signing will be more meaningful, useful, and successful if you have these *Signing Smart* strategies in your toolbox as you start—or even as you continue—your baby sign language journey.

The tips we offer will make the difference between having to wait months versus only days or weeks to see your child look you in the eye, raise her little hand, and tell you what she's thinking about!

Welcome to the world of *Signing Smart*!

CHAPTER 1:

Get Ready, Get Set, Go ... On Your Way!

GET READY . . .

RESEARCH AND EXPERIENCE have demonstrated that *Signing Smart* with very young children advances many aspects of development.

Cognitive/Linguistic Benefits

EARLY SIGNED AND SPOKEN VOCABULARIES

Wide-Eyed Learning, LLC, is currently examining the development of both signs and words in hearing *Signing Smart* children. While this is a work in progress, the preliminary results are exciting. For example, developmental norms tell us that, on average, a nonsigning child at twelve months will have two to three words; at eighteen months, a nonsigning child will have, on average, a vocabulary of ten to fifty spoken words, and he or she may be on the cusp of combining words into minisentences (e.g., "Bye-bye, Dada."). In our *Signing Smart* programs, however, we see these same language abilities appear months (and, for some children, years) earlier with signs. In terms of *spoken word* development, *Signing Smart* children are *ahead* of what these developmental averages would predict.

Specifically, results from our recent research demonstrate that *Signing Smart* children have an average of *twenty-five signs* and *sixteen spoken words* at twelve months; at eighteen months, they have an average of *79 signs and 105 words*. In addition, *Signing*

Our research demonstrates that *Signing Smart* children are ahead of developmental norms in terms of vocabulary size and the ability to communicate in sentences. Here, ten-month-old Bailey tells her mom about the **BEAUTIFUL FLOWERS** she sees.

Smart children can begin combining signs as young as six months old, and at eleven to fourteen months, a majority will begin to use signed/spoken sentences. In this way, many *Signing Smart* children not only have extensive *sign* vocabularies and are able to form minisentences with signs at a remarkably young age, but they are also often early and prolific *talkers*.

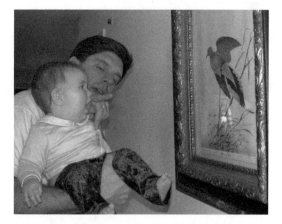

Signing Smart strategies give parents the tools to integrate signs when children are most able to learn them. Here, Scott uses signs and words to help eight-month-old Maya learn more about her favorite **BIRD** portrait.

FACILITATED SPEECH

In our programs, we give parents the tools to heighten children's attention and to integrate signs when children are most primed for learning. Families learn ways to use language in many of its forms (signing, speaking, singing, reading, conversing, and storytelling) to engage children in supported interactions that are rich, complex, varied, and meaningful. *Signing Smart* strategies teach parents to use signs to highlight (and draw children's attention to) a particular word/concept. Through such techniques, parents give their child a "picture" or "image" of that concept (i.e., action, object, or idea). In all these ways, *Signing Smart* methods help adults pull concepts out of the stream of complex English grammar that children need to decipher, and thereby give children multiple access points for learning these concepts at the exact moment(s) they are most able to do so.

In providing such rich communicative and learning environments for children at very young ages, *Signing Smart* helps "wire" the brain for linguistic and conceptual understanding. Each time a parent engages his child in *Signing Smart* interactions, neural connections are formed that pave the way for increasingly complex connections to develop. As a result, *Signing Smart* children learn a broad range of signs, words, and their underlying concepts more easily and quickly.

CHILD-INITIATED CONVERSATIONS/COMMUNICATIONS

Signing Smart's emphasis on child-initiated conversations and communications not only facilitates children's signed and spoken vocabulary, but also gives children the means to exert developmentally appropriate,

Sixteen-month-old Vincent, who has Down syndrome, excitedly asks for **MORE**. With fifteen signs and eight words, communication is easy.

Fifteen-month-old Rachel signs **HURT** along with her mother, recollecting a time she had hurt herself.

positive control over their environment. While many parents make a point of talking a great deal to their young children, *Signing Smart* teaches parents to pay special attention to the many ways—signed and nonsigned—that children *initiate* conversations. Recognizing these "conversation initiators" requires no additional work on the part of parents, just a new way of looking at what their child does naturally. Once parents recognize these conversation initiators, *Signing Smart* gives families the tools to engage their child, showering her with words about topics that are of immediate interest to *her.* For example, as any parent can tell you, having your toddler

enthusiastically sign **PHONE** upon hearing one is far better than the whines and cries that would otherwise be necessary to get your attention and convey her excitement. And, with this positive conversation initiator, the parent is easily able to build on her child's interest.

Signing Smart children are also able to talk about abstract ideas (like saying they feel **SICK** or need **HELP**) from a very young age. This allows children to cue their parents into their specific thought processes.

Eight-month-old Maya lets us know in no uncertain terms that she needs **HELP** getting out of her snow pants.

FACILITATED MEMORY

Signing Smart children are precocious in having a means to "talk about" past or non-present objects and experiences (e.g., talking about the time they got **HURT** or about the **AIRPLANE** they remember seeing). Parents also learn techniques to engage children in such discussions. As a result, *Signing Smart*

Signing Smart allows children to "talk" about events that captivate them. Here, sixteen-month-old Grace shares her fascination with **PUMPKINS** with her mom.

learn to *sign* over forty words by her first birthday, and can have a vocabulary of over three hundred words/signs used in two-, three-, and four-word/sign "sentences" before she is eighteen months old. In addition, regardless of age, *Signing Smart* children can use signs for complex words that they are not yet able to say (e.g., signing **ALLIGATOR** or **PUMPKIN** or **MEDICINE**).

Emotional Benefits

REDUCED FRUSTRATION

Through *Signing Smart*, children and parents develop two-way communication from very early on. In addition, *Signing Smart* allows parents to facilitate *long-term learning*, using signs and *Signing Smart* strategies to support their child's spoken-language development and to clarify their child's ambiguous early words. Through these techniques,

facilitates children's access to and expression of their memories.

EXPANDED VOCABULARY

Signing Smart strategies facilitate a tremendous early vocabulary. Between eight and twelve months a child may begin to *say* a few words. Our research has shown that by using *Signing Smart* techniques, a child can

Thirteen-month-old Sydney asks her mom for **MILK** after play class.

Even very young children can talk about complex ideas. At only eight months, Maya is able to comment on the diaper-rash **MEDICINE** Michelle is holding.

adult-child miscommunications (and the child's frustration and tantrums that often follow suit) are drastically reduced.

As a result, the number of times *Signing Smart* parents must ask "What-do-you-want, this-or-this-or-this-or-this?" is greatly diminished. *Signing Smart* children are thus able to keep interactions positive, rather than needing to end a warm and loving play session with a tantrum because they have no other way to convey what they want.

Reyna's doctoral research demonstrates that signing facilitates two-way communication between parents and children. This was certainly true for eighteen-month-old Kylie, who from a very early age was able to talk and sign about the **DREAMS** she had while in **BED.** This took the guesswork out of her middle-of-the-night tears and allowed Michelle and Scott to help her work out her fears.

INCREASED INTIMACY, ATTACHMENT, SELF-ESTEEM, AND EMPOWERMENT

Reyna's dissertation research on signing toddlers' and preschoolers' interactions with their mothers indicates that ASL enhances communication between parents and children.[2] By using ASL signs with children who have no other form of shared communication with their families, parents are able to capture and maintain children's interest in a topic, which in turn fosters extended interactions about common themes. These extended interactions empower children to see the impact communication has on their world, facilitate closeness between parents and children, and foster the sense of intimacy that shared communication brings.

Similarly, because *Signing Smart* children experience a great number of positive child-initiated interactions, they are able to influence their environment in a productive manner, and are able to get their needs met. They are also able to more easily engage in and maintain interactions that foster intimacy, attachment, and self-esteem.

Long-Term Benefits

Additional research by ourselves and by others documents the long-term benefits that signing brings to children. Research funded by the National Institutes of Health demonstrates that by age four, children who used baby sign language as infants and toddlers are linguistically advanced compared to children who did not.[3] Recent follow-up studies of these same children in the second grade reveals that children who signed as babies have an average IQ advantage of twelve points compared to their counterparts who never signed.[4]

Research conducted at Pennsylvania State University shows that even those hearing children who are not exposed to signs until the preschool years go on to display literacy advancements over nonsigning children. Specifically, these children evidence enhanced vocabulary, spelling, and reading skills.[5]

Michelle's doctoral research—a longitudinal study[6] of signing elementary school children—shows that signing facilitates the integration of a child's linguistic and cognitive systems.[7] By linking visual/gestural and linguistic representations to form unified ideas, a child is able to create a word/concept "package" in memory. A child's facility with creating word/concept "packages" is further related to his or her later ability to clarify, unify, and organize both oral and written stories. As you can see, signing is the gift that keeps on giving, from infancy into the elementary school years and beyond.

Signing Smart in Everyday Life

While starting something new or different is never easy, there are many rewards for undertaking this journey. Once you have implemented the general plan that we outline in this chapter, you will find that the amount of "additional work" is negligible, and the payoffs immense. In fact, once you become comfortable integrating *Signing Smart* into your interactions with your child, you will find the "additional work" in your life drastically diminishes! And, please know that integrating *even a small handful* of the great many strategies and techniques within these pages is enough to allow your family to benefit from what *Signing Smart* has to offer.

GET SET . . .

Regardless of where you are on your baby sign language journey, you will want to familiarize yourself with the *Signing Smart* Start and the Four Keys to *Signing Smart* Success, to allow you and your child to take full advantage of all the strategies, techniques, and activities in this book. Understanding each of these aspects of our program will allow your child to sign back as quickly and as prolifically as possible.

The *Signing Smart* Start

Our research and applied work with thousands of families has demonstrated that it does matter *how many* signs you start with, *which* signs you use, and the *kinds of contexts* in which you use them. If you have already started signing with your child, it is worth taking stock of the signs you are using and how you are using them. Many parents start signing in a way that is not the most effective for encouraging their child to sign back as quickly and as extensively as possible. The *Signing Smart* Start will help you effectively choose the number and kinds of signs you use, and the Four Keys to *Signing Smart* Success will help you recognize and take advantage of the kinds of interactions that lead to a successful signing experience as quickly as possible.

THE *SIGNING SMART* START: HOW MANY SIGNS TO START WITH?

You will find that we developed our techniques and strategies with children's development in mind. *We strongly encourage you to choose six as your minimum number of signs* to start with. Why? For your child's sake. It is important that your child see you signing in various contexts, to allow him to understand the usefulness of signs in his world. When you choose only a couple of signs to start with, you limit the number of contexts in which you are able to sign, lengthening the time it will take your child to sign back and develop an extensive vocabulary.

We strongly encourage you to choose twelve as your maximum number of signs to start with. Using too many signs initially will actually slow your child's signing back in that, instead of signing *supplementing* and *highlighting* English, it becomes a new code system to decipher *in addition to* English.

Once your child begins to show strong evidence of comprehension or begins to sign back, you can add to this initial set of six to twelve signs (see page 41 for more on this). Remember, the purpose of *Signing Smart* is highlighting English words/concepts with visual information (signs).

CHOOSING YOUR *SIGNING SMART* STARTER SIGNS

As we mentioned above, parents' best intentions sometimes unknowingly work against what we know about children's development, and can thereby greatly lengthen the time it takes children to begin signing or to build up a sizable sign vocabulary. One way this happens is when parents choose to use mostly what we call See A Lot / Do A Lot Signs—signs that *parents* are particularly interested in having their children use ("parent-oriented" signs such as **MILK**, **MORE**, and **EAT**).

As you know all too well, children *have* the ability to indicate these desires to parents. We may not appreciate the grunts and whines children often use to express their needs, but—from the child's perspective at least—they are effective. (It is for this very reason that "eat," "milk," and "more" are rarely children's first *spoken* words.)

By introducing what we call Highly Motivating Signs ("child-oriented" signs such as **MUSIC**, **FAN**, or **BALL**) from the beginning, we give our children the means and the *motivation* to begin "conversations" about topics of interest and importance to *them*—topics they have little way of communicating about without signs. Be aware that choosing to use only these more "motivating" signs also has its limitations in that, even if your child is very excited about, for example, bubbles, it is not likely that you and she will interact around **BUBBLES** numerous times a day (or week).

SIGNING SMART: FINDING A BALANCE

Our research with thousands of families has demonstrated that when families choose three to six See A Lot / Do A Lot Starter Signs ("parent-oriented" signs), *as well as* three to six Highly Motivating Starter Signs ("child-oriented" signs), it will significantly shorten the time frame for children signing back and developing a sizable vocabulary. Exciting findings from our recent research demonstrate that you can further shorten this time frame by choosing *some* Starter Signs that are general enough to be used in many contexts, thereby greatly extending the number of situations in which you can sign meaningfully. Examples of General See A Lot / Do A Lot Signs are: **EAT**, **MORE**, **FINISH**, **WHAT**, **HELP**, **WHERE**, and **PLAY**; see the *Signing Smart* Illustrated Dictionary on page 192 for more. These General Signs can be used during almost every interaction you have with your child.

Signing Smart Starter Signs

SEE A LOT / DO A LOT SIGNS

- Decide on three to six signs for *words you use often enough in your day* so that your child has ample opportunity to see them in context and to connect the hand movements with the meaning.

- Choose signs that are *versatile* enough to use in a great many contexts with young children.

- Choose *events that happen often* during the day, so your child will see you sign during these routines (see Part I, "*Signing Smart* Activities for Every Day" for more).

- Suggested signs:

WHAT; HELP; PLAY; EAT; WHERE; MORE; FINISHED; MILK; DRINK; SILLY; BED; BATH; CLEAN-UP

I'm **FINISHED** eating (sixteen months).

HIGHLY MOTIVATING SIGNS

- Decide on three to six signs of interest to your *child*, to motivate her signing back sooner.

- Choose signs for *objects* or *actions* your child is very interested in (see Part II, "*Signing Smart* Activities for Play" for more).

- Choose signs for items that are *abundant* (*and fascinating*) in the lives of young children.

- Many families find that children who begin using Highly Motivating Signs relatively quickly come to understand the power that signing holds in their world. They then begin signing the more "useful" signs as well.

- Suggested signs:

LIGHT; FAN; MUSIC; KEY; BALL; DOG/CAT; CAR; BABY; JUMP; DANCE

I see the camera **LIGHT** (ten months).

REMEMBER—*Signing Smart* means keeping a *balance* between these two kinds of signs.

Our recent research has demonstrated that using
General Signs such as **EAT**, **MORE**, **FINISH**, **WHAT**,
HELP, **MUSIC**, **LIGHT**, and **BALL** will greatly extend
the number of contexts in which parents can sign
meaningfully, thereby shortening the time frame for your
child to sign back and develop a sizable vocabulary.
Here, seventeen-month-old Lincoln tells his mom he wants
MORE of the game.

When you do not know *the* sign for the object your child is playing with, General Signs such as **WHAT**, **WHERE**, **HELP**, **MORE**, **FINISH**, and/or **PLAY** allow you to use *a* sign. By having *a few* such "all-purpose" signs in your early repertoire, even if these are not the signs you expect (or want) your child to sign back first, you help your child learn that hand motions are useful and can fit into his world in lots of different contexts. Remember that signs like **EAT** and **MORE** are extremely versatile (e.g., to comment on your child mouthing a toy or wanting to hear the same song over and over again).

This same principle applies to Highly Motivating Signs. Including signs such as

LIGHT, BALL, and/or MUSIC in your set of Starter Signs will allow you to talk about interesting items that are abundant in a young child's life (think of how many of today's toys have lights, play music, or contain balls!) in a large variety of play situations. We describe how to use these more General Signs throughout this guide.

Signing Smart Starter Signs

Below is a list of eighteen suggested Starter Signs. There are many more possible signs to choose from in the *Signing Smart* Illustrated Dictionary; see Appendix 1, page 192. Feel free to replace any of the signs below with others that are more relevant, useful, or interesting to you or your child. Just remember to choose *some* General Signs *as well as* a balance between See A Lot / Do A Lot and Highly Motivating Signs.

Highly Motivating Signs allow children to talk about the things they find fascinating. They are often the signs children sign back first. Here, nine-month-old Naia signs **LIGHT** to initiate a conversation with her mom about something that captivates her.

Suggested General Starter Signs

Choose at least two from each category. These are signs that you can use in almost any interaction to easily create *Signing Smart* Opportunities around topics of interest or importance. Please see the *Signing Smart* Illustrated Dictionary on page 192 for more.

SEE A LOT/DO A LOT SIGNS

HELP
Bottom palm helps lift other hand

MORE
Tap fingertips repeatedly, as if adding two things together

WHAT
Shake hands back and forth in natural questioning gesture

HIGHLY MOTIVATING SIGNS

BALL
Bounce curved hands toward each other, in the shape of a ball

LIGHT
LIGHT-ON
LIGHT-OFF
L: Repeatedly close and open fingers, like light rays shining
ON: Open hand once
OFF: Close hand once

MUSIC
Swing hand over forearm repeatedly, as if conducting

Suggested See A Lot / Do A Lot Starter Signs

Add in two to four of these "parent-oriented" signs to help you meet your child's needs while signing.

BED
Tap side of head with palm, as if laying head on pillow

FINISH/ ALL-DONE
Flip hands over, as if dropping something you're done with

DRINK
Tip "cup" hand to mouth

MILK
Open and close fist, as if milking a cow

EAT/FOOD
E: Bring imaginary food to mouth
F: Tap hand to mouth repeatedly

WHERE
Move finger in a pendulum motion, as if asking if it's here or there

Suggested Highly Motivating Starter Signs

Add in two to four of these "child-oriented" signs to motivate your child to sign back.

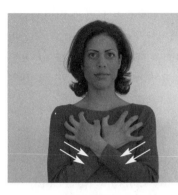

BEAR
Scratch chest
repeatedly

DOG
Slap leg, then
bring fingers to
a snap, as if
calling a dog
to you

CAR/DRIVE
C: "Steer" your
car
D: Stationary
"steering"
hands go for-
ward

FAN
Trace the way
fan blades
circle

CAT
Fingers pinch
and trace
"cat's
whiskers" out-
wards

KEY
Twist "key"
hand in palm,
as if turning a
key in a lock

SIGNING SMART MILESTONES

There are few greater joys than seeing your child reach the first milestone—her first sign. However, most parents (mistakenly) assume that once their child produces her first sign, life will get easier instantaneously. Unfortunately, they are only half correct—life will get easier, but not instantaneously. Remember, the definition of "development" is "change over time." This means that children who have one sign will *slowly and gradually* build up their number of signs until the next two milestones are reached—the Sign Cluster and the Language Explosion.

THE SIGN CLUSTER

Somewhere between five and ten signs, children hit what we call the Sign Cluster—the solidification of a critical mass of signs (used however inconsistently), after which sign vocabulary increases more rapidly and children begin combining signs and/or words into short sentences. *Our research has shown that how soon a child will sign back and when she will hit her Sign Cluster is greatly influenced by the family's use of Signing Smart strategies and techniques.* In general, parents can anticipate their child reaching the Sign Cluster four to twelve weeks after their child's first sign ap-

pears. Some *Signing Smart* children will reach their Sign Cluster as early as six months of age; others will reach it at twelve months or later. However, our research has shown that, on average, *Signing Smart* children hit their Sign Cluster when they are eight to ten months old. In one example, a family began attending a *Signing Smart* class when their son was only five months old. Despite the fact that he was not yet sitting up, within two weeks of using *Signing Smart* strategies, he had two signs. Shortly thereafter, at only six months, he had five signs and was nearing his Sign Cluster at a remarkably young age.

THE LANGUAGE EXPLOSION

Our recent research indicates that there is a third milestone in young children's language development—the Language Explosion. The Language Explosion is the time when children's spoken and signed vocabulary increases *in conjunction with* a notable increase in cognitive skills and social awareness and determination. It is after the Language Explosion is reached that parents feel as if they are communicating with a whole new child—their child picks up signs effortlessly (sometimes three to ten signs/words in a single day!), initiates and extends conversations, signs much more spontaneously, and seems more determined in his communication. If a child is older than twelve months when he reaches his Sign Cluster, it will often seem as if he simultaneously reaches his Language Explosion. If a child is under twelve months when he reaches his Sign Cluster, it will take a number of weeks before he then reaches his Language Explosion. On average, *Signing Smart* children reach the developmental "turning point" marked by the Language Explosion between eleven and thirteen months.

How quickly a child reaches his Language Explosion is again influenced by when a family begins *Signing Smart,* as well as how often the family uses *Signing Smart* techniques. It is through the Four Keys to *Signing Smart* Success that children are engaged in interactions that facilitate the coordination of the two necessary components of the Language Explosion—the vocabulary component and the social/cognitive component (the development of conceptual understanding and social awareness/determination).

Once children reach their Language Explosion, the doors to extensive communication are flung wide open and children will learn the vast majority of the signs they see, many after only a single showing. In fact, we hear time and again how amazed parents are to see their child sign something they themselves have not signed in a long time! And once children reach the Language Explosion, parents often will see their child's burst in sign vocabulary followed relatively quickly by a burst in spoken vocabulary as well.

Signing Smart Time Frame for Signing by Your Child

LESS THAN 8 MONTHS OLD:	8–12 MONTHS OLD:	13 MONTHS–2 YEARS:
• Families that begin *Signing Smart* with their less-than-8-month-old child can anticipate that their child will sign back (on average) in about 4–12 weeks.	• Families that begin *Signing Smart* with their 8–12-month-old child can anticipate that their child will sign back (on average) in about 2–8 weeks.	• Families that begin *Signing Smart* with their 13-month to 2-year-old child can anticipate that their child will sign back (on average) in about 1 day to 6 weeks.
• In fact, these children can learn to use over 40 signs by the time they are 1 year old. Many of these children also begin to combine signs well before their first birthday.	• Again, once the child reaches his Sign Cluster, many new signs and the beginnings of short signed and/or spoken sentences will appear. The child's Language Explosion is soon to follow.	• These children generally reach their Sign Cluster and Language Explosion relatively quickly. Very often, their sign use is followed by a burst of spoken words as well.

Signing Smart will significantly shorten the time frame for signing back, and for reaching both the Sign Cluster and the Language Explosion:

The time frame for signing back is influenced by more than just chronological age or the amount of time an individual family has been signing. A family's use of the *Signing Smart* Start and the Four Keys to *Signing Smart* Success plays a large role in the length of time it takes for a child to reach all three milestones. In one example, a thirteen-month-old's family had been signing for about eight months with small increments of success. *Within a single hour* after learning *only a small handful* of the *Signing Smart* techniques we describe in this guide, the little boy began using three new signs and four new words—hitting his Sign Cluster and his Language Explosion simultaneously!

THE FOUR KEYS TO *SIGNING SMART* SUCCESS

Our research indicates that, in addition to the *Signing Smart* Start, using the Four Keys to *Signing Smart* Success will not only greatly reduce the wait for signing back but will also allow your child's sign and word development to become as prolific as possible, as quickly as possible. In this section, we introduce you to the Four Keys, which will be described in more detail in the "Go" and "On your Way" sections of this chapter. As you use your Chosen Signs (whether they be your Starter Signs or additions to this collection), keep these Keys in mind:

The Four Keys to *Signing Smart* Success

1. Create *Signing Smart* Opportunities

2. Bring signs into your child's world

3. Recognize your child's versions of signs

4. Facilitate *both* early communication and long-term learning

1. Creating *Signing Smart* Opportunities

- Children learn best in interactions that are "meaning-full." We have developed all of the activities in this book with this understanding in mind. *Signing Smart* Opportunities are developmentally appropriate experiences that allow parents and children to interact in playful, engaging ways that are also conducive to learning. This entire guide contains endless possibilities for creating *Signing Smart* Opportunities at home.

- Through recognizing, capitalizing on, and creating these *Signing Smart* Opportunities, parents are able to notice the many ways their child already initiates interactions; respond to their child's unintentional movements in meaningful ways; make interactions more conversational; introduce signs at moments their child is most primed for learning; and structure interactions that foster intimacy, concept development, and language skill. This may seem like a tall order, but for those armed with the many *Signing Smart* tools in this book, it will quickly and easily become second nature. We describe these interactions more thoroughly beginning on page 20.

- Common characteristics of *Signing Smart* Opportunities:

  * *Variety:* In creating or responding to such Opportunities, parents are able to use their Chosen Signs in various contexts, emphasizing the *quality* of the interactions over the *quantity* of signs.

  * *Motivation:* The more motivated your child is to communicate, the sooner he or she will sign back. Motivation is

strongly influenced by *Signing Smart* techniques, including this first Key.

  * *Invitation:* Part of *Signing Smart* is learning how to provide your child with Opportunities to *participate* in interactions. Equally important is learning to notice and respond to the ways your child will "invite" *you* into interaction with *her.*

Seventeen-month-old Lincoln's mom taps his hand and invites him into an interaction around the toy that interests him, seamlessly creating a *Signing Smart* Opportunity.

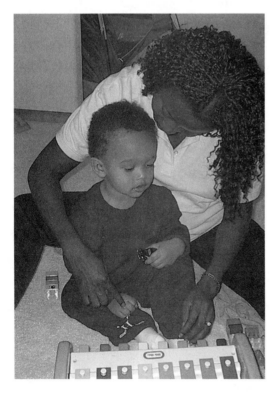

2. Bringing Signs into Your Child's World

- An important aspect of *Signing Smart* is helping parents become partners in their child's development. One effective way to do this is to work *with* your child's developmentally appropriate desire to explore her world and bring your signs *to her.* In fact, she will learn signs faster and appreciate their usefulness more readily if you employ *some* of the *Signing Smart* Attention-Getters and Adaptation Strategies (descriptions beginning on page 28) that will allow signing, interacting, and exploring to go hand in hand. We have developed all of the at-home activities in this book to make this Key easy and fun.

Recognizing your child's version of signs is the Third Key to *Signing Smart* Success. Here, seventeen-month-old Lincoln signs his own version of **PLEASE,** asking his mom to play more music with him.

The Second Key to *Signing Smart* Success is bringing signs into your child's world. Here, ten-month-old Gracie feels her mother sign **BATH** on her, using hand-over-hand signing, while she *also* sees a classmate's mother's sign.

3. Recognizing Your Child's Versions of Signs

- For many parents, developing their *Signing Smart* eyes—noticing their child's early signs—*seeing signs as signs*—is a challenge at first. When we hear stories of families who say signing "didn't work," this is one of the first things we look into, as it is possible that a child is signing but the parents aren't "seeing" the signs. With the *Signing Smart* tools we provide in this guide, you will be well prepared to recognize and respond to your child's earliest signs.

4. Facilitating *Both* Early Communication and Long-Term Learning

- *Signing Smart* will give you the tools to integrate signs into all kinds of interactions, which will foster *both* early communication and long-term learning. Through maintaining the balance of See A Lot / Do A Lot (parent-oriented) and Highly Motivating (child-oriented) Signs, you will be best able to use signs and *Signing Smart* techniques to facilitate interactions, support vocabulary and conceptual development, and promote long-term learning. At the same time, using both kinds of signs in all kinds of interactions encourages and enables your child to share with you the many things she finds fascinating and important in her world—a critical component in promoting the continued development of intimacy and bonding between you and your child.

SIGNING SMART: GO!

At this point, you may be raring to go but wondering how you are going to take advantage of the Four Keys to *Signing Smart* Success. The first thing to remember is that *Signing Smart* does not mean signing every time you say the corresponding words—not by any stretch! *Signing Smart* success is about the *kinds of signs you use* and the *kinds of interactions and experiences in which you use them.*

Key 1: Creating *Signing Smart* Opportunities

Children learn best in interactions stemming from their own interests. When parents create or respond to *Signing Smart* Opportunities, they work *with* their child's interests, engaging her in two-way communication.

RESPONDING TO CHILDREN'S NON-SIGNED "INVITATIONS"

Young children have many ways of letting us know they are eager to interact. They may stare intently at an object of interest, they may move toward a toy or person, they may start manipulating an object, or they may exhibit a marked change in affect (e.g., from happy to neutral, or the reverse). *Signing Smart* teaches parents to view all these behav-

iors as invitations to create *Signing Smart* Opportunities. Remember, you need not feel obligated to turn *all* of these situations into *Signing Smart* Opportunities; just notice that they all *could* be, and then take advantage of *some* of them by engaging your child with a quick comment supported by a sign.

So, a parent may choose to create a *Signing Smart* Opportunity when her child crawls over to her ("Oh, you want **MOMMY**? Let's **PLAY BALL**."), throws the ball he's been mouthing ("You threw your **BALL**, are you **ALL-DONE EATING** it?"), looks up from playing with her feet and smiles ("**WHAT** are

Signing Smart Opportunities are simply moments that present themselves where parents integrate one of their Chosen Signs. Here, thirteen-month-old Eli's mom notices that he's looking at the fire truck, so she engages him by picking up the truck and asking him **WHAT** he sees.

you doing with your feet? Are you **PLAYING** with your toes?"), or topples over and starts fussing ("**WHAT** happened? Do you need **HELP**?"). Will a parent do all of these things in any given interaction? Absolutely not! The parent would be overwhelmed, the child overstimulated, and none of the chores would get done. However, by creating such *Signing Smart* Opportunities from *some* of these situations *at some points* during the day, parents tell their child that they notice his invitations to communicate, and take advantage of them by engaging him with some of their Chosen Signs. The child, in turn, gets to see relevant signs during moments in which he is most primed for learning and is eager to be engaged by his parents.

Signing Smart strategies will arm you with many tools to be able to sign in any situation, even with just a handful of signs. Here, seventeen-month-old Lincoln's mom uses Conceptual Grouping to extend her vocabulary, interacting with him about his xylophone while signing **MUSIC**.

SITUATION: Parent sees her child happily playing with a xylophone.

In this situation, parents may feel stumped because the sign for "xylophone" is not among their Chosen Signs. Parents may wonder if they should simply forgo signing in this situation or if they should try to take advantage of their child's good mood by bringing over a toy that they *do* know the sign for. But because *Signing Smart* is flexible, parents can use signs they already know to continue to engage their child with her chosen toy! Even if you do not know *the* sign, you can use *a* sign to create a *Signing Smart* Opportunity.

Signing Smart Opportunity—Option 1: Instead of using the sign "xylophone," draw on another related sign you know. For instance, say, "I see you playing with your xylophone. You are making wonderful **MUSIC**! Can Mommy make **MUSIC** with you as well?" For more on the *Signing Smart* strategy of "plugging in" related signs, which we call Conceptual Grouping, see pages 58 and 70.

Signing Smart Opportunity—Option 2: If you can't remember or don't know the sign for **MUSIC**, plug in a more General Sign. So, for instance, ask your child **WHAT** he is playing with and then fill in the answer (xylophone) verbally; or ask him if he wants **MORE** music and begin to bang away; or comment on the fact that he is **EATING** the mallet and ask him if it is yummy. When you notice his interest waning, ask him if he's **FINISHED** and if he would like to play with his **BALL** now. Regardless of his choice at that point, think of the wonderful interaction(s) you had with him about the thing that was most interesting in his world during those few moments.

In addition to responding to your child's "invitation" (object manipulation), *Signing Smart* allows you to extend the exchange by inviting him to participate even more. Notice how the above interchanges move beyond simply labeling the object, and, in this way, enable you to engage your child in rich and stimulating interactions. Using a single, more generalized sign opens the door to enriched conversations about anything under the sun. More important than the extent of your vocabulary are the *engaging contexts* in which you and your child are interacting—contexts in which signs are seen, internalized, understood, and eventually used by both of you.

RESPONDING TO CHILDREN'S NATURAL MOVEMENTS AND BABBLING

Recent research conducted at Franklin and Marshall College indicates that when a mother responds to her baby's random babbles by smiling at, moving closer to, and touching him, the child's vocalizations become more advanced.[8] In a similar way, creat-ing *Signing Smart* Opportunities from your child's nonintentional movements *or* babbles will benefit both sign *and* word development! The beauty of *Signing Smart* Opportunities is that they exist whether or not children's movements or vocalizations are actually deliberate.

For instance, when your child flaps his arms up and down—even for no apparent reason—we call that a *Signing Smart* Opportunity. There are several *possible* signs this movement may resemble (e.g., **BALL, FINISH, RAIN**), and when you react to even seemingly random movements in meaningful ways, your child will come to understand that his hands can convey meaning. Here, creating a *Signing Smart* Opportunity involves deciding on a *possible* meaning for your child's movements—if your child flaps his arms happily, you might respond by initiating an interaction around a **BALL** you can play with together; if your child makes the same type of "flapping" movement while fussing, you might respond by commenting on how your child is **FINISHED** playing and bring him over to his high chair for a snack. In this way, the same unintentional movement might "initiate" different interactions, because you as the parent choose to reinforce different signs, depending on how you read your child's emotions and interests. As you can see, there is no "right" way to create a *Signing Smart* Opportunity.

You can also create *Signing Smart* Oppor-

Michelle notices twelve-month-old Elle (not a thumb sucker) put her thumb in her mouth. Taking advantage of this *Signing Smart* Opportunity, Michelle asks her if she wants a **DRINK** from her bottle.

tunities in response to completely accidental hand positions. For instance, if you notice your child sucking his fist or thumb (especially if he is not usually a thumb sucker), this is a *Signing Smart* Opportunity to reinforce his movements as a *possible* sign for **DRINK** or **BOTTLE**.

We want to stress that we are *not* suggesting that a child's meaningless movements are signs. What we are saying is that our *responses* to these meaningless movements will help turn them *into* meaningful and purposeful signs *over time*. Note that the same can be said for reinforcing your child's "meaningless" vocalizations. When we hear our child say "bu-bu-bu," even if we *know* it is not intentional, we instinctively reinforce the word as "bye-bye." Doing so allows your child to more quickly turn that "random" sound pattern into a purposeful word. By creating these kinds of *Signing Smart* Opportunities, parents

allow children to "initiate" and participate in rich and meaningful interactions from the start—*even before children are signing back.*

SITUATION: Child excitedly flaps his arms up and down for no apparent reason.

Initially, parents may feel silly assigning meaning to these natural movements. Or they may feel comfortable commenting on their child's excitement but be reluctant to treat the movements as a "sign." Remember, we are not trying to convince you that these natural movements *are* signs. Rather, we are asking you to interact with your child as if these movements are *precursors* to signs.

Signing Smart Opportunity—Option 1: Engage your child with words, signs, actions, and experiences around the *possible* meaning of his movements—in this case, maybe **BALL**. Thus, a *Signing Smart* response might be "**BALL**? Are you saying **BALL** with your hands? Let's go get your **BALL**—great idea!" The parent would then play ball with his child, continuing the interaction the child "started" through his accidental hand movements.

While it is the *parent* who mapped meaning onto the child's meaningless movements, this does not diminish the vital information the *child* received. In creating these *Signing Smart* Opportunities, the child learns that his hands can (and in fact do!) convey ideas that initiate interactions and lead to getting objects or having experiences.

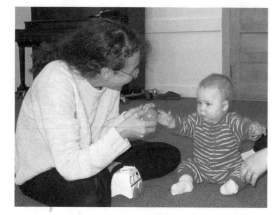

Kegan had a natural hand-flapping motion that his mother consistently reinforced as the sign **BALL**. Just before he turned seven months, he began using the sign **BALL** intentionally. Here, seven-month-old Kegan flaps his arms to initiate a conversation with Michelle about the **BALL**.

Signing Smart Opportunity—Option 2: If you notice your child is eagerly watching your pet dog while simultaneously making arm-flapping motions that could be the sign **BALL**, you may choose to *go with your child's interest* while still commenting on and reinforcing his use of signlike natural movements. Therefore, you might say, "I see you saying **BALL** with your hands. You're looking at the **DOGGIE**, woof, woof! Let's go say 'hi' to the **DOG**."

Again, there is no "right" way to create a *Signing Smart* Opportunity—experiences such as this one will multiply and give your child the message that you are attuned to his natural movements *as well as* his interests.

Over time he will come to refine his hand motions; but until then, he is still experiencing the power that his natural movements have to influence his world—both in getting your attention and in leading him to interesting interactions. Notice again that these interchanges do much more than simply label objects—they include discussions, interactions, and experiences.

RESPONDING TO SIGNED/SPOKEN INVITATIONS

Perhaps the most obvious *Signing Smart* Opportunity to create is the one in which your child clearly uses a sign/word in an appropriate situation, such as when she crawls over to her high chair and signs **EAT**. In this case the interchange will likely proceed without a hitch, especially if you use *Signing Smart* tools to enrich your interaction.

SITUATION: Your child looks up at the lamp and excitedly signs **LIGHT**.

In situations such as this one, parents will often take advantage of Key 3 (Recognizing your child's signs) and comment briefly on the **LIGHT** their child noticed. Brief interactions like this are important and necessary—they allow your child to continue interacting with the world on his own terms, and they let you continue your chores after a brief interchange. However, when you have the time to engage more fully with your child, it is in moments like this one that a great deal of learning and play can happen.

Signing Smart Opportunity: You excitedly say to your child, "I see you signing **LIGHT** with your hand. **WHAT** happens when I turn the **LIGHT-OFF**?" You then proceed to "play with" the lamp, interacting with your child over the very thing that she told you interested her at that exact moment. With these behaviors, you not only recognized your child's sign (Key 3) but you also extended the interaction and created a learning environment through experiences, words, and a balance of signs (Keys 1 and 4). And, if you used any *Signing Smart* Attention-Getters or Adaptation Strategies (Key 2) (such as signing **LIGHT** in the rays of the light), you will have hit all Four Keys to *Signing Smart* Success in a single interchange. *This is a wonderful example of the flexibility and usefulness of Signing Smart techniques.* And, what a rich interaction your child just experienced on so many levels: cognitive—the cause and effect of flipping the lamp switch; social/emotional—when I communicate, Mommy responds to and interacts with me; and linguistic—I've seen and heard lots of signs and words that I'm coming to understand and use myself.

While we have emphasized the fact that *Signing Smart* Opportunities are often short but rich interactions, do not let this discourage you from extending these interactions if your child's interest and your time permit. So if your child is engaged in your game with the lights and you have the time and energy to take the interaction further, by all means, do so. One way is by going on a **LIGHT** walk, as suggested on page 90 or 146. Let these interactions go as far as both you and your child can take them, but do not measure their success on length alone.

Unfortunately, not all signed/spoken invitations are as clear as we might like. Children often use signs (and words) very differently

Sometimes a child's sign does not fit the situation. *Signing Smart* in this context involves responding to your child's *intent*, even if that contradicts the sign she uses. Here, eleven-month-old Rachel tells her mother about the rabbit she is holding by signing **DUCK**.

than we do. Sometimes parents are unsure how to respond—do we work from what our child signed or from what we think she really meant? Our research has shown that we make the most of a potential *Signing Smart* Opportunity when we work from what our child *means,* while still acknowledging and applauding what was actually *signed.*

SITUATION: Parent sees her child sign **LIGHT** while looking at the vase of flowers on the table.

Families often bring stories such as this one to our play classes and workshops. In this type of situation, parents cannot help but wonder whether their child is confused, whether they were just imagining that their child understood, or whether they were just imagining that their child was signing purposefully. Trust us, everyone feels this way sometimes. Even we, as developers of the program, have gone through these "crises of faith" about our children's abilities/intentions. We encourage you to overcome your own doubts and give your child the credit she so richly deserves, while creating a *Signing Smart* Opportunity in the process.

Signing Smart Opportunity: Recognize your child's attempt, but then work from her *interest* rather than her sign. For instance, tell her, "Yes, you're telling me with your hands; you're signing **LIGHT**. But I see you looking at the **FLOWERS**. You really like those **FLOWERS**." Don't know the sign for

FLOWER? Say, "**WHAT** are you looking at? I see you looking at the flowers. Do you want **MORE** of the flowers? Let's go see those flowers some **MORE** [as you lift your child]." If you discover your child is captivated by flowers, add **FLOWER** to your set of Chosen Signs.

GOING BEYOND BASIC LABELING

An important difference between *Signing Smart* Opportunities and other types of interactions is the level of engagement between the parent and child. While an Opportunity may be short, it still engages and stimulates in meaningful ways. Take a look at the situation below and see the richness, intimacy, and learning that come with simple *Signing Smart* techniques, which can take any interchange far beyond basic pointing and naming.

SITUATION: Parent sees child playing with a horse.

Basic pointing and naming: "Oh, you have a **HORSE**. Can you say **HORSE**? Look at Mommy. That's a **HORSE**. Carlos, sweetie, look at Mommy. That's a **HORSE**, say **HORSE**."

The only information the child is getting is that the object he is playing with is called a horse.

Basic pointing and naming with a Signing Smart invitation: "Oh, you have a **HORSE**. Can you say **HORSE**? That's a **HORSE**.

Mommy is saying **HORSE** with her hands. Can you say **HORSE** with your hands? Carlos does it, Carlos says **HORSE** with his hands."

This basic interaction goes beyond the previous one in that it invites the child into the conversation through signs. However, additional *Signing Smart* techniques can bring much more.

Signing Smart Opportunities in action:

Animating the interaction with pretend play:

- "**WHAT** are you **PLAYING** with? Do you have a **HORSE**? 'Neigh' [Language Clustering] says the **HORSE**."

- "Look! You have a **HORSE**. **WHAT** is your **HORSE** doing? Is it **JUMPING**? **MOMMY** is making the **HORSE JUMP**. Can *you* make the **HORSE JUMP**?"

Fostering intimacy:

- "The **HORSE** is giving you **KISSES** [with Language Clustering]. Hee, hee, are you **EATING** your **HORSE** now?"

- "Who else **KISSES**? Your **BEAR**! Your **BEAR** is giving you **KISSES**! Oops. **WHERE** did **MOMMY HIDE** your **BEAR**? Can you **LOOK-FOR** it? Do you need **HELP**?"

Additional ways to extend the interaction:

- "Oh, you have a **HORSE**. Are you **PLAYING** with that **HORSE**? Can **MOMMY PLAY** too?"

- "You have a **HORSE** [parent hides horse]. **WHERE'S** the **HORSE**? She's **HIDING**! Can you **LOOK-FOR** the **HORSE**? **SURPRISE**! You can have a **TURN**. Do you want to **PLAY** with the **HORSE** some **MORE**?"

- "Let's **LOOK-FOR MORE HORSES**! Oh, here is a **BOOK** with **HORSES** in it. We can read the **BOOK**."

While you will only engage your child in a smattering of such interchanges, and any given interchange may include fewer signs, *even the most basic of interactions can be easily made more three-dimensional and meaningful to your child with almost no extra work.*

SIGNING SMART OPPORTUNITIES SUMMED UP

Remember, *Signing Smart* is not a list of prescribed responses for every one of a hundred possible scenarios. It doesn't involve signing all day, or dancing around your child and bringing over balls, or even engaging him every time he seems interested in something. Understanding *Signing Smart* Opportunities helps you to realize *possible* times and *possible* ways to interact. It is not the number of signs you use—or even the number of times you sign—in any given day that will have the greatest impact on your communication with your child.

Signing Smart creates short but meaningful interactions at various points, integrating select and relevant signs where comfortable and feasible. It teaches you to *notice the possibilities* and use new eyes and new tools to *enrich what you are already doing.* The fact that *Signing Smart* Opportunities *can* happen in many different contexts simply means you have the *opportunity* to create such interactions one hundred times a day. It does not mean you *should* do so. But what a relief to know that any missed opportunity only means another will pop up in short order. Believe us when we say there are *whole days* that go by when we do not sign with our own babies. Life is just like that! So we have developed a program that reflects and allows for the realities of real-time parenting!

Key 2: Bringing Signs into Your Child's World

By now you are armed with your six to twelve Starter Signs and with an understanding of the multitude of *possible Signing Smart* Opportunities in which to use them. However, many parents wonder how to best get their child to look at them and to see their signs. Have you ever tried to get an active

Signing Smart Attention-Getters and Adaptation Strategies

- *Verbal:*
  - ✓ Make attention-getting noises
  - ✓ *Signing Smart* Language Clustering

- *Nonverbal:*
  - ✓ Touch or pat your child
  - ✓ Vary proximity
  - ✓ Sensory attention-getting
  - ✓ Bring object to you
  - ✓ "Tell me with your hands"

- *Using signs to get attention:*
  - ✓ *Signing Smart* Baby-Talk
  - ✓ Hand-over-hand signing
  - ✓ Sign on your child's body
  - ✓ Sign in your child's line of sight
  - ✓ Make two-handed signs one-handed
  - ✓ Sign on an object of interest
  - ✓ Change the angle of the sign

fourteen-month-old to glance over at you, let alone to stare you in the face, so he can see you sign **BALL** or **LIGHT**?

Take heart and know that once your child understands the power of *Signing Smart*, she will often look to you for these visual highlights. But discovering the wonders of her world is one of your child's most pressing and developmentally appropriate jobs, and the worst thing that you can do is to make her choose between looking at you for signs and exploring her environment.

To make signing and interacting as successful as possible as quickly as possible, *Signing Smart* has developed a great number of Attention-Getters and Adaptation Strategies for hearing families. These give children access to sign information without their ever having to stop what they are doing to look up at the signs. We call this *bringing signs into your child's world,* and it is the Second Key to *Signing Smart* Success. Rest assured, by using even *a few* of the following *Signing Smart* strategies, both you and your child will feel the joy and success of signing without the frustration. In short order these strategies will become second nature to you! *And once you have your child's attention, don't forget to extend the Signing Smart Opportunity beyond basic labeling: Engage your child with words, actions, or experiences that involve the object that holds his attention!*

SIGNING SMART ATTENTION-GETTERS: VERBAL

Diversify your verbal requests for attention (beyond just calling your child's name) by incorporating some of these *Signing Smart* strategies, developed to capture your child's attention through creative use of your voice.

Make Attention-Getting Noises
One way to do this is to play up the "silly

factor." No child can resist turning to Daddy when he suddenly makes a strange noise (e.g., "doo-wop") or couples a funny sound with an exaggerated movement or sign!

Signing Smart Language Clustering
One wonderfully effective verbal strategy is what we call *Signing Smart* Language Clustering. Put simply, Language Clustering entails joining a word with a sound and with a sign, and it is a strategy we developed for many learning and interaction forums. To use

Signing Smart Language Clustering is a wonderful way to get your child's attention. Here, fourteen-month-old Alma enjoys watching her mother combine two *Signing Smart* strategies: signing **EAT** directly on the puppet while also making eating sounds to further engage Alma in the interaction.

this technique for attention-getting, exaggerate and extend the sound of the object you're talking and signing about, to capture your child's interest and attention. For instance, make an exaggerated "rrrrroaring" sound for a lion; "beeeeep-beeeeping" for a car; a high-pitched "Hi, I love you" for a doll, and so on. These sounds are compelling attention-getters for your child and are sure not only to draw his eye gaze over to you but also to initiate or extend wonderfully playful interactions.

SIGNING SMART ATTENTION-GETTERS: NONVERBAL

Another *Signing Smart* strategy is to use nonverbal means of getting your child's attention before you sign. The more you vary the ways you ask your child for his attention, the more likely it is that he will not only give it to you but also realize what he gains by doing so.

Touch or pat your child

The most basic nonverbal *Signing Smart* Attention-Getters are those that involve a gentle tactile signal. Touch, tap, or rub your child's arm, leg, cheek, or foot. When your child looks over to you, take advantage of the *Signing Smart* Opportunity you have created.

Vary Proximity

A simple but highly effective nonverbal *Signing Smart* Attention-Getter is to vary your proximity to your child. Moving closer to—or moving away from—your child is sure to grab her attention and cause her to look at you. This creates the perfect *Signing Smart* Opportunity: Initiate an interaction about an object of interest by using a sign.

Sensory Attention-Getting

Another wonderful *Signing Smart* Attention-Getter involves using a sensory quality of the object itself to get your child's attention. For instance, turn on the fan and let the blowing wind entice your child to look over. Turn a light on and off until your child notices. Use the squeaker of a toy to get your child's attention, without *you* having to utter

Mom brings the toy dog up near her face, catching twelve-month-old Elle's attention. She also ends the snapping part of the sign **DOG** up in Elle's line of sight, where she knows her daughter can see both the toy and her sign at the same time.

a sound. This strategy is a wonderful one to combine with others, such as signing on the object, described below.

Bring the object to your body or face

Another *Signing Smart* nonverbal strategy is to bring an object that is holding your child's interest toward your body or face, drawing his attention to you while allowing him to continue looking at the object. Once his eyes are on you, sign, but be sure to return the interesting object to him afterward.

"Tell me with your hands"

One very effective *Signing Smart* technique is a combination of both verbal and nonverbal cues. Tap your child's hand and encourage her: "Tell me with your hands," or ask, "Can you make your hands say **LIGHT**?" You can then either sign away or employ another *Signing Smart* technique, such as signing on your child's body or using hand-over-hand signing (see below).

The "tell me with your hands" technique is one of the most successful *Signing Smart* strategies because it gives children a clear means of understanding what we are asking them to do: use their hands to communicate. When you open the door to, and specifically encourage, "alternative" communication, many children tune in eagerly and quickly begin to sign back.

You can extend the effectiveness of this strategy by adding, "Daddy's hands are saying **LIGHT**. Can Rakeesh's hands say **LIGHT**? Ra-

keesh does it. Rakeesh says **LIGHT** with his hands [as you tap them]." From there take advantage of the *Signing Smart* Opportunity you have created. Such interchanges not only help *bring signs into your child's world* but also make the early stages of learning more interactive.

SIGNING SMART ADAPTATION STRATEGIES: USING SIGNS TO GET YOUR CHILD'S ATTENTION

Based on our knowledge of the way Deaf[9] parents interact with their Deaf children, *Signing Smart* has developed a great number of strategies to help hearing families work within their child's developmental level, follow their child's lead, and literally move signs into their child's world. Using real ASL signs gives you great flexibility to adapt and exaggerate signs to your advantage in each of the ways described as follows.

SIGNING SMART BABY-TALK

While Deaf adults use ASL "baby talk" when signing with young children, *Signing Smart* adapts this technique for use within hearing families. To do this, make movements somewhat bigger and more repetitive than one would in adult sign conversation. The larger movements attract and maintain children's attention; the repeated movements allow children to see the sign produced a number of times in a very short period. An additional benefit of this strategy is that, by repeating a single sign throughout an entire spoken sentence, you highlight that one concept, making it easier for your child to attend to and learn it. For example, asking, "Do you need **HELP** pulling your bear out?" with repetitions of **HELP** spanning the entire spoken question, focuses your child's language-learning energy on the sign/concept **HELP**.

Hand-over-hand signing gives your child a kinesthetic feeling of how a sign is produced. Here, Malena's mom notices seven-month-old Charlie's fascination with her **SHOES** and helps him sign "for himself" using this technique.

Hand-over-hand signing

Another wonderful *Signing Smart* Adaptation Strategy is to move your child's hands/arms to help him get a feel for the sign. The goal here is a very gross movement—a clapping for **MORE**, a hand bumping the mouth for **BIRD**, an arm lifting for **LIGHT**. Developmentally, children experience these parent-guided movements as "their own" and can therefore readily learn the basic movement patterns necessary for sign production through this technique. However, do not try to place your child's fingers into position or make them move as the sign might (e.g., opening and closing the fingers for **DUCK**) as this is too difficult and frustrating for young children. In addition, when you help your child create fine movements, he is more likely to become a passive participant in the signing. Why? His fine motor skills won't be developed enough to form very specific, smaller movements until weeks, months, and maybe even years into the future; therefore, manipulating his hands to create particular fine motor patterns makes him dependent on *you* to make the sign *for him*. On the other hand, because he will be able to produce his own rough version of the sign(s) relatively quickly, when you help him experience the general way signs feel, you empower him to make the sign himself.

You can extend this *Signing Smart* strategy by combining it with the "Tell me with your hands" technique described previously. For example, as you clap your child's hands together, say to him, "Do you see the **SHOES**? *Michael's* hands are saying **SHOES**. Good work!"

Some children find it frustrating to have their hands held and manipulated. Some re-

One very effective way to bring signs into your child's world is to sign on your child's body, allowing him to feel the sign while looking at the interesting object. Here, Dad signs **HAT** directly on sixteen-month-old Liam, who has Down syndrome, enabling Liam to feel the sign while looking at and enjoying the book they are reading together.

Moving signs into your child's sight makes the learning process easier. Here, five-month-old Luke is still learning to sit, but has no trouble seeing and learning his mother's sign **BALL**.

spond well on certain days and not others. If your child seems to tense up when you use this technique, choose from the other *Signing Smart* strategies instead.

Sign on your child's body

Instead of doing a sign on *your* body where your child may not be able to see it (e.g., when your child is sitting on your lap as you read a book together), do it on *her* body. This literally gives your child a feel for the sign. Don't worry that she won't see the exact hand shape or movement; she will *feel* it on her body and have plenty of opportunities to see it in other contexts. Signs that easily lend themselves to

being done directly on your child are those that you produce on your head or torso.

Sign in your child's line of sight

Another *Signing Smart* Adaptation Strategy is to move your sign so that it is in your child's line of vision (e.g., above the toy she's playing with or between her body and the object that holds her attention). If there is no specific object your child is watching, sign in front of *his* body. Any sign that is not "anchored" to your body can move into your child's line of sight.

Having one hand occupied does not have to stop you from *Signing Smart*. Here, Reyna signs **HELP** one-handed, using the top of the shape sorter as her "other hand." Doing so allows her to continue to hold thirteen-month-old Nadia and the toy, and allows Nadia to both see the sign and continue playing.

Signing on the object of interest is a wonderful *Signing Smart* strategy for reading. Here, Michelle signs **RABBIT** directly on the book eight-month-old Maya is transfixed by.

Make two-handed signs one-handed

Life with a baby will keep your hands busy. There will therefore be many times when you will only have one hand free for signing. There are two ways to make a two-handed sign into a one-handed sign. One is to simply drop the use of the other hand (e.g., **CAT**, **BATH**, or even **BALL**). While the sign may look different, it is still discernible to your child. For signs that *require* the other hand (e.g., **MORE**, **HELP**, or **BOOK**), brace the one hand you are signing with against something else—your child's body, the book you are reading, a toy you are holding, and so on.

Sign on an object of interest

Another way to move signs into your child's line of sight is to sign directly on an object that your child is looking at. If your child is looking at a doll, sign **DOLL** on the *doll's* nose. Or if you're pretending to feed a rubber ducky, sign **EAT** by tapping your hand on the *duck's* bill. One especially useful way to use this strategy is to sign directly on the book that your child is looking at. For instance, sign **COW** directly on the picture of the cow in the book. *Signing Smart* strategies such as this keep the learning cycle intact (your child sees the object, sees the sign, and

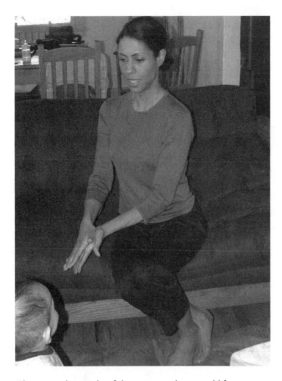

Changing the angle of the sign can be a real lifesaver. Here, thirteen-month-old Eli's mom reminds him to **CLEAN-UP**. Notice how she tips her hands downward while signing.

Getting down on your child's level will allow him to easily see and learn your signs. Here, Mom picks up on five-month-old Luke's natural hand movements and creates a *Signing Smart* Opportunity, reinforcing the "sign" while talking about the soft **CAT**.

hears the word *simultaneously*), thereby shortening the time frame for your child to sign back and develop a sizable vocabulary.

Change the angle of the sign/ Get down on your child's level

If you are standing above your child and sign the "regular" way, your child only sees the underside of the sign. If you tip your hands downward, your child can see the sign "head-on," in its most accessible form. For instance, if your child is sitting on the floor while you are standing, sign **CLEAN-UP** with your hands tilted downward toward him. Another strategy is to get down on your child's level when you sign.

Combining Strategies

Don't forget, you can combine these strategies for even greater flexibility. For instance, you can use the strategies one after the other, allowing you double the opportunity to capture and maintain your child's attention (e.g., repeat a sign on the object of interest and then on your child's body). Similarly, you can employ two or more *Signing Smart* strategies simultaneously, thereby ex-

Combining *Signing Smart* Strategies will not only deepen and extend interactions, but will also shorten the wait time for signing back. Here, Michelle signs **BIRD** on eight-month-old Maya while *simultaneously* inviting Maya to sign by tapping her hand and asking her to "tell Mommy with your hands." Maya then looks over to the cameraperson and tells him about the **BIRD** she sees in the book.

On Your Way

- Key 3: Recognizing your child's versions of signs

- Key 4: Facilitating both early communication and long-term learning

tending the means by which your child can access the sign information (e.g., signing on your child while engaging in Language Clustering, tapping his hands, and so on).

On Your Way with *Signing Smart*

With your *Signing Smart* Starter Signs and your chosen Attention-Getters and Adaptation Strategies, you are ready to be *on your way.* At this point you may wonder how you will know when your child is "really signing," when you should add onto your Starter Signs, and how you should integrate signs into your interactions, at present and in the future. The two final Keys to *Signing Smart* Success address these specific concerns.

Key 3: Recognizing Your Child's Versions of Signs

When parents ask us, "How will I know if something is *really* a sign, as opposed to a natural movement or a happy accident?" we tell them it doesn't matter! That is, whether or not your child *intended* to sign **DOG** will not change the *Signing Smart* Opportunity such a movement presents. That being said, it is important for parents to have tools to recognize "real signs."

As parents, we all know that when children begin talking, their early words will be approximations of the words they hear us say (e.g., "ba-ba" for "bottle," "da" for "dog"). The same is true for signing—children's early productions of any given sign (regardless of how many signs they may already have) will usually be their own version—an approximation of the sign we have been showing them. For this reason, part of *Signing Smart* is learning the "how" and "why" of children's sign "errors."

For instance, you will see your child produce some two-handed signs with only one hand. This happens because she has seen you produce so many signs with only one hand (when you carry her, for instance), or because her other hand is occupied with the object she is describing/playing with. Alternatively, your child will sometimes produce one-handed signs with both hands because she has less control over moving each hand individually (when both are free) than you do.

Being able to recognize and respond to your child's version of a sign will make a tremendous difference in how many signs your child will use and the time frame in

Be Alert to Children's Signs

Likely Hand shapes

- Loose index finger
- Loose fist
- Relaxed open hand

Likely Movements

- Jabbing/bouncing
- Clapping/colliding
- Bigger hitting/slapping

Likely Locations

- In front of the body
- On the head or body but not in the correct spot
- Beside the shoulder (instead of on the face/head)

Overlapping Movement Patterns

- Signs produced the same way that actually refer to different concepts (e.g., **MORE/SHOES**)

Be aware: Children will create their own versions of signs even if you try and give them "baby-friendly" signs.

- Instead of trying to "figure out" which signs will be "easy enough" for your child (really, they all will be), learn the *Signing Smart* strategies that will help you see and respond to whatever your child's version may be.

which she will use them. Knowing this, *Signing Smart* has researched and documented the predictable ways young children are likely to adapt any given sign's three main components.

Children will make these same "mistakes" no matter how much you try and "simplify" the signs that you show them. Rather than spending time and energy trying to figure out how to make a sign "easy enough" (when your child will then create his own version anyway), learning these *Signing Smart* strategies will help you see and respond to whatever his version may be, thereby speeding the process along.

CHILDREN'S SIGNS: LIKELY HAND SHAPES

Taking advantage of our training in both child development and sign language linguistics, we know that children's early signs are likely to be produced with one of three handshapes: a loose index finger, a loose fist, or a

Reyna knows just how to interpret seven-month-old Nadia's "clapping"—she is asking for **MORE** playtime with the squeaky mouse!

relaxed open hand. For example, children will often sign **MORE** with open palms (like clapping), **BIRD** or **DUCK** with an opening and closing of the fist (like waving), and so on.

CHILDREN'S SIGNS: LIKELY MOVEMENTS

Children are also likely to simplify the movements of signs, eliminate the movement completely, and/or make much more exaggerated motions than adults would. Their early signs are likely to be larger and less controlled than yours (jabbing, clapping, hitting, as opposed to tight, small movements). For example, **MORE** might be done with a bigger slapping motion than the light tapping you will do or with a stationary hand clasp, **PLEASE** with a large swiping as opposed to a crisp circling, and so on.

CHILDREN'S SIGNS: LIKELY LOCATIONS

Children also modify the locations of signs, but our research with *Signing Smart* children indicates that some locations are more likely to be altered than others. In general your child will most accurately produce locations for "free-floating" signs. For instance, **BALL** will likely be done in front of him, **LIGHT** up above his ears, and so on. For signs anchored on the body, you may see the general location preserved, but not the specific one. So, for example, **CRACKER** may in-

Part of *Signing Smart* is knowing what to look for in children's versions of signs. Here, nineteen-month-old Kylie signs and talks about an **ELEPHANT** by signing out by her shoulder—a very common approximation for face signs such as this.

volve a pounding on the opposite *hand* rather than the elbow, **BEAR** a swiping on the belly or legs rather than the chest, and so on.

The signs children are most likely to produce in an incorrect location are those that are supposed to be done on the face. This happens because anchoring her hand on her face *and* producing an accurate movement is a later developmental accomplishment. So a sign like **ELEPHANT** might be produced with a flipping motion beside the shoulder. Knowing this, *Signing Smart* parents can be on the lookout for other face signs like **DUCK** or **DRINK** to be produced free-floating, beside the shoulder. However, note that some children will accurately produce the location of face signs but will alter the hand shape and/or movement. For these children, **ELEPHANT** may look like a palm tap to the nose, **BIRD** or **DUCK** like a grab/bump of the mouth, and so on.

CHILDREN'S SIGNS: OVERLAPPING MOVEMENT PATTERNS

As a young child's vocabulary increases, her parents are likely to notice that she seems to be making the "exact same movement" to talk about very different things. This happens with spoken language as well, when a child uses the "exact same sounds" to talk about more than one thing (e.g., when a child says "ba-ba" to refer to both his bottle and blanket). At *Signing Smart,* we call these *sign* approximations Overlapping Movement Patterns. You may see your child signing "the same exact thing" when asking for **MORE** and when commenting on his **SHOES** (e.g., by clapping). In such contexts, our research has shown that children are not confused— they really do have two signs, one for each concept. The children just haven't yet developed the motor control to distinguish these two productions. Despite the fact that the adult productions of some of the following signs look very different, children's versions of these signs often look the same (i.e., they often show Overlapping Movement Patterns for the following sign groupings): **MORE/BALL/SHOES**; **DUCK/BIRD**; **PLEASE/BEAR/BLANKET/BATH/MONKEY**; **BED/PHONE**; **FROG/PIG**; **MUSIC/FINISH**. Please see the *Signing Smart* Illustrated Dictionary on page 192 for the adult forms of these signs. Techniques such as *Signing Smart* Body Leans, Assorted Cues, and Opposite-

How will I know it is *really* a sign?

It does not matter!

- Whether your child's hand movements are accidental or intentional, what is most important is the *interaction* you create when you respond. It teaches your child that such movements have meaning and initiate experiences.

Cues your child is making purposeful attempts to sign:

- If he makes "signlike" movements

  * while he is looking directly at you

  * while he is looking directly at his hands

  * while he is looking directly at the object

- If he produces a similar (approximate) movement over time

Don't forget that young children often sign *very inconsistently. Not signing* in one context says nothing about what she *may have signed* in another context.

Handed Signing (described later in this guide) will go a long way toward helping you help your child develop distinct movements for each of his signs over time. For more on similar-looking signs, see pages 64, 103, 149, and 169.

HOW WILL I KNOW IT IS REALLY A SIGN?

No parent is immune from sometimes wondering whether her child is "really signing." While of course we recommend that you interact with any signlike movement as if it is intentional, there are several cues that will help you know whether or not your child is "really" signing. One cue is her gaze: Is she looking directly at you? Is she looking intently at something? Is she focusing on her hands? Another cue is her use of the same "sign" over time. Has she repeated this same (approximate) movement at various points over a period of time? If you answer yes to any of these questions, you have a strong indication that your child is intentionally signing.

And while the above checklist can help, we know that we are all vulnerable to the confusion and uncertainty that arise from trying to "read" our own child's version of a sign or to understand his "confusing" signing. Even Michelle was in disbelief when—at not yet four-and-a-half months—Maya began banging her fist into the side of her head (too many times to be accidental) when her sister was nearby, in a very "signlike" attempt to produce the name sign Michelle and Scott had been using for Kylie (a "K" hand beside the eye). It was only through Maya's continued use of this same movement in enough ap-

Watching very young children sign can sometimes feel as if you are talking with Mr. Ed. It takes many months before children's signs become consistent, but that does not mean they are not "real," even early on. Here, four-and-a-half-month-old Maya signs **KYLIE** while watching her favorite thing in the world—her sister!

Key 4: Facilitating *Both* Early Communication and Long-Term Learning

Signing Smart will give you the means to facilitate both early communication and long-term learning. When you use signs to foster both communication and learning, you allow your child to "break into" signing more quickly and allow your family to take full advantage of all that *Signing Smart* has to offer, from the very first day into the preschool years. In fact, as you continue *on your way* with *Signing Smart*, in relatively short order you will want to add to your initial set of Starter Signs, and you may wonder when and how to do so. Let Key 4 be your guide.

WHEN TO ADD TO YOUR STARTER SIGNS

Add on to your set of Starter Signs when your child seems to understand your signs and/or begins to produce even one "real" sign himself. From there, your goal is to "stay ahead" of your child, using a few more signs than he is using (e.g., go from your set of six to twelve signs to twelve to twenty-four signs, or whatever pace your own learning curve will allow). From there, there is no reason to limit your vocabulary, as long as you strive to maintain the balance of See A Lot / Do A Lot

propriate contexts *over time* that Michelle was able to "really know" it was an intentional sign. Reyna felt a similar way about Nadia's first attempts at **BALL** until she saw Nadia's arm bouncing in enough contexts over enough days. One word of warning, however: *Very young children sign very inconsistently.* Do not expect your child to sign **BALL** every time she sees one, or even many of the times you think she might be inclined to sign. *Not signing* in one context says nothing about what she *may have signed* previously. All this is to say, if you think it *could* be a sign, interact with it as if it *is*. Then watch it over time and see what develops.

and Highly Motivating Signs. Add any new number with confidence—your child understands the role signing plays in your interactions and is ready for more sign input. *Signing Smart* gives you the tools to highlight concepts and ideas as well as to engage in topics of interest to you or your child. For this reason continue expanding your Chosen Signs when you notice your child developing new interests, when you want to help prepare him for new experiences, or when you wish to take advantage of *Signing Smart* strategies for long-term learning.

HOW TO ADD TO YOUR CHOSEN SIGNS

While it may be tempting to add a slew of new animal signs, part of the Fourth Key to *Signing Smart* Success is to maintain the balance of Highly Motivating and See A Lot / Do A Lot Signs. This will allow you to sign in all kinds of interactions and to continue to provide your child with tools to talk about his interests as well as his needs. It will also enable you to use signs to support your child's learning now and into the future.

To expand your repertoire of Highly Motivating Signs, pay attention to your child's developing interests: Is she fascinated by city **BUSES**, does he notice every **BIRD** at the park? Think about the change in seasons: Are you likely to start seeing a lot of brightly col-

Signing Smart fosters both early communication and long-term learning, allowing parents to see even very young children make sophisticated connections. Here, twelve-month-old Maya "reads" to herself, signing **BED** to comment on the sleeping animals in *Goodnight Gorilla* by Peggy Rathman.

ored **FLOWERS** or beautifully decorated **TREES** with **LIGHTS**?

To add to your See A Lot / Do A Lot collection, consider new or upcoming family experiences: Are you expecting relatives or going on a family vacation? Is your toddler interested in potty training? Don't forget to choose signs for concepts you'd like to help your child learn. Key 4 is about using signs for *both* early communication *and* long-term learning. So regardless of whether or not your goal is to have your *child* sign a particular word, *Signing Smart* will allow *you* to use signs to help your child to understand abstract ideas. You just may be surprised by what your child wants and needs to talk about!

So think about including Opposite signs such as **IN** and **OUT**, Social Interaction signs such as **TAKE-TURNS** or **STOP**, or Health and Safety signs such as **HOT**, **COLD**, **MEDI-CINE**, **HURT**, or **WET** in your growing set of Chosen Signs. These kinds of signs will allow you to highlight conceptual aspects of your activities, thereby facilitating your child's understanding of relatively abstract ideas—especially if you forgo using other signs in your repertoire to highlight a particular concept and focus your child's attention on the new information (see Spoon Fun on page 124 for more on this learning strategy).

The Four Keys to *Signing Smart* Success Summed Up

We hope you can now see how each of the Four Keys to *Signing Smart* Success builds off of, or becomes a component of, the others—with little or no additional work required from the parent. For example, suppose you notice your child clapping her hands as her own version for **MORE** (Key 3: Recognizing your child's sign). You engage her in an interaction about the toy that excited her (Key 1: Creating a *Signing Smart* Opportunity) by asking her if she wants **MORE MUSIC** or **HELP** putting the toys **IN** the music box (Key 4: Facilitating communication and learning). Bring signs into your child's world (Key 2) by signing **MUSIC** above the toy she is looking at or by signing **IN** directly into the container, and you will have hit on all four Keys in one very short and simple, but incredibly rich, interaction.

We wish you well on your upcoming adventure—and remember, *Signing Smart* should always feel like a welcome addition to your life with your child. If you find yourself frustrated or overwhelmed, we encourage you to reread this chapter; frustrations are most often the result of things you're doing (or not doing) that can be changed with a little guidance from the *Signing Smart* strategies we have offered. You will also learn about some common frustrations and suggested solutions alongside the activities that follow. Be confident in the wonderful gift you are giving your child, yourself, and your whole family—and *have fun* interacting, playing, learning, nuzzling, and *Signing Smart* with your child in exciting and engaging new ways.

PART I

Signing Smart Activities for Every Day

CHAPTER 2:

Diaper and Dressing Activities

LIFE WITH AN INFANT OR TODDLER is often defined by routines. And it is the reoccurrence of these various routines that makes them wonderful times to integrate *Signing Smart* strategies and techniques, and to take advantage of the Four Keys to *Signing Smart* Success. Of all the routines that happen over and over, changing diapers and dressing children are the ones that we as parents and caregivers probably enjoy the least. The same could be said for our children. In many families, especially as children get older, distraction and speed are the names of the game. What follows in this chapter are a number of games and activities to help fill these restless moments with learning, interaction, and playful communication.

In thinking about diaper-changing signs, we recommend using the sign **CHANGE** as opposed to diaper. The sign for diaper is done on the hips and is therefore hard for your child to see when you are most likely to use it—as you carry your child to the changing table. In addition, the bulkiness of diapers often makes the sign hard to feel, even if you

sign directly on your child's body. You can extend your vocabulary by using the *Signing Smart* strategy of Conceptual Grouping (signing the larger category while *saying* the specific name) to talk about how he is playing with his diaper, while you sign **CHANGE**. And don't forget—it's fine to sign **CHANGE** with one hand by anchoring it on your child's leg or arm or belly as you carry him to the changing table.

To help you move beyond simply naming actions (e.g., "Now we're going to **CHANGE** your diaper"), we have designed activities for creating *Signing Smart* Opportunities that will also give your child developmentally appropriate control over an experience that, in general, affords her little control. For similar reasons, you will likely find that incorporating our *Signing Smart* strategies while dressing your child is just the distraction she needs to allow you to finish the process smoothly. How much nicer it is to see your child commenting on the **HAT** as opposed to merely ripping it off her head and throwing it down!

WHEN YOU NEED TO GET OUT THE DOOR

Let's face it. Some days are busier than others. Some days we just need to get our children dressed and out of the house. Rather than feel guilty for not having the time to sign in these moments, remember that *Signing Smart* is not about signing at every *possible* opportunity. Instead, it is about *noticing* the opportunities when they present themselves and finding the ones that work for you. Trying to squeeze signing in when you are pressed for time, distracted, or stressed simply throws signs into the air. While of course it is great if you are able to sign when you are hurrying, what you want are those snippets of less harried time that multipy together to benefit both you and your child. So what do you do when you are too pressed for time to create or respond to potential *Signing Smart* Opportunities? Let them go! Don't worry; there will always be another chance to interact and engage.

Sing a Song of Diaper Changes

Possible signs: **CHANGE, BABY, CLEAN.** Please see the *Signing Smart* Illustrated Dictionary on page 192.

These two songs are meant to be simple and easy to remember. The last thing you need when you are trying to keep your child still and distract her is a set of complicated lyrics. Use either song to help move your child to the changing table or while you are actually changing her diaper.

Why sing and sign at moments such as these? Part of *Signing Smart* is surrounding your child with language-rich interactions in their many forms. Signing while singing is a wonderful way to allow your child to be surrounded by language *and* the visual highlights that signs provide. Most likely, you are comfortable with children's songs and the finger plays that often accompany them; thus, integrating signing into singing often feels "natural." Songs allow children to hear the rhythm of language, often involve language play (e.g., rhymes), and are engaging for young children to listen to.

Although we advocate singing to your child at various points throughout the day, and integrating signs when you do, it is im-portant to realize the limitations of singing in helping your child break into signing (and communication in general). Learning a sign from a song is a great deal of additional work for your child; it requires her to pull both the sign and the word from the "unit" that is the entire stanza or song. Children can indeed do this; it just takes a lot *longer* than learning signs and words from more communicative interactions.

Accordingly, *Signing Smart* involves finding a *balance* in how you present signing to your child. Integrating signs into everyday interactions *in addition* to singing will ensure that your child sees the signs in more "accessible" formats as well.

♫ S O N G ♫

"Change the Diaper"
(TUNE: "LONDON BRIDGE")

CHANGE the diaper, just like this, just like this, just like this,
CHANGE the diaper, just like this,
Now **BABY** [or: Nadia] is nice and **CLEAN**

Fifteen-month-old Jack and his nanny tell his classmates about the **BABY** she is getting ready to change.

♪ SONG ♪

"*This Is the Way . . .*"

(TUNE: "MULBERRY BUSH")

This is the way we **CHANGE** the diaper,
   CHANGE the diaper, **CHANGE** the diaper,
This is the way we **CHANGE** the diaper,
In the **BED**room
   (or)
On your **CHANGING** pad
   (or)
Right before your **BATH**

SIGNING SMART
FOR BUSY PARENTS:

If you can't remember all the words or signs in a given song, focus on one sign to start, make up your own lyrics, and don't worry if the words don't rhyme. What you are striving for is your child's fleeting attention for the few moments it takes to accomplish the task at hand. Using a single sign per song is also a wonderful *Signing Smart* Learning Strategy that brings that one sign to the forefront and makes learning it that much easier.

Family Dressing

Possible signs: **TURN, LOOK-FOR, WHERE,** clothing signs. Please see the *Signing Smart Illustrated Dictionary* on page 192.

Needing to get dressed and ready to go is a fact of life in all families. On some days we can be casual and nonchalant about how long it takes; on others, time is of the essence. Because children often break down when they sense a "hurry-it-up-already" tone in our voices, it can help to build structure around such times of transition and intensity. You will be amazed at how much more you get done, and how much more fun you have, when you work *with* your child's interests and become *partners* in interchanges rather than trying to convince her "it's time to put on your socks because Daddy needs to go."

One way to do this is to finish dressing *yourself* as you dress your child. Alternate pulling on his **SOCKS** and **SHOES** and your own, his **COAT** and yours, and so on. Ham it up! Exaggerate how hard you have to pull on your and his socks, pretend to lose your and his arms in the sleeves, then **SURPRISE**—pop them out, and so on.

Another wonderful way to use this activity is to introduce the idea of turn-taking. To do this, announce that it is **DADDY**'s **TURN** as you put on your **SOCKS**. Then give your child a role in the interaction by telling her she can have a **TURN**, while you help her complete the activity. By making the activity about **TAKING-TURNS**, you change the dynamic from one of parental control to one of parent-child interaction. In doing so you give your child an important role, and (on most days) she will participate in the interaction positively and productively.

SIGNING SMART FOR LONG-TERM LEARNING:
HELPING CHILDREN WITH TURN-TAKING

Part of *Signing Smart* is using signs to facilitate development beyond the point when children become fluent talkers. One way to do this is continuing to use the sign **TURN**, which gives more control to your older toddler or preschooler and helps her more fully understand what it means to take turns. As your child grows, tell her it is her **TURN** to **LOOK-FOR** her **SHOES** after you pick up your shoes, or to bring you your **COAT** after you find hers, and so on. Remember to allow time for your child to complete her **TURN** in

Signing Smart strategies allow signs to be used for concept learning long past when children are talking. These strategies allow young children to understand and talk about developmentally advanced topics. Here, nineteen-month-old Sophie (with almost two hundred words and signs) and her mom tell twenty-month-old Anna (with almost three hundred signs and words) that she can have a **TURN** with the hat.

the activity with lots of encouragement from you. If you are in a hurry, you can talk about how fast you can take your **TURNS**—set a visually compelling timer (such as those that drip colored water) and challenge her to beat the clock.

Find the Frog

Possible signs: **HIDE, WHERE, LOOK-FOR**, animal signs, vehicle signs, or other Highly Motivating Signs. Please see the *Signing Smart* Illustrated Dictionary on page 192.

*S*igning Smart can help you turn your toddler's healthy rebellion at getting dressed into a playful learning opportunity. Choose a few baby-safe stuffed animals or other objects of interest from among your *Signing Smart* Chosen Signs. Play peek-a-boo with your child, **HIDING** the **FROG** behind his or your back, or under his shirt. Use *Signing Smart* Language Clustering as you engage and distract your child, asking, "**WHERE** is your **FROG**, ribbit, ribbit!" While you encourage your child to **LOOK-FOR** the **FROG**, or as you pop the **FROG** out with a healthy, "**SUR-PRISE**!" slip one arm into a sleeve. You may choose to switch the animals with each transition, grounding the interaction through Language Clustering. For instance, you might say, "Neigh! Here comes the **HORSE**!" as you replace the frog with a horse while slipping his other arm into his sleeve. If your child is more active, ask *him* to **HIDE** the animal under his shirt while you slip on his pants.

SIGNING SMART FOR BUSY PARENTS

If you have to get ready in a hurry, don't miss the *Signing Smart* Opportunities even busy schedules can afford! In such moments, hand your child one of the animals, encouraging him to hold it in the hand you're not working on getting through the sleeve. Use Language Clustering as you engage and distract your child, so that you can get everyone ready and out the door faster.

TROUBLESHOOTING:
DRAWING ON MULTIPLE STRATEGIES

This activity is a wonderful one for any number of *Signing Smart* Adaptation Strategies. For example, you can sign **FROG** *on your child's body*. Sign directly on the **HORSE** you are handing your child. Or *bring the horse to your face* to draw your child's gaze up to you and sign normally before you give it to her. Combine *Language Clustering* with *tapping your child's hands*, saying, "Neigh! Mommy has a **HORSE**. Can you say **HORSE** with your hands? Soo-Jin does it. Soo-Jin says **HORSE** with her hands." If you then gently bump your child's hand against her temple, you will have furthered your interaction with *hand-over-hand signing*. There are any number of simple but effective *Signing Smart* strategies that you can use within a single interaction.

nique into interactions, we encourage children to use this very natural, salient, and easy means of expression in many different situations.

DEVELOPMENTAL DETAILS:
SIGNING SMART LANGUAGE CLUSTERING
AND EARLY WORDS

Language Clustering is an attention-getting and language development technique developed by *Signing Smart*, which involves pairing signs with words and sound effects. It is a wonderful way to provide multiple avenues for children to express their fascination with animals, objects, or actions, thereby speeding the acquisition of both signs and words. For example, clustering "neigh" with the word and the sign **HORSE**, "vrrmm, vrrmm" with **CAR**, or "ch-ch-ch" with **TOOTH-BRUSH** helps children communicate with us as soon and as extensively as possible. Children will often use sounds as word "substitutes" long before they can say the words themselves. By integrating this tech-

Language Clustering is a tool that will allow your child to use all available resources to communicate as early and as extensively as possible. Here, just-turned-two-year-old Nicolas, who has apraxia of speech, tells us about the "oink, oink" **PIG**.

I Want to Be Just like Mommy and Daddy

Possible signs: **MOMMY/DADDY, SISTER/ BROTHER**, signs for items used in dressing routines. Please see the *Signing Smart* Illustrated Dictionary on page 192.

Signs and songs during transitions help prepare children for change and give them developmentally appropriate control over times of uncertainty. Here, nineteen-month-old Sophie and her mom sing and sign the **CLEAN-UP** song, announcing to her classmates that it is time to put the toys away.

You may have heard the phrase "You are your child's first teacher"; truer words have never been said. Your child looks to you for love and safety, information and security. He seeks to emulate what you do—whether those behaviors are conscious or not. This happens in part because very young children identify with their parents, seeing them as actual extensions of themselves. We can take advantage of this developmentally appropriate identification by emphasizing the things we do that we also would *like* our child to do, thereby becoming role models for our child and creating a *Signing Smart* Opportunity along the way. One way to do this is through the activity below.

This song can be used during the actual event or as you lead your child to the dresser, closet, sink, bath, and so on. We developed activities such as this to help prepare children for transitions—alerting them in a comforting way that a given activity is ending while another is beginning. By using such transi-tional songs, we as parents provide something familiar at a time of change that, for children, is a time of uncertainty. For many children this familiarity is all they need to seamlessly exit one activity and enter another without incident. For example, we are constantly surprised when many children in our play classes begin signing CLEAN-UP as one of their first signs! The CLEAN-UP song we sing at the end of Center Time provides familiarity and continuity at a time of change, and as such is an invitation for children to take positive control in an out-of-control experience.

The goal here is to use a simple tune that does not require you to remember complicated words, allowing you (and your child) to focus on the interaction and the signs. So let your creative juices flow and use any of your *Signing Smart* Chosen Signs to engage your child in playful sign interchanges (**EAT, EAT, EAT** your **VEGGIES**, or **BATH, BATH**, take a **BATH**); the possibilities are endless.

♪ **SONG** ♪

"Shoes, Shoes, Put On Your Shoes"
(TUNE: "CLAP, CLAP, CLAP YOUR HANDS")

SHOES, SHOES, put on your **SHOES**,
Put on your **SHOES** like **MOMMY**,
SHOES, SHOES, put on your **SHOES**,
Put on your **SHOES** like **DADDY**

This song can be used with any number of other routines:

CLEAN, CLEAN, CLEAN your hands,
CLEAN your hands like **BROTHER**
  (or)
BRUSH, BRUSH, BRUSH your teeth,
BRUSH your teeth like **SISTER**

CHAPTER 3:

Mealtime Activities

MEALTIMES ARE PERFECT TIMES to notice, create, and respond to *Signing Smart* Opportunities. Not only do mealtimes tend to be somewhat slower than other parts of the day, but they are also often marked by one-on-one interaction and increased eye contact from your child. Children are also highly communicative at mealtime, using various points, cries, body wiggles, or other means to indicate what they want. Therefore, mealtimes are good times to "stack the deck" in your favor; remind yourself of your balanced set of Chosen Signs and your *Signing Smart* Adaptation Strategies to help your child understand more about the flavors and foods you provide.

MOTIVATING YOUR CHILD TO SIGN

While we never deny our child a necessity (such as food), it is important that we allow her the opportunity to develop and identify a desire, and to then ask for what she wants or needs. Mealtimes are a perfect time to use

Signing Smart strategies to provide structured motivation that will encourage your child to use signs to do just this. Some easy ways to invite your child to sign:

- Tap his hands and ask him to say **MORE** with his hands.

- Allow the food to be eaten without being replenished, or pause between spoonfuls. When your child looks over to you expectantly, ask him if he wants **MORE VEGGIES** and *wait* to see whether you get a response.

- Encourage your child to communicate by using Forced Choices: Ask him whether he wants something to **EAT** or something to **DRINK**.

Of course if your child fails to sign back or seems unusually hungry or otherwise out of sorts, don't delay feeding him. *Signing Smart* is for enhancing communication, not denying necessary gratification.

Just as important as increasing your child's motivation and opportunities to sign is knowing what to look for as evidence of her participation and comprehension. As we have emphasized before, signs are just one way your child will communicate with you. You will actually increase the likelihood that your child sees you sign as well as help build his confidence and motivation to communicate with signs and words if you are also able to recognize and respond to his nonsigned "invitation" behaviors such as:

- gazing at the object desired

- reaching for the spoon as you ask whether he wants **MORE**

- head nodding/shaking, pointing, gesturing, or babbling

- body wiggling

Many parents wonder how to sign **MORE** while holding a spoon or jar of baby food. One wonderful aspect of *Signing Smart* is the Adaptation Strategies we have developed to make signing seamless and successful. Here, eight-month-old Nadia watches Reyna sign **MORE** directly on the jar of food that she is looking at.

Use signs yourself to comment on what your child is communicating by his behaviors—this gives him a label and a means to express himself with language as soon as he is ready.

I Like to Eat

Possible signs: **MORE, EAT, PLEASE,** food signs. Please see the *Signing Smart* Illustrated Dictionary on p. 192.

A s you sing and sign this song, offer some of the signed food to your child. You may choose to adapt the speed of your singing to match your child's eating pace or you may sing normally, irrespective of your child's pace, offering food at intermittent points. This is also a nice time to allow food to be eaten without replenishment (to create desire and motivation) and to ask your child if he wants **MORE** before beginning to sing, sign, and eat again. Building in a delay heightens desire and invites your child to sign. Such *Signing Smart* strategies shorten the time frame for signing back. Another way to invite participation is by pausing before naming the second item in the song. Tap your child's hands and ask him to "sing with Daddy," accepting words, signs, or body wiggles as evidence of participation on your child's part.

TROUBLESHOOTING:

WHICH FOOD SIGNS TO START WITH: CONCEPTUAL GROUPING

When starting to sign with your child, we recommend that you limit your early food signs to general categories such as **CEREAL** (e.g., infant cereal), **CRACKER, FRUIT, VEGETABLE,** and **FINGER-FOODS.**

- It is very easy for parents to "load up" on food signs at the expense of other more useful (and more motivating) signs. Of course, when your child obviously enjoys specific items, do add these to your group of Chosen Signs. This transition will be seamless if you pair the new, specific food sign with the broader category sign you have been using (e.g., "You like that **FRUIT.** Do you want **MORE PEAR?**")

- Baby food requires that children make a somewhat abstract leap to connect the flavor with the actual food item they may see in other (unrelated) contexts. Therefore, broader categories of food items are more useful at this stage.

- We do our children a greater service if we help them learn to categorize these early *tastes* (**FRUITS** are sweet, **CRACKERS** are hard and crunchy, and so on), giving them a good understanding of the variety of *kinds* of foods.

- Don't forget to use the *Signing Smart* Strategy of Conceptual Grouping; say the actual spoken word, but sign the larger category sign. For instance, say, "Do you want more pears?" while signing **MORE FRUIT**. In this way, you allow your child to *hear* the specific word (pear) but also allow her to *see* the broader category label (**FRUIT**). This helps her to better understand "pear" is a specific kind of fruit that is sweet in the way other items labeled "fruit" are also sweet (apples, peaches, and so on).

- Emphasize kinds (e.g., categorize both whole peas and pureed peas as **VEGGIES**) or emphasize how a food is eaten (e.g., categorize bits of cheese, meat, cereal, scrambled eggs, pasta, or chunks of fruit and veggies as **FINGER-FOOD**).

♪ SONG ♪

"Fruits and Veggies"

(TUNE: "FRÈRE JACQUES")

FRUITS and **VEGGIES**, **FRUITS** and **VEGGIES**; good to **EAT**, good to **EAT**;
Put-them-in-your-mouth [natural action], Put-them-in-your-mouth;
Yum, yum, yum [natural gesture];
Yum, yum, yum

Other possible versions:

CER-E-AL, **CER-E-AL**; on the **SPOON**, on the **SPOON** . . .
(or)
Crunchy **CRACKERS**, crunchy **CRACKERS**; **PLEASE** give me some, **PLEASE** give me some . . .

Food Surprises

Possible signs: **WHERE, HELP, EAT, MORE, HIDE, LOOK-FOR,** food signs. Please see the *Signing Smart* Illustrated Dictionary on page 192.

L ooking for a way to distract your child, make eating more enjoyable, and create a *Signing Smart* Opportunity all at the same time? Give Food Surprises a try! Take two to three small food-storage containers (fewer for younger children, more for older children) and place them upside down on your child's high-chair tray. You may choose to have them be see-through or not. Under one, slip in some peas or other finger foods. Ask your child **WHERE** the **VEGGIES/FINGER-FOODS** are **HIDING**. If your child lifts, bats at, or knocks over the correct container, her reward is a well-earned nibble.

This activity allows you to come in and out of interaction with your child. As your child is **LOOKING-FOR** the peas, you can take a break from interacting with her directly to prepare the rest of her meal or your own. When you return, begin interacting with her again by commenting on her success or encouraging her to keep trying with some strategic sign use (e.g., "Do you need **HELP** getting that cup off?"; "Look at you **EAT** your peas [signing **VEGGIES** or **FINGER-FOODS**]."; "Do you want **MORE** to **EAT** [as you set up the game again]?"). For more on coming in and out of interactions, see page 68.

For more on coming in and out of interactions, see page 68.

TROUBLESHOOTING:

LEARNING STRATEGIES FOR MEALTIMES

Another way to take advantage of mealtime *Signing Smart* Opportunities is through *Signing Smart* Body Leans and Language Clustering. You can do this by asking your child if she wants more to **DRINK** (with an exaggerated Body Lean to the right) or to **EAT** (with an exaggerated Body Lean to the left). Doing so will visually set off the two choices and make your child's options more clear. Use your tone of voice and Language Clustering (adding "slurp" with **DRINK** and "mmm" with **EAT**) to get your child's attention and to further clarify the conceptual difference between the two choices. Additional visual distinctions, such as Opposite-Handed Signing (signing **DRINK** with your right hand as you do a Body Lean to the right and signing **EAT** with your left hand as you do a Body Lean to

Here, Mom uses Opposite-Handed Signing in conjunction with *Signing Smart* Body Leans and Language Clustering to help thirteen-month-old Eli understand his choices: Does he want something to **DRINK** (slurp, slurp) or to **EAT** (mmm, mmm)? With the possibilities clear, Eli is easily able to make his decision—he wants something to **EAT**!

the left), helps children literally *see* the contrast between the signs/words/concepts. With all of these strategies, you are helping to make clear the choices and to structure your child's set of possible responses, thereby shortening the signing back time frame.

The Silly Puppet

Possible signs: **CLEAN, MORE, FINISH, SILLY, TAKE-TURNS, HELP, EAT**. Please see the *Signing Smart* Illustrated Dictionary on page 192.

Please see the *Signing Smart* Illustrated Dictionary on page 192.

Meals are messy, but children tend to dislike the process of getting clean. Since there is no escaping its necessity, here is an activity that will allow you to introduce an element of playfulness to the drudgery of getting clean. Turn a damp napkin or diaper wipe into a puppet by draping it over your index finger and holding it in place with your thumb and middle finger. You now have a new friend for your child to meet! Ham it up and make silly noises or have the puppet start a playful dialogue with your child. When your child reaches for this captivating creature, swoop in for a quick wipe of his face or neck. Pull your hand away and resume the puppet's playful dialogue (this will help distract your child from his dislike of having just been wiped). After a moment, ask your child if he wants to see **MORE** of his new friend, and if so, come in again for a playful face wiping from the **SILLY** puppet.

TROUBLESHOOTING:

WORKING WITH DEVELOPMENTAL IMPERATIVES

At mealtimes, children want and need to exert control, making a tremendous mess as they try to feed or clean themselves. *Signing Smart* can help you work *with* your child's developmental imperative, providing manageable structured independence. One way is to offer your child her own spoon, empty bowl, or cup, keeping the actual food out of reach. Comment that she is **EATING** all by herself. **TAKE-TURNS** with each spoon, trading your spoon for hers after each mouthful. Your child can also "**HELP**" **CLEAN** with *her* wipe as you continue to use yours. Tell her it is **MOMMY**'s **TURN** with the **SILLY** puppet as you go in for a final wipe (or two), adding what a nice job she is doing **CLEANING** by herself. These strategies create wonderful *Signing Smart* Opportunities by inviting your child into interactions and motivating her to sign about what matters to her; they also give your child developmentally appropriate control in a way that feels manageable to you.

"MY CHILD WILL ONLY SIGN 'MORE' WHILE EATING, NEVER ANYWHERE ELSE."

Children often use a particular sign in only one context. In this case, your child has created a definition of **MORE** that is not broad enough. Contrary to how it may seem, he is not merely confused; rather, he is making a natural "mistake" that is a necessary component of learning to form categories.

SIGNING SMART PARENT STRATEGY:

To better respond to the "mistake," first ask yourself whether *you* are only using **MORE** while eating; often children's under-use of a sign reflects the way we ourselves use it! When you emphasize how **MORE** is relevant in multiple contexts (including play), you encourage your child to *gradually* expand her own sign use (over time). Remember, these kinds of "mistakes" give you insight into your child's development as well as allow you the opportunity to enhance your role as a source of knowledge and support in her life. The

length of time it takes a child to "correct" her "mistake" is irrelevant to the importance of the *Signing Smart* Opportunities presented during the process itself.

High Chair Pull-Up Toys

Possible signs: **HELP, WHAT,** animal signs, vehicle signs, or other Highly Motivating Signs. Please see the *Signing Smart* Illustrated Dictionary on page 192.

Children experiment with cause and effect to develop an understanding of how the world works. One way we see this with babies is the delight they take in dropping objects off their high-chair tray. While we as parents are usually happy to indulge this developmentally appropriate exploration any number of times, at a certain point we are done. We offer you this activity to allow your child to drop or throw to his heart's content while simultaneously allowing you to get some nearby chores done. Of course you will still want to pop in and out of meaningful interaction with your child while you attend to your chores. (For more on coming in and out of interactions, see page 68.)

Take some ribbons of various lengths and tape them securely to your child's high-chair tray with clear packing tape. Be sure your child can reach the hanging ribbons. Securely attach lightweight items from your *Signing Smart* Chosen Signs (e.g., **SPOON**, toy **PHONE**, rubber **DUCK**, even **CRACKERS**) to the ends of the ribbons. Show your child how to pull the items up onto the tray. While your child is engaged in the activity you are free to go about your business in close proximity—commenting on your child's progress from a nearby table or across the room (e.g., "**WHAT** do you have? You got your **DUCK**! Are you going to throw it down some **MORE**?").

If your child is unable to get the toys up on his own, this is a wonderful activity to reinforce the concept of **HELP**. And even if your child merely fiddles with the ribbon or is engaged in a developmentally appropriate struggle to bring up the items (increasing his motivation to communicate along the way), you will have bought yourself some time to get things done.

Caution: Do not leave your child unattended during this activity.

DEVELOPMENTAL DETAILS:

"MY CHILD SEEMS TO BE CONFUSED AND WILL SIGN 'DUCK' AND 'LIGHT' THE SAME WAY. WHAT SHOULD I DO?"

Just as children's early words can be a challenge to decipher, the same can be true for their early signs. Children will sometimes produce what seems to be the "same sign" to refer to different items. And in all likelihood, your child is not confused; rather, she has produced what we call an Overlapping Movement Pattern—using the same movement for two distinct signs.

for "light," "du" for "duck"). Regardless of how "rough" (or wrong!) the attempted sign seems, turn your child's "invitation" into a *Signing Smart* Opportunity!

SIGNING SMART PARENT STRATEGY:

Look for slight variations in the location of the two signs: **DUCK** may be beside her shoulder and **LIGHT** may be near her head. Recall that location is one of the three main components of any sign, and children's "similar" signs may in reality vary slightly along these lines. In addition, use *Signing Smart* Body Leans to emphasize the two signs, asking your child whether she means **LIGHT** with a Body Lean to the left or **DUCK** with a Body Lean to the right. Over time she will better distinguish between the signs. Context will also help distinguish such similar-looking signs. For instance, if your child looks up at the ceiling while signing, she is most likely signing **LIGHT**. Finally, listen carefully; she may "talk" when signing ("ay"

The WHERE Game

Possible signs: **WHERE, SURPRISE, MORE, HIDE, LOOK-FOR.** Please see the *Signing Smart* Illustrated Dictionary on page 192.

Perhaps the most frustrating part of mealtimes is the time it takes for you to prepare the food. So let *Signing Smart* help you turn meal preparation into a playful time, taking advantage of short but meaningful *Signing Smart* Opportunities where integrating signs is just part of the fun.

For this activity get out a number of interesting kitchen items that have holes in them (a colander, a funnel, a slatted spoon). Select thin items that will fit through the holes (feathers, strips of brightly colored paper, scarves, pipe cleaners, even your finger may work for some items). As you go about cooking and preparing, play an ad hoc game of peekaboo: Ask your child **WHERE** the (scarf, paper, and so on) is and then—**SURPRISE**—push the item of interest through a slat for your child to see. If your child is older, encourage him to pull the "treasure" out himself while supervising him for safety. You may also **HIDE** the items (fully or partially) under a towel, in the cupboard, or under a mixing bowl. You can also enjoy this game by popping your head out from behind a baking tray or colander with a playful "**SURPRISE!**" Ask your child if he wants **MORE** of the **WHERE** game / **HIDING** game. (By labeling the game you give him the tools to ask for it by name.) Each rendition takes only a moment, which will allow you to cook as well as play with your child. For more on coming in and out of interactions, see page 68.

TROUBLESHOOTING:

WHY INTRODUCE THE ASL 'WHERE' SIGN?

Most people naturally use the gesture for "where" or "I don't know" (tossing their hands to their sides in a movement very similar to the sign **WHAT**). The drawback to this gesture is that when children produce it (and they will!), parents will not know if their child is asking "**WHAT** is it?"—meaning she wants more information about something, or "**WHERE** is it?"—meaning she wants to find something. As mommies, we learned first-hand the benefits of using the ASL sign **WHERE**. While we don't discourage the natural gesture—knowing we all continue to use it—we recommend parents add the official

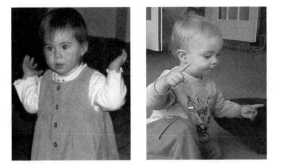

Experience has taught us the benefits of using the ASL sign for **WHERE**. Here, fifteen-month-old Natasha gestures to Reyna. It takes some investigation to find out she is looking for her bear, not asking about the nearby toys. By using the ASL sign **WHERE**, we can easily understand what fifteen-month-old Joey is asking— **WHERE** is the magic penny his mother is hiding?

WHERE sign to their repertoire. To do this, you might say, "Your **BALL** fell down. Where did it go [with the natural gesture]? I wonder **WHERE** it is." By adding **WHERE**, parents give their children the tools to ask *different* questions about the world around them. Furthermore, with both **WHAT** and **WHERE**, *parents* can more fully understand the intent behind their child's questions and therefore respond more specifically.

Mini-Me Cooking

Possible signs: **SPOON, EAT, HELP, CLEAN, TAKE-TURNS, WHAT, CUP.** Please see the *Signing Smart* Illustrated Dictionary on page 192.

As any parent of a young child knows, preparing meals with your child nearby is often a challenge, especially as he gets older and wants to be more involved in household operations. Try these *Signing Smart* suggestions to allow your child to do his part while you cook and pop in and out of interactions with him. For this activity, put down a towel or sheet to keep cleanup to a minimum. Get out some plastic bowls, measuring spoons, and other interesting containers. Empty and clean some baby-safe spice containers and put infant cereal or instant mashed potatoes in them (you may need to widen the holes). While you prepare the meal, your child can make his own "dinner" alongside. At various points briefly engage in interactions by asking **WHAT** he is making you; by talking about how he can have a **TURN** to make **FOOD**; by commenting on the **SPOON** he is **EATING** with; or by asking if he needs **HELP CLEANING**.

As Children Grow: Use colored sugar or water to talk about different colors. Use spices with interesting smells (be sure they are baby-safe). Use water and flour to make a paste; add food coloring and turn his creation into an art activity or his own "side dish" to the main meal.

TROUBLESHOOTING:

COMING IN AND OUT OF INTERACTIONS

Life with young children can feel harried and busy. Take heart and know that, developmentally, children benefit immensely when they learn to explore and discover their world without a parent's constant barrage of running commentary on their every move. We know what it is like when you see your child happily playing; you think to yourself, now is my chance to get some things done! So, yes, please, attend to your chores. But when your child complains because he can't reach a toy, or crawls over to show you a car—take advantage of that *Signing Smart* Opportunity by popping in and out of the interaction. It may be a brief comment about the **BOOK** he is looking at, or the **BALL** you roll to him, after which you go back to your work.

More than simply distracting your child while you work, you are helping him learn independent play and how to manage intermittent adult interaction. Children do not start out being able to play independently for much more than thirty to sixty seconds (on a good day), and they do not intuitively know how to "allow" adults to enter and leave their play easily. Both of these important skills take time to learn.

So don't be surprised if your child plays happily for fifteen seconds and then needs you; or if your child is energetically mixing his creation until you briefly interact with him ("Oh, **MOMMY** sees your **FOOD**. **MOMMY** is making **FOOD** too!") and then he suddenly wants nothing more than to be in your arms. The definition of "development" is "change over time." It will take many attempts to refocus him on his own activity (with or without your having engaged him) before he will comfortably reengage *himself* for longer periods. But rather than avoid this strategy, both you and your child gain tremendously as you each develop the ability to "work" alongside each other, pausing at either child- or adult-initiated intervals to connect around topics of meaning, with each of you then able to return to your respective "work." As two work-from-home mommies can tell you, these are skills that are worth developing, for both of you!

Pots and Pans Band

Possible signs: **MUSIC, FOOD, COOK, DANCE, MORE, HELP**. Please see the *Signing Smart* Illustrated Dictionary on page 192.

Looking for another activity that will allow you a moment or two—but hopefully longer—to get dinner ready? Well, pull out your earplugs and open your cabinets to your child's rendition of the tried-and-true Pots and Pans Band. Simply turn some pots and pans upside down (or plastic storage containers for a quieter version) and hand your child a wooden mixing spoon or two. If necessary, **HELP** her to hit the spoon against the pan to make a sound. Proceed going about your business, pausing at various moments to notice or comment on her industry and then going back to your own. For instance, tell her how much you like making **FOOD** to her **MUSIC** and then return to your **COOKING**.

As her interest wanes, ask her if she wants **MORE** pots as you bring out bigger pots, or smaller ones. Or trade her pots for the metal colander; trade the wooden spoon for the potato masher. Variety is the spice of life, and keeping such "new" items of interest close by will guarantee you a few extra moments of preparation time, even as her initial enthusiasm begins to wane.

TROUBLESHOOTING:

USING *A* SIGN EVEN IF YOU DON'T KNOW *THE* SIGN: CONCEPTUAL GROUPING

If you look in the dictionary of this guide, you will not find "pot" or "pan" among the sign choices. So how will you have anything to say as you enter and leave the brief but meaningful interactions suggested above? Remember, *Signing Smart* means using *a* sign, even if you do not know *the* sign. One wonderful tool we have developed to help you do this is Conceptual Grouping. Conceptual Grouping involves using a single related sign when talking about multiple, similar concepts to unify them for your child (e.g., signing **BABY** when talking about a doll). One way to do this with the above activity is to sign **MUSIC** when talking about the ruckus she is making with her spoon and pot. You can also use **MU-SIC** when talking about songs and instruments (such as drums, tambourines, pianos,

Signing Smart Conceptual Grouping allows you to use *a* sign, even if it is not *the* sign. Doing so will not only allow you to use a small number of signs in many different contexts, but it is also a wonderful way to use signs for long-term learning. Here, twelve-month-old Nadia tells Nick about the lion she sees in the Busy Box, using the sign **CAT** that Reyna had Conceptually Grouped for lion.

and so on). You might also sign **DANCE** when talking to your child about how she is bouncing, wiggling, or rocking while playing.

Note that you will continue to use the specific *word* while using the larger category *sign*. In this way Conceptual Grouping does more than simply expand your ability to use the limited number of signs you may know; it also facilitates learning and vocabulary development. When caregivers use the strategy of Conceptual Grouping to facilitate learning, they choose a sign their child *knows,* and then they pair it with new, unfamiliar, or more difficult words/concepts. For your child, you have just grounded the new/unfamiliar/more difficult concept in a familiar one, allowing

him to more easily and more quickly *learn* and *use* that new concept himself. For more on using Conceptual Grouping for long-term learning, see page 187.

Signing Smart for Busy Parents

Signing Smart is about enriching interactions in the midst of real-time parenting, including getting the laundry done, preparing meals, answering e-mails, making phone calls, or doing other projects. Certainly there will be times when getting your projects done will prevent you from having even a second to think about signing. But don't let the mere fact that you are busy prevent you from *Signing Smart*. Build on the suggestions below and see how easy it is to come in and out of interactions; while signing and playing along the way you can also get your chores done. See page 68 for more on this strategy.

DOING LAUNDRY/ROOM STRAIGHTENING

- *Dual Labeling PeekaBoo:* As you remove and fold laundry, cover your child or yourself with items from the dryer, playing an ad hoc game of **WHERE's MOMMY?** Don't forget signs like **SILLY**, **PLAY**, **MORE**, **SURPRISE**, **WARM**, **COLD**, and so on. For activity extensions, see page 112.

- *Sock Toss:* Turn your laundry basket into a basketball hoop and have your toddler try and toss his **SOCKS** (or other clothing items) **IN.** You have bought yourself some time to collect laundry or straighten the room while he plays.

- *Sock Tickle Monster:* Put a sock on your nondominant hand, creating a portable "tickle machine." Ask your baby if she wants **MORE** between each tickle fest. Meanwhile, you can fold or clean as you come in and out of the interaction.

- *Tent Hideaway:* Even very young children love to be inside smaller spaces. So turn the sheets you just stripped from the bed into a tent and ask your child **WHERE** she is **HIDING.** Pretend to **LOOK-FOR** her, even in plain sight, and see how many giggles you get as you put on fresh linens or straighten the room.

MOVING AROUND THE HOUSE

- *Where oh where has my little dog gone?*: As you go about vacuuming or straightening any number of rooms, bring your child along on a "**DOG** Hunt" (Conceptual Grouping: **LOOK-FOR**). Sing the song as you periodically lift a pillow or peek under a blanket, trying to find **WHERE** the toy **DOG** is **HIDING**. When you feel you are losing your child's interest, **SURPRISE** your child by finding the toy **DOG** that you previously planted somewhere on your route. Repeat this as long as she stays engaged.

- *Going on a Bear Hunt:* This activity will not only allow you to move from room to room, cleaning, straightening, or putting toys away but it also serves as a wonderful literacy extension to the book of the same name by Bill Rosen. So ham it up and pretend to be trudging through sticky mud, climbing over treacherous mountains, swimming through murky swamps, all to **LOOK-FOR** the **HIDING BEAR**. Ask your child **WHAT** he will do when you find it!

- *See Also:* Silly Scarves (page 122); Three in the Bed (page 144); Magic Mirror (page 166).

KITCHEN ACTIVITIES

- Designate a drawer and/or a low cabinet for Tupperware or other nonbreakables and allow your child to see **WHAT** she can take **IN** and **OUT**, all while you are cooking.

- Invest in a small broom or dustpan and allow your child to help **CLEAN-UP**.

- Look for fridge magnets that match your Chosen Signs to engage your child.

- *See Also:* Mini-Me Cooking, page 68; Pots and Pans Band, page 70.

CHAPTER 4:

Bathtime Activities

BATH TIME IS THE PERFECT TIME to incorporate the Four Keys to *Signing Smart* Success by introducing playful songs and interactions that foster intimacy and provide opportunities for learning. Don't worry if your hands are full during tub time. We developed our *Signing Smart* Adaptation Strategies for just such "busy Mommy/Daddy moments." You might sign with one hand or sign directly on your child. He will love the intimacy it engenders, as will you. If things feel hectic when you first start *Signing Smart*, don't panic. Remember, there's no such thing as a lost opportunity. *Signing Smart* is about creating meaningful interchanges when you are able—your child won't know that you "forgot" to sign previously. In fact, what you *forgot* to do in any past moment is irrelevant to your child's learning in the *present* moment.

Safety tip: Be sure to have all the necessary supplies or props on hand before you begin.

If you go a whole bath without fitting in a single sign, have no fear—there is always the next time. However, in short order you are likely to find (as we have) that your child will remind you by signing that he wants the **DUCK** song or another **BATH** activity again and again.

Signing Smart is easy for the whole family. Here, two-year-old Ian signs **BATH** on ten-month-old Amber, and she signs **BATH** back, allowing each of them to be a part of the interaction.

Part of *Signing Smart* is becoming a partner in your child's development. We as parents can facilitate this process by better understanding why our child behaves the way she does. One curious aspect of development is our child's need for and love of repetition. Developmentally, however, this desire for repetition makes sense:

• Repetition is the means by which children come to understand what to expect in their world. It gives them some sense of reliability, and it allows them the sense of control that comes from knowing what will happen next.

• In this way, repetition is a key element of learning. While it seems boring to us, it holds a great deal of mental stimulation for your child—think of all the prediction and confirmation skills you are fostering in him (e.g., "I think the clown will pop up at the end of the song. Yes, it did!"). In addition, when an environment is understandable and stable, your child is able to refocus his learning energies on new aspects of the situation (such as the signs).

SIGNING SMART
PARENT STRATEGY:

One aspect of Signing Smart is to break expectations in safe but meaningful ways: Pretend you are the clown popping out of the box; sign the actions in the book instead of the objects, wait a moment before you tickle your child, and let her delight at the break in expectation.

Bath, Bath, Take a Bath

Possible signs: **CLEAN, BATH, MORE, SILLY, WATER, WET, TOWEL.** Please see the *Signing Smart* Illustrated Dictionary on page 192.

This activity is perfect for the tub, for helping your child anticipate (and transition into) bath time, or even for distraction while washing his hands, hair, or face. (Have soap on your washcloth before you start.) This song is wonderful for using your *Signing Smart* Adaptation Strategies. For instance, begin the song by signing **BATH** on yourself as you normally would, and then sign on your child. If you are holding a washcloth, sign **BATH** one-handed on yourself or your child. You can also sign **CLEAN** with the washcloth in your hand—your child will still hear the word and will become skilled at "reading" this type of "distorted" sign.

When you get to "Scrubby, Scrubby . . . ," use the washcloth and scrub your child's torso or other body parts. You can also make this activity a family affair, inviting an older sibling to get involved in the action. Or, playfully sing this song during nonbath times—tickle your child while pretending to scrub and ask if she wants **MORE.** Your child will love to experience this activity over and over, and she will soon be signing and singing along!

TROUBLESHOOTING:

"HOW CAN I ENCOURAGE MY CHILD TO PARTICIPATE MORE IN THE ACTIVITIES?"

Part of *Signing Smart* is inviting your child to become an active participant in your interactions. To help you do this, use what we call

Bathtime is a wonderful time for *Signing Smart*—integrating fun, intimacy, and learning. Here, eighteen-month-old Rachel signs **BROTHER** to big brother T.R. as he scrubs little Rachel **CLEAN.**

Signing Smart Pregnant Pauses as both Attention-Getters and invitations. One way to use Pregnant Pauses is to place your hands in the beginning position for **CLEAN**, but *pause* before you actually sing the word and finish the sign. This lets your child know you're "holding" her place in the interaction and inviting her to sign along.

Another important part of the Pregnant Pause is drawing in a "noisy breath." This helps you remember to pause, helps get your child's attention, and lets her know that you are asking her to sign *with* you. If she doesn't join in after a moment or two, continue on.

While initially she may look at you with a puzzled expression (or blankly), if you give your child plenty of chances like these to participate, she will soon begin to look to you for invitations into the interaction. And after that, it's only a matter of time before she accepts your invitation and adds to the conversation by signing (or singing) herself.

♪ SONG ♪

"Bath, Bath, Take a Bath"

(TUNE: "ROW YOUR BOAT")

BATH, **BATH**, take a **BATH**,
Get so nice and **CLEAN**,
Scrubby, Scrubby, Scrubby, Scrubby [rub your child all over],
Now you're nice and **CLEAN**

Try adding other verses that start with:

Wash, Wash, Wash your hands [mime washing your hands] . . .
Wipe, Wipe, Wipe your face [mime wiping your face] . . .

Bathing the Doll

Possible signs: **CHANGE, WET, WATER, BATH, TOWEL, RAIN, DOLL, BABY.** Please see the *Signing Smart* Illustrated Dictionary on page 192.

As children enter the toddler years, they become increasingly interested in controlling the world around them. Suddenly, even trying to help your child wipe his face can ignite a tantrum. To work with this developmentally appropriate (although frustrating) need for autonomy, it is important to provide your child with positive control. While it would be inappropriate and unsafe to allow your child to bathe himself alone, it is easy to allow him to help you wash his body and to be the boss of bathing a doll friend.

Encourage your child to **LOOK-FOR** a collection of washcloths or bath toys for his **DOLL** and be prepared for a laughing, playful mess as your child splashes and washes his own arms, hands, and face as well as the doll's! Bring out cups with holes in the bottom to make it **RAIN** on both the doll and your child. Sing "**RAIN, RAIN,** Go Away" (use Conceptual Grouping and sign **FINISH** while singing "go away") as you wash your

child and he washes his doll. Because many children dislike having their hair washed, this is a nice place to give your child a developmentally appropriate say in the experience (e.g., he can decide how much to lather up his **DOLL**, how much **RAIN** to pour down, and so on).

SIGNING SMART LITERACY EXTENSION:

Part of *Signing Smart* is surrounding your child with language in its many forms. One wonderful way to do this is to use books to extend activities and to use activities to bring books and stories to life. For instance, in this activity, you might bring out a book such as *Duck is Dirty* by Satoshi Kitamura and use the story as an "invitation" to take a bath / get a shampoo. After reading the book, say, "Look how **WET** and dirty **DUCK** got when the **RAIN** came down. We can make it **RAIN** right here at **HOME**! Let's get in the **BATH** and see if you [or your **DOLL**] can get **WET** too." Then drip "rain" as you sing "Rain, Rain, Go Away," engaging your child with activities, words, signs, songs, and stories.

TROUBLESHOOTING:

"HOW CAN I EXTEND INTERACTIONS WITH SIGNS?"

With the suggestions below, this activity is easily taken to the "next level" of interaction. Note that the suggestions below are phrased so that you can offer your child as much control as possible during his bath experience.

- Ask your child if the **DOLL** is dirty, needs to get **CLEAN**, and how to **HELP**.

- Ask your child **WHAT** he wants: **BUBBLES**, or to **CHANGE** the color of the **WATER**. Reinforce his choice through words, signs, and actions.

- Tell your child that the **DOLL** is **WET**. Splash so that your child gets **WET** as well. Suggest that your child use a **TOWEL** to dry the **DOLL** and himself.

- Give your child the choice of a **BOAT** or a **DUCK** for him and the **DOLL** to **PLAY** with. Wait to see if your child answers.

- You can also pretend to ask the doll if she's **CLEAN**, answer for the doll, and then encourage your child to continue to wash the

DOLL or to offer the **DOLL** a **TOWEL** (depending on the "answer").

- Ask your child if he is **FINISHED** or wants to play **MORE** in the **BATH**.

Pop and Drop

Possible signs: **MORE, WET, WATER, SUR-PRISE, TOWEL, WHAT,** Chosen Signs. Please see the *Signing Smart* Illustrated Dictionary on page 192.

This activity is a wonderful one for reinforcing Chosen Signs. Use familiar toys to allow your child to focus on the new element of the interaction (the addition of signs) as opposed to simply being intrigued by the objects themselves.

Choose three to five target toys that will pop back up to the surface when held underwater. While holding down the toy, ask your child "**WHERE**'s the **DUCK**?" Then let the duck pop up to the surface. Ask your child if he wants to see the **DUCK** pop up some **MORE**. You can structure his choice (and invite him to sign) by asking him if he wants the **BOAT** or the **DUCK** to pop up. Children love the **SURPRISE** (again and again). You can use this activity into the preschool years and extend the learning by using *Signing Smart* Body Leans to help your child better distinguish between similar-sounding words (e.g., "Do you want the **DOLL** or the **BALL** to pop up?").

Variation: Hold the toys over the water and say, "Ready, set, go! Let's drop the **BOAT**, **DUCK**, or **FISH**." Put toys in your baby's hand and ask your child if he wants to drop the **BOAT** or the **DUCK**. Help your child let go of the toy if necessary; if he resists, move on to a different interaction. For instance, pick up another toy, drop it into the water, and comment that it makes a splash and gets your child **WET**.

TROUBLESHOOTING:

"HOW CAN I HELP MY CHILD TO SIGN BACK MORE?"

Asking your child open-ended questions such as **WHAT** he wants is a wonderful way to let him know he has a place in the conversation. However, children can sometimes feel overwhelmed at the great number of *possible* answers to such questions. So as time goes by and you feel more confident in using your growing collection of Chosen Signs, give your child a set of limited options from which to choose.

By asking him **WHAT** he wants, the **BOAT** (with a *Signing Smart* Body Lean to the left) or the **DUCK** (with a *Signing Smart* Body Lean to the right), you help clarify the spe-

Despite having over two hundred words, twenty-one-month-old Isabel continues to benefit from her family's use of *Signing Smart*. Here, Grandma pairs **DOLL** with a *Signing Smart* Body Lean to the left and **BALL** with a Body Lean to the right. This gives Isabel a "forced choice" of which toy she wants to splash into the pool, while it also visually emphasizes the difference between these two similar-sounding words. Isabel answers with a hearty "ball!"

cific question you are asking. In addition, you model for your child two of the possible responses you are seeking, which not only structures the interaction but also gives him the tools necessary to take his rightful place in the conversation by responding with one of your two signs. Top it off with a *Signing Smart* Attention-Getter and invitation, such as tapping your child's hands and asking him to "show Daddy with your hands," and you will find your child signing back or expanding his vocabulary in no time.

Three Little Ducks

Possible signs: **MOMMY, DUCK, OUT, MORE, HELP, BABY, LOOK-FOR.** Please see the *Signing Smart* Illustrated Dictionary on page 192.

While the "real" version of this song has five ducks, you may find that your child's attention span is better suited to this shorter, three-duck version. Remember that you don't need a CD player to expose your child to songs. Your child loves to hear you sing, and there is no such thing as "off-key" in the world of young children; to your child, there is no sweeter music than the sound of your own voice.

So set up the bath with three small **DUCKS** and one large **MOMMY** duck in it. As you sing the song, take the **BABY DUCKS** one by one from the tub and **HIDE** them. Alternatively, set the **DUCK** family on the ledge of the tub, tipping each baby off and onto the floor in turn. When all three ducks are gone, ask your child, "Is **MOMMY DUCK** happy or sad without her **BABIES**?" Pause and see if your child responds. If your child does not reply, fill in the blanks for her. Tell her, "The **MOMMY DUCK** is sad without her **BABIES**.

♪ SONG ♪

"Three Little Ducks"

Three little **DUCKS GO-OUT** to **PLAY**, over the hills and far away.
MOMMA DUCK says, "Quack, quack, quack, quack," but only two little **DUCKS** come back.
Two little **DUCKS** . . . One little **DUCK** . . .
Sad **MOMMA DUCK** . . . And all of her three little **DUCKS** come back!

Let's **HELP** her **LOOK-FOR** her **BABIES**." Then resume with the last verse of the song as you and your child find the babies.

SIGNING SMART LITERACY EXTENSION:

You will easily find *Five Little Ducks* in board-book form. So pull it out during nonbath times and read aloud or enact the story. For example, after reading the tale, bring it to life

Using signs in grounded, meaningful contexts facilitates learning and communication. Here, seventeen-month-old Clay and his nanny sign and talk about getting the ducks (and themselves!) **WET**.

Signing Smart lets your child ask for specific activities. Here, fifteen-month-old Rachel asks to sing the **MOMMY** duck song.

by setting up a small basin as a pond for the ducks. Be sure to dress for a splashing playful mess!

DEVELOPMENTAL DETAILS:
"I TRY AND SIGN BEFORE, DURING, AND AFTER EVERY ACTIVITY BUT I HAVE FOUND IT IMPOSSIBLE. I'M READY TO GIVE UP!"

Don't give up! Our research on the development of signs and words in young hearing children demonstrates that signing each time you say the word, or signing before, during, and after each event is not necessary to experience success. More important than the number of times you sign in a given day are the *contexts* in which you sign. For example,

when you build off of your child's love of his rubber duck by singing this song, reading the book, enacting the story, or engaging in conversation about the ducks without singing, you are using *Signing Smart* techniques for meaningful communication and extended learning. A *few* of these interactions allow learning to happen more easily, more quickly, and more prolifically than do *dozens* of "before, during, and afters" that follow your own (rather than your child's) agenda. Rather than having sign monologues *add* together *slowly* over time, our research has shown that taking advantage of the Four Keys to *Signing Smart* Success will allow experiences to *multiply* together for *more rapid* success.

Soap Scientists

Possible signs: **CHANGE, BATH, BUBBLES, CLEAN, WET, WATER**, signs for bath toys or books. Please see the *Signing Smart* Illustrated Dictionary on page 192.

Signing Smart creates collections of short but meaningful interactions in which children are actively engaged and thereby motivated to participate with signs and words. Here, twenty-month-old Grace signs **BUBBLES** as she delights in the wondrous array of experiences in her bath.

From your child's perspective, bathtime is a great time to explore the properties of water and how objects are affected by this intriguing medium. So when you have the time and patience, open the door to some messy baby science experiments in the tub. Let your child discover how **WATER CHANGES** color with child-friendly food coloring; how **BUBBLES** pop atop **WATER**; that no matter how **WET BATH BOOKS** get, they still float; and so on. Give your child permission to "paint" the walls of the tub with soap crayons or to color her **DUCK** green.

You may find it easier to get your agenda met (e.g., give your child a shampoo) while she is happily engaged in looking up to catch the **BUBBLES** (be careful they don't get in her eyes). When the fun is done, break into the "**BATH, BATH,** take a **BATH**" song and scrubby, scrubby, scrubby, scrubby your little scientist **CLEAN**.

TROUBLESHOOTING:

TAKING ADVANTAGE OF OUR *SIGNING SMART* ADAPTATION STRATEGIES

Our *Signing Smart* Attention-Getters and Adaptation Strategies are easily integrated into any activity. For instance, as your child watches the water turn colors, move the sign **CHANGE** between his gaze and the changing water. Bring a duck to *your face,* drawing your child's gaze upward before signing **DUCK.** Tap your child's hands while saying, "**DADDY** is saying **DUCK** with his hands. Can Antonio say **DUCK** with his hands also?" Or use Language Clustering and begin quacking; when your child looks over, sign. You can also sign **DUCK** directly on the *duck's bill* or *your child's face* so that he never has to look over to you to see/feel the sign. Or try hand-over-hand signing: Take your child's hand and gently bump it against his mouth while saying **DUCK.**

DEVELOPMENTAL DETAILS:

"MY BABY HAS NO SIGNS AND DOESN'T SEEM TO SEE ME SIGNING—WILL SHE EVER SIGN BACK?"

• Take stock of your Starter Signs—are you using six to twelve and keeping a balance between See A Lot / Do A Lot and Highly Motivating Signs; are you also including a few General Signs in each category, to allow you to sign in any situation (the *Signing Smart* Start)?

• Watch your child for even accidental hand movements; use these to create *Signing Smart* Opportunities and invite her to interact.

• Bring signs into your child's world—this will allow her to continue to explore and still have access to the sign information.

• Remember that children's signs often look very different than ours; observe your child carefully—she may in fact be signing.

• Don't forget the learning cycle. The time before children produce signs is important for conceptual development and understanding. Regardless of how much your child is signing, she is benefiting from the visual highlights that *Signing Smart* provides.

CHAPTER 5:

Bedtime Activities

BEDTIME IS PERHAPS the quintessential time for snuggles, quiet games, whispered words, and hugs and kisses. At least, these are what we parents seek. Children, however, often have very different ideas about bedtime, deciding it's the perfect time to bounce on Daddy, be tickled by Mommy, or chase the dog around the house.

Let *Signing Smart* help your child transition from more active games to more quiet play as you settle down for the night. The following activities include rituals that signal either the transition to bedtime or the end of the bedtime routine—the time when it's your child's job to relax, close her eyes, and fall asleep. Draw on this guide to incorporate the Four Keys to *Signing Smart* Success into your bedtime routines. After all, what better way to leave your child for the night than with the closeness, intimacy, and understanding that *Signing Smart* brings?

♫ SONG ♫

"For Kylie"

(TUNE: "FROSTY THE SNOWMAN")

Mommy loves her Kylie, she loves her all the
  time,
And 'cause she loves her Kylie, she made up
  this rhyme,
She loves her when she's happy, she loves her
  when she's sad,
She loves her when she's feeling good, and
  when she's feeling bad

A NOTE ABOUT RITUALS AND LULLABIES

Bedtime routines help your child prepare for and understand the transition from being together to being apart, and different children need different things in order to wind down. For Kylie, it was twenty minutes of out-and-

Signing Smart has given fifteen-month-old Alma a way to anticipate **BED**, making this a smoother transition for her.

♪ **SONG** ♪

"For Maya"

(TUNE: "OH MY DARLING")

Little Maya, little Maya, Mommy loves her
  Maya so,
And she'll hold her, and she'll rock her, and
  she'll love her, don't you know,
Through the days, and through the nights, and
  through the months, and through the years,
Mommy loves her little Maya, loves her little
  Maya dear

out roughhousing with Daddy; for Natasha, the same three books in the glider with her special bear. Knowing that each child's needs are unique, we have developed various types of activities to integrate into that special time before bed.

Along with bedtime rituals come nighttime lullabies. While *you* may feel you have a terrible voice, there is no sound more soothing to your *child,* no matter how off-key you sing (and believe us, no one is more off-key than Michelle!). If you are worried about forgetting the words, make up your own. Michelle created a "special song" for each of her girls that she sings to each right before bed (or whenever one needs comforting). Each knows that the song is "just for and about her" and signals the outpouring of love only a parent or trusted caretaker can offer.

Feel free to adapt these songs, or make up your own. As for signing the words—don't worry! Using *Signing Smart* Conceptual Grouping, you can tell your child it's time for her special song while signing **MUSIC**; **I-LOVE-YOU** when singing "love"; **BABY** while singing your child's name; and then you can gently sign **BED** on your child as you come to the end, signaling that the time for sleep has come. So scoop your child into your arms and enjoy the intimacy of the *Signing Smart* bedtime activities that follow.

Good Night Walk

Possible signs: **BED, KISS,** signs for objects to say good night to (e.g., **DOG, BLANKET,** etc.). Please see the *Signing Smart* Illustrated Dictionary on page 192.

One activity that is particularly effective in helping your child let go of playing and transition to bedtime is to take him on a "good night" walk, stopping to **KISS** each important item (e.g., his toys, his high chair, the dog, even the moon) good night. Your child will more easily accept bedtime when he thinks others are going to bed as well. So comment that the **DOG** is going to sleep (Conceptual Grouping: **BED**), that the high chair is taking a rest (Conceptual Grouping: **BED**), and that everything will be there when he **WAKES-UP.** When possible, say good night to the same items in the same order. The repetition and predictability will allow your child to anticipate what is coming and will allow him to focus on the signs and thereby participate in the interaction sooner. Such predictability also allows your child to anticipate the end to the activity and begin to "prepare" to say that final good night more willingly.

The sign **KISS** is wonderful for this activity because, while the formal sign goes from the side of your mouth to end resembling the sign **MORE**, it can easily be adapted. That is, your (or your child's) "kiss hand" can move from the side of your (or his) mouth to land on the dog or your child's tummy rather than your (or his) other hand. And while it would be tough to **KISS** the moon, repeated bounces of the "kiss hand" toward the moon will work just as well. In this same way, your child can **KISS DADDY** even if Daddy is not physically present to nuzzle (by moving the "kiss hand" toward a photo of Daddy, for example, or toward Daddy's favorite chair in the living room). Your child will also love the extra **KISSES** he can get—even while lying in his crib—and you don't have to make that back-breaking lean over the crib rail! Also, don't forget *Signing Smart* Language Clustering—make kissing noises to extend the **KISSING.**

TROUBLESHOOTING:
ADAPTATION STRATEGIES FOR FULL HANDS

Because we suggest that you carry your child for this activity, draw on your various *Signing Smart* Adaptation Strategies:

Good Night Walk is a wonderful activity to combine *Signing Smart* Adaptation Strategies. Here, Maya's babysitter signs **BLANKET** one-handed *on Maya;* nine-month-old Maya shows she understands what comes next by signing **BED**.

- Make your two-handed signs into one-handed ones.

- Use your child's *body* to serve as a "second hand." For example, instead of ending the sign **CHAIR** on *your* fingers, end the sign on your *child's* hand, arm, or even knee or thigh.

- Sign **DOG** or **BLANKET** on *your child's* body, giving him both visual and tactile access to the signs.

Turn Off the Lights

Possible signs: **LIGHT, LIGHT-ON, LIGHT-OFF, MORE, FINISH, BED.** Please see the *Signing Smart* Illustrated Dictionary on page 192.

After spending many months lying on her back, your child has great curiosity about these fascinating and magical things called lights. She directly experiences their wondrous effect—making things light or dark—and yet no one ever talks about them. This is another great transitional activity that will not only allow your child to explore these fascinating objects but will also help her to let go of playing and to move into getting ready for bed. For young children, transitions are very difficult as they involve the loss of an activity as well as a loss of control. Bedtime can be trying, especially because it involves the loss of connection with a parent or caregiver for a (relatively) long period; thus, many children resist giving up daytime play for the events that signal the night.

Knowing this, we developed an activity to give positive control back to children, while allowing parents to support them in the necessary transition to bedtime. So scoop your child into your arms and tell him it is time to put all the **LIGHTS** to **BED.** For young children, giving them the "power" to literally put *other* things to bed makes them less resistant to go to bed themselves. So walk around your house, turning on and then off many different kinds of lights (**LIGHT-ON/LIGHT-OFF**)— overhead lights, lamps, night-lights, toys with lights, even flashlights. Brush your child's teeth with the "Brush, Brush, Brush Your Teeth" song (see page 92), turning off the bathroom light and finally their own room's light.

TROUBLESHOOTING:

CONCEPTUAL ADAPTATIONS OF THE SIGN 'LIGHT'

The ASL sign for light shows the light beams splaying outward from the "light source" that is your hand. Because this sign is conceptually based, it can be adapted to show how any individual light splays its beams, allowing you to move the sign so your child can see the actual light and see the sign at the same time.

Twelve-month-old Joey and his mom have great fun going around the house, signing and talking about turning on and off the **LIGHTS**.

SIGNING SMART
ADAPTATIONS
FOR THE SIGN 'LIGHT':

- *Overhead light or table lamp:* as pictured in the dictionary

- *Lights in baby toys, balls, on Christmas trees:* done with your palm upward (because the light rays splay up and out from these items) and your hand directly on, near, or in the direction of the light source

- *Flashlights:* hold your hand horizontal and sign **LIGHT** in the beam of the flashlight or at the place on the floor where the beam is shone

Brush, Brush, Brush Your Teeth

Possible signs: **BRUSH-TEETH, LIGHT-OFF, HELP, FINISH.** Please see the *Signing Smart Illustrated Dictionary* on page 192.

While children love to play with toothbrushes, it is common for toddlers to resist having their teeth actually brushed. Children often accept toothbrushing as part of the bedtime routine when they're distracted by a rhyme or song. It is important that the song be familiar enough to feel comforting, yet novel enough to hold their interest. We adapted this song to satisfy both criteria. Re-

peat this song as many times as necessary to complete the **TOOTH-BRUSHING** process. After the last repetition, scoop your child up, bring him over to the light switch, and let him (or help him) turn the **LIGHT-OFF.**

♪ SONG ♪

"Brush, Brush, Brush Your Teeth"

(TUNE: "ROW YOUR BOAT")

BRUSH, BRUSH, BRUSH your teeth,
BRUSH your teeth tonight,
Back and forth, back and forth,
Before we turn out the **LIGHT** [sign: **LIGHT-OFF**]

DEVELOPMENTAL DETAILS:

"WHENEVER I SING THIS SONG, MY CHILD OPENS AND CLOSES BOTH HIS HANDS BY HIS EARS. COULD HE BE SIGNING 'LIGHT' EVEN THOUGH HIS SIGN LOOKS NOTHING LIKE MINE?"

Just like children's early *words* are their own versions of our words ("baba" for "bottle"), their early *signs* will follow suit. For example, it is common for children to produce one-handed signs with both of their hands—they often have difficulty isolating a single hand (if both are free) when they produce a sign. It is also common that, when children produce a sign that involves opening and closing their hands, their movements are less precise and crisp than ours are.

Recognizing your child's versions of signs is the Third Key to *Signing Smart* Success, and we cannot emphasize it enough: If you see something that remotely resembles a sign, take advantage of that *Signing Smart* Opportunity and react as if it is one! "Yes, you're right. We do sing about a **LIGHT** [supply the correct sign] in this song! Good remembering!" If you recognize your child's versions of a sign and continue to respond by reinforcing the "correct" sign, your child's sign will develop closer to the standard form. This may happen over weeks or months, but more important is the fact that the two of you understand each other!

Fourteen-month-old Nadia signs a two-handed version of **LIGHT** as she also *says* "light." Recognizing your child's versions of signs is the Third Key to *Signing Smart* Success and will go a long way to facilitating word development as well.

Tickle to Touching

Possible signs: **GENTLE, MORE, BED, KISS.** Please see the *Signing Smart* Illustrated Dictionary on page 192.

If you have a child like Kylie, who tends to ask for active play right when it's time to wind down for the evening, this activity is for you. (If your child easily transitions into quiet activities at night, try this at other times of day.)

Start by tickling your child from head to toe—neck, belly, thighs, and feet. Next, transition into a less "stimulating" kind of touch. Tell your child you are going to **KISS** her whole body and follow the same path with soft, light kisses. You can actually kiss your child, or use the sign itself to kiss your child more quickly all over (e.g., bounce the "**KISS**" hand all over your child's body while making kissing noises [Language Clustering]). Last, tell your child you are going to give **GENTLE** touches to help her relax. Rub your hands in soothing circles starting at her forehead, going down her arms and legs, and ending at her feet. Let her know that now it is time to get ready for **BED**.

DEVELOPMENTAL DETAILS: "ALL I HAVE TO DO IS PUT MY SON DOWN ON HIS BACK AND HE IMMEDIATELY SIGNS 'MORE,' EVEN WHEN I HAVEN'T TICKLED HIM YET. DOES HE REALLY KNOW WHAT 'MORE' MEANS?"

When your child signs **MORE** before you've even begun the activity, he is using the sign to mean "I want that game" rather than "I want *more* of that game." This is a very common type of *overgeneralization*—when a child uses a word or sign more broadly than an adult would.

SIGNING SMART PARENT STRATEGY:

Initially, when you ask your child if he wants **MORE** and then give him what he desires, what is salient for him is that he received what he was hoping for. Your child needs your help to understand that specific signs have specific meanings. So, draw on your *Signing Smart* knowledge base and tell him, "I see you saying **MORE** with your hands, I think you want me to play the tickle/GENTLE game you love so much!"

Fourteen-month-old Kylie reminds Michelle that the Tickle Game ends with **GENTLE** touches.

Over time your child will distinguish "more" from "want," but it will take weeks to months before he has enough experience and awareness to make this distinction. More important is your patient message that specific signs have specific meanings (and that the two of you understand each other)!

Bedtime Books

While reading with your baby is one of the most wonderful long-term gifts you can give to him, it can often feel like an exercise in futility. Reading can and will be a magic time in your house if you have some *Signing Smart* Reading Strategies under your belt.

Select a handful of books that highlight your *Signing Smart* Chosen Signs.

- Choose those that have one character or action that repeats on every page (e.g., a book with a bunny character, to highlight **RABBIT** or **JUMP**).

- For bedtime, look for books that are also lullabies, to allow you to read, sign, and sing your child to sleepiness.

- Choose books that allow you to not only tell the story, but also allow you to "read" the pictures, or to invent your own tale, highlighting the actions or objects of interest to *your child*.

- Take advantage of signing board books to make reading and signing seamless and fun. Some of these books state they are ASL-based but also depict invented gestures, so be sure to investigate before you

purchase any of them. See www.signing smart.com for more on board books that use true ASL signs.

- Be alert to your child's versions of signs and create *Signing Smart* Opportunities from them. Encourage any and all attempts at active participation (e.g., signs, glances, points, babbles, page turnings, book switching, and so on). Doing so gives your child control of the reading session and allows him to participate more fully.

TROUBLESHOOTING:
READING FAVORITE BOOKS WITH VERY YOUNG CHILDREN

Signing Smart makes it easy to follow your child's interest, so there is no need to shy away from books that do not fit the above characteristics. If you want to read a bedtime classic such as *Goodnight Moon* by Margaret Wise Brown (Natasha and Nadia's favorite), take advantage of all your *Signing Smart* resources!

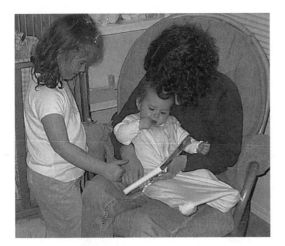

Bedtime stories are the perfect time to snuggle and take advantage of some *Signing Smart* Adaptation Strategies. Here, reading is a family affair, with five-year-old Natasha signing **PHONE** directly on the book that nine-month-old Nadia is mesmerized by.

- To use the book as a soothing ritual and transition maker, read the text in a soft voice, sprinkling in your *Signing Smart* Chosen Signs along the way (e.g., **PHONE**, **BEAR**, **LIGHT**, etc.).

- To use this story more interactively, use your General Signs to ask **WHERE** the mouse is **HIDING** on each green room page and then **HELP** your child **LOOK-FOR** it. Or ask **WHAT** she sees and watch her gaze—then talk about what she is looking at.

- Use *Signing Smart* Adaptation Strategies to allow your child to look at the pictures, hear the story, and experience your signs simultaneously. For example, sign **CAT** directly on the picture or on your child. En-gage your child with *Signing Smart* strategies such as Language Clustering and Conceptual Grouping. For instance, sign **PHONE**, making it "ring" (Language Clustering) literally off the page or off your child's ear, or blow up the balloon with blowing noises (Language Clustering) as you sign **BALL** (Conceptual Grouping) directly over the red balloon. Or sign **LIGHT-OFF** directly above the lamp, while talking about how night is coming and it's time for **BED**.

These techniques are not applicable only to *Goodnight Moon*—with them, you can read and sign almost any bedtime book, and you will enrich your intimate reading time at the end of a busy day.

Bears (and Children) Are Sleeping

Possible signs: **BEAR, WAKE-UP, KISS, BED.** Please see the *Signing Smart* Illustrated Dictionary on page 192.

Probably the most important part of your bedtime ritual is the way you leave your child when it's time to fall asleep. Many parents mistakenly avoid letting their child know that bedtime is coming, fearing it will make the transition more difficult. However, if you give your child enough experience anticipating the last thing you say or do before you leave his room, he is much *less likely* to be surprised or upset when that leave-taking happens. Knowing this, we designed an activity to help children transition from a last bit of parent-child playtime to falling asleep.

Start the interaction by putting a stuffed bear to bed. As you sing the accompanying song, lay the **BEAR** (or other security item) on the bed (you may cover it with a small **BLANKIE**). After the **BEAR** is snuggled in for **BED**, tell your child it is his **TURN**. Get your child nestled into bed; sing the song again, substituting his name for "bear." Soften your voice as you sing through the verse, and end the song with light kisses (real or with your "**KISS**" hand) on his cheek or belly.

SIGNING SMART LITERACY EXTENSION:

To extend the activity and give your child more time to prepare for the leave-taking transition, begin the interaction with a book such as *Corduroy* by Don Freeman. Connect the story to your child's bear, commenting on how his **BEAR** is going to go to **BED** just like when Corduroy was in the furniture department. Proceed with the activity as described.

DEVELOPMENTAL DETAILS:

"MY CHILD SIGNS 'BED' WHEN I KNOW HE IS NOT TIRED. I PUT HIM IN ANYWAY, AND HE CRIES AND CRIES! SHOULD I JUST IGNORE HIS SIGN?"

Children are such interesting (and confusing) creatures! Enhancing communication with your child requires that you attend to two pieces of information at the same time. The first is deciphering the *actual sign* your child produces. But part of *Signing Smart* is also determining his intended *meaning*. For instance, if your child signs **BED** and then balks when you put him into his crib, it may be the *meaning* you have misunderstood. Rather than asking to be put to sleep, your child may instead be asking for his pacifier or blanket that he *associates* with his bed. Your child may have "overgrouped" blanket or pacifier into his understanding of **BED**, and from his perspective, he is communicating very clearly about what he is looking for—"those other comfy things that I love that are in my bed." So when your child uses signs in such "confusing" ways, draw on your knowledge of development and look for his *meaning* as opposed to simply his *words*.

Children are endlessly fascinated by bears. Here, twelve-month-old Natalie signs **BEAR** while playing with fourteen-month-old Sarah in their *Signing Smart* Beginner Play Class.

♫ SONG ♫

"*Bears Are Sleeping*"

(TUNE: "FRÈRE JACQUES")

BEARS are sleeping, **BEARS** are sleeping,
In their **BED**s, in their **BED**s,
Waiting to **WAKE-UP** again, waiting to
    WAKE-UP again,
Shh, shh, shh [gesture: finger across lips],
    Shh, shh, shh

PART II

Signing Smart Activities
for Play

CHAPTER 6:

Floor-Time Play

NEVER UNDERESTIMATE the importance of getting down on your child's level and playing with her on the floor. All of the activities we developed for this section are wonderful ways to turn floor time into *Signing Smart* Opportunities that multiply the fun and extend the learning your child does through play. So grab a bucket of balls, a pile of books, or other appealing objects and plop down on the ground beside your child, using these activities as a starting place to engage your child with words, signs, actions, and experiences.

Getting down on the floor with your child is a surefire way to engage him in interaction. Here, sixteen-month-old Liam, who has Down syndrome, enjoys taking turns with the **PHONE** he and his dad are playing with.

TROUBLESHOOTING:
KEEPING YOUR SIGN BALANCE

Some families' first inclination is to use their Highly Motivating Signs during playtime and reserve their See A Lot / Do A Lot Signs for routines. As we have stressed throughout this book, the Fourth Key to *Signing Smart* Success is using signs for both early communication and long-term learning, and this involves using *both kinds of signs during all kinds of activi-* ties. Doing so will also allow you to interact over a greater variety of items in a wider variety of contexts. Remember, asking your child if he wants **MORE** is just as relevant for a fun activity as it is for his quickly disappearing crackers. Commenting on a toy your child is mouthing is a wonderful way to integrate **EAT** into playtime. And giving your child the means to say he is **ALL-DONE** looking at a book is very powerful for a young child.

"MY CHILD SIGNS THE SAME SIGN TO ALMOST EVERYTHING!"

The road to communication is not without its bumps and hurdles. Along the way some children choose a particular hand movement (even one that you've never actually shown them) and use it often to refer to various items. For some, this sign will mean "**I-WANT-THAT**" (e.g., moving their fist in the direction of a desirable object). For others: "**GIVE-ME-ATTENTION**" (e.g., waving their fist in front of them while watching you intently). However, children often hear their parents say, "Do you want that car?" or "Is that the book you want?" or "That's a cow." In this way, parents may be unknowingly "creating" or "reinforcing" a **THAT** sign, which children then use to refer to any number of items or to get their parents to *talk* about interesting objects.

Because your *child* initiated an interaction, this is the moment he is most primed to learn; it is the perfect time to create a *Signing Smart* Opportunity and respond with additional signs/words/experiences. Use the *Signing Smart* strategy of Dual Labeling, adding the additional reference to your child's invented **THAT** sign (e.g., "Do you want **THAT CAR**?"). By using both signs, you visually demonstrate to your child that the sign **THAT** is not a synonym for **CAR**. Remember, it may take several weeks or months for your child to expand his sign vocabulary.

Streamer Fun

Possible signs: **FAN, MORE, WHAT, STOP, FINISH, WIND, SILLY, PLAY.** Please see the *Signing Smart* Illustrated Dictionary on page 192.

Signing Smart interactions can be enjoyed by the whole family. Here, Nick and nine-month-old Nadia enjoy the spoon with blowing streamers, while five-year-old Natasha adapts the sign **FAN** to be in Nadia's line of sight.

Have you ever noticed how ceiling fans are magical to young children? In this activity, we build off of young children's fascination with fans to create a wonderful sensory learning experience. Tape streamers or ribbons to the blades of a ceiling fan. You can either lay your child under the fan or hold him up to it in your arms. Remember, *Signing Smart* is about moving beyond simple point-and-name interchanges, so turn the fan on and interact both about the familiar ("Do you see the **FAN**? The **FAN** is going around!") as well as the novel ("**WHAT** is on that **FAN**? Are those streamers on the **FAN**? Should I make them turn some **MORE**?"). Turn the fan off and comment that the **FAN STOPPED**, asking your child if he wants **MORE**.

You can also use a tabletop fan with streamers taped to the grate, or bring over a streamer-laden object (e.g., a straw), or baby-safe pinwheels. Get your child's attention with the *sensory aspect of the fan* (the feeling of the wind), and move the sign into his line of sight, asking him, "Do you feel the **FAN**? It's making **WIND** on you!" Before turning the fan on, create a moment of Heightened Anticipation for your child (e.g., asking "**WHAT** will the **FAN** do to the streamers/pinwheel?").

Caution: Be sure to keep your child's hands away from any moving parts, watch that the streamers/pinwheels are not a choking or strangulation hazard, and keep streamers away from the motor of the fan.

TROUBLESHOOTING:
"UGH! MY CHILD HAS ONLY ONE SIGN: 'FAN'!"

It is frustrating to feel as if you are "waiting" for your child to add more signs—especially if he does what many children do and signs only one sign, often. Some children use their one sign correctly and some use it as an Attention-Getter (e.g., "Look at me, Mommy, I'm using my hands"). When Nadia first started signing **BALL**, she used it all the time to talk about anything she found interesting. By using *Signing Smart* strategies such as those suggested below, Reyna was able to help Nadia expand her vocabulary and reach her Sign Cluster at only nine months of age.

for your child to learn more signs and reach his Sign Cluster or his Language Explosion. But we promise it will happen, and when it does, you will not remember this frustrating time. The other thing to remember is that talking about the **FAN** for the 150th time may not be interesting to *us*. But to our children, it is a key to opening up the world of interaction. If you think about it, by just moving that little hand, your child gets your attention and gets to talk about things that matter to him, whenever *he* wants. How great is that?

SIGNING SMART PARENT STRATEGY:

When your child signs, he is initiating a conversation with you, so extend it with additional signs. By adding *other* signs at these moments, your child is more likely to learn them; he is primed to absorb new information because *he* initiated the interaction. Sometimes it will feel as if it is taking forever

Hiding Tower

Possible signs: **WHAT, WHERE, MORE, PLAY, HIDE, LOOK-FOR, SURPRISE,** Highly Motivating Signs. Please see the *Signing Smart* Illustrated Dictionary on page 192.

In this game we use a childhood favorite—nesting cups. But instead of placing the cups inside one another, we turn the cups over so that you can stack them like a tower (smallest cup at the top). Keep your towers short —unless the goal is a "topple the tower" game (which is great for signing **WHAT, MORE, PLAY, SILLY,** and **CLEAN-UP**). Choose baby-safe toys that match your Chosen Signs and can be hidden under the cups. Place one object on the floor and cover it with the largest cup. Place the next toy atop the upside-down cup, and then put the next largest stacking cup on, so that it is hiding the second toy, and so on. (Keep the tower out of your baby's reach until you're ready to play; and once you begin the game, hold the lower cups so that your baby is more likely to be successful at taking one off at a time.) An alternative to creating a tower (especially for children particularly interested in knocking it down in one fell swoop) is to hide each of the toys under its own cup on the floor. To add interesting variety, use see-through Tupperware of various sizes for stacking or arranging next to one another.

You can focus on discovering the toys under each cup by asking your child, "**WHAT**'s under here? Oh, look, you found the **BEAR**! Should we **LOOK-FOR MORE** animals? **WHAT**'s **HIDING** under this one?" You can mix up the game by looking for a single item. For instance, ask your child, "**WHERE** is the **CAR**? Let's **LOOK-FOR** it! Wow, the **CAR** was all the way at the bottom of the tower!" If you're hiding objects under individual cups (rather than in a tower), an ad hoc game of hide-and-seek can ensue: "Let's **HIDE** the **KEYS**. Can Jason do it? **WHERE** are those **KEYS**? **SURPRISE**! You found the **KEYS**!" or "**WHERE** is **DOGGIE HIDING**? Oh! You found the **CAT**. Let's **LOOK-FOR** that **DOG**!"

TROUBLESHOOTING:
PLAYING WITH ACTIVE CHILDREN

As you have undoubtedly discovered, all infants and toddlers have very short attention spans, but some children are simply more active than others. Believe us, Kylie was an extremely busy toddler and wasn't still for a moment! But have no fear; it only takes a second for your child to see/feel the sign, hear the word, and to be drawn (for a moment) into the playful interchange. *Signing Smart* helps you to go with *your child's* interest rather than your own. So if your child's delight is simply to knock down the tower (again and again!), change the focus of the activity and alter your expectations. The goal of *Signing Smart* is for you and your child to explore, discover, and create together, and your child may have his own definition of "interaction." Ask your child if he wants to knock down the tower some **MORE**, comment on how **SILLY** he is, or ask him to **LOOK-FOR** the **DOG** among the fallen toys. Enjoy your child for who he is and what he brings to your interactions. Doing so will not only extend the fun (for both of you), but will also allow you to take advantage of your child's individual interests, allowing learning to happen seamlessly. If you have a very active child, don't forget the *Signing Smart* Active Play Activities in Chapter 7.

Itsy-Bitsy Spider

Possible signs: **SPIDER, MORE, RAIN, SUN.**
Please see the *Signing Smart* Illustrated Dictionary on page 192.

Songs that rely on repetition allow children to "participate" early on. Here, nine-month-old Nadia looks upward, anticipating Reyna's adapted **SUN**, making the song a "duet" of sorts.

Using *Signing Smart* strategies, we transform "The Itsy-Bitsy Spider" into a language-rich experience that is sure to engage and delight even the youngest of children. To make the song kinesthetic, use the sign **SPIDER** to tickle your child's tummy. You can facilitate your child's tactile understanding of the concepts of "up" and "down" by crawling your "**SPIDER** hands" up your child's body during "climbed up the water spout," and by wooshing your hands down and off your child's torso when singing "washed the spider out." Adapt the sign SUN so that the beams (your splayed fingers) are directed *at your child*. If you are consistent with where you sign SUN, you may just notice your child do what four-month-old Nadia did—"participate" from a very young age by glancing upward in anticipation of the sign. Extend the activity by reading a book based on the song or by enacting the "story" with relevant props. What a wonderful way to communicate and interact, even before your child is signing back on his own!

TROUBLESHOOTING:

"I WOULD LOVE TO DO MORE SINGING AND SIGNING, BUT I KNOW SO FEW SONGS. WHAT SHOULD I DO?"

Another wonderful *Signing Smart* language learning tool is to take a familiar song and sing new words with it. In doing so, we alert our children to the melody while refocusing their language-learning attention on the new and unexpected words—thus helping them attend to the interaction in a new way. This

Language-learning attention is enhanced when we take a familiar song (such as "The Itsy-Bitsy Spider") and then change the words, heightening our child's awareness of what stays the same (the tune) and what differs (the words). Here, Michelle leads the Intermediate Play Class in a festive rendition of "The Great **BIG** Elephant," using signs, creative lyrics, and the "ham-it-up" factor to capture and engage children's attention.

song has many possible adaptations (e.g., singing about the great big **LION** who went out to **PLAY** in the grass and made a splash when the **RAIN** came down, etc.). In this way language learning is enhanced when we incorporate the familiar (and build up expecta-

tion) and then vary the expectation (to reengage interest and heighten language awareness). Draw on both of these *Signing Smart* strategies with the words to any familiar song.

Car Wash

Possible signs: **MORE, PLAY, WET, WATER, BATH, CLEAN, RAIN,** vehicle signs. Please see the *Signing Smart* Illustrated Dictionary on page 192.

Children love to play with and in water—sometimes much to our dismay! However, one aspect of the *Signing Smart* partnership between parents and children is facilitating developmentally appropriate exploration in a way that remains manageable to parents. Thus, we give you the Car Wash! Do this activity outside on a sunny day or in the bathtub any time of year.

LOOK-FOR several baby-safe vehicles, baby soap (if your child is likely to mouth the washcloths, skip the soapy part), a few washcloths, and a watering can (to rinse the vehicles). Help your child lather/scrub the cars. "**WHAT** are you doing? You're giving the **CAR** a **BATH**!" or "**WHERE** should we pour the **WATER**? Do you need **HELP**? Now the **CAR** is nice and **CLEAN**!" or "Look! The **WATER** coming down is like **RAIN** on the **CAR**!" Don't have many vehicles among your Chosen Signs? Incorporate any items of interest that allow you to take advantage of your

Chosen Signs and the Four Keys to *Signing Smart* Success while engaging and playing with your child. For example, ask your child, "Should we **PLAY** with **MORE CARS** or does your **DOLL** or your **DUCK** need a **BATH**?"

TROUBLESHOOTING:

TAKING ADVANTAGE OF THE FOUR KEYS TO *SIGNING SMART* SUCCESS

As we described previously, the goal of *Signing Smart* is to give parents new tools to enhance what they are already doing with their child. While all the activities in this guide were developed to take advantage of the Four Keys to *Signing Smart* Success, we want to take a moment to show you exactly what this looks like in the context of a specific activity. Note that these same strategies can be used in any activity.

1. *Creating Signing Smart Opportunities:* Watch your child's interest. Is he more invested in getting the **CARS WET, PLAYING** with the various toys, dumping **OUT** the **WATER**, or something else entirely? Whatever it is that engages him, enter his

play and sprinkle in a sign or two along the way!

2. *Bringing Signs into Your Child's World:* Sign **BATH** or **WATER** directly on your child's body, sign **CAR** right above the toy car he is looking at, tap his hands, and ask him to tell you with his hands if he wants **MORE**. Use Language Clustering to get his attention (e.g., say "beep, beep" while signing **CAR**).

3. *Recognizing Your Child's Versions of Signs:* Recognizing your child's version of the sign or responding even to accidental hand movements that resemble signs takes no extra work, just extra attention. Remember to create a *Signing Smart* Opportunity out of these hand movements to encourage your child's increasingly purposeful signs.

4. *Facilitating Both Early Communication and Long-Term Learning:* In this activity, you can facilitate communication and learning by using both See A Lot / Do A Lot Signs such as **WHAT**, **WHERE**, **MORE**, **ALL-DONE**, **BATH**, **CLEAN**, and **PLAY**, and Highly Motivating Signs such as **CAR**, **BUS**, **AIRPLANE**, **TRAIN**, **KEYS**, and **DOLL**. Don't forget to also use signs such

as **OUT**, **IN**, **COLD**, **HELP**, and **WARM** and ground these more "abstract" concepts in a playful and meaningful context, giving your child the tools to better understand them.

Sense-ational Toys

Possible signs: **HOT, COLD, WARM,** Highly Motivating Signs. Please see the *Signing Smart* Illustrated Dictionary on page 192.

One way to facilitate both early communication and long-term learning is by grounding abstract concepts such as hot and cold in the context of children's play, where children can directly explore or experience these concepts and therefore more easily learn them. Choose a handful of toys, preferably pairs (e.g., two bears or two rubber ducks), placing one in the dryer/sunlight and the other in the freezer. If you're using your dryer, be sure to set it on low and be sure your toys are dryer-safe!

Take one pair of toys out of the dryer and freezer, letting your child touch and mouth the **COLD** and **WARM** objects. Be sure to test them first, commenting to your child if the **DUCK** is too **HOT** to **PLAY** with right now. If the temperature is right, use the toy's warmth or coldness against your child's skin to get his attention. For more sensitive children, place the items atop their clothing; for less sensitive ones, place the toys directly on their skin. To further the learning opportunities, add *Signing Smart* Assorted Cues: Use tone of voice,

Dual Labeling (e.g., **WARM DUCK**), Body Leans, and Language Clustering (e.g., "quack, quack") while describing both the temperature and the toys themselves. Ask your child, "Are you **EATING** the **COLD DUCK** [Body Lean to the left]? Here comes the **WARM DUCK** on your arm [Body Lean to the right]. Quack, quack!" When your child loses interest in the pair or when the temperature regulates, choose another pair or call it quits.

VARIATION:

Use washcloths, wrapping your child's hand in a **WET, COLD** cloth and then a **WARM** one. Move on to her feet, belly, cheeks, and back of the neck, allowing her to better understand the concepts of **WARM** and **COLD** through the direct experience of feeling the sensations on different parts of her body.

TROUBLESHOOTING:
THE VALUE OF DUAL LABELING

As you take advantage of Key 4 and add more signs to your repertoire (especially those that

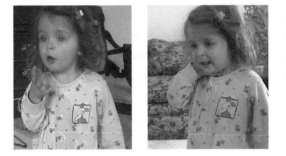

Signing Smart strategies such as Dual Labeling help children better understand concepts and expand their vocabulary. Here, nineteen-month-old Kylie comments on her **WARM PIG** pajamas, fresh from the dryer.

will facilitate learning, such as signs that describe qualities of objects), recall the *Signing Smart* strategy of Dual Labeling. That is, when using an adjective (e.g., **WARM**) that describes an object (e.g., **DUCK**), use *both* signs. Why? This helps your child realize that your new sign (**WARM**) is not a *synonym* for the sign he's more familiar with (**DUCK**). Dual Labeling also lets him see the new sign *and* the familiar one, allowing him to focus his language-learning energy on the *new* sign. This will help him realize that he has a **WARM** *DUCK,* not just a **WARM**. Using Dual Labels in this way will help your child understand abstract concepts such as temperature more easily—e.g., lots of things can be warm (a **WARM DUCK**, a **WARM BLANKIE**, a **WARM DRINK**, etc.).

Hide-and-Seek Hands

Possible signs: **HIDE, MORE, EAT, LOOK-FOR, WHERE,** Highly Motivating Signs. Please see the *Signing Smart* Illustrated Dictionary on page 192.

Babies are truly little scientists, actively exploring their world and seeking to understand how things work. One developmental challenge is learning to understand object permanence—that objects and people exist even when we cannot see them. While a budding awareness of object permanence occurs at around eight months (when children begin to protest our leaving because they know we continue to exist even after we go), it is not fully developed until somewhere between eighteen to twenty-four months.

One playful way to support your child's developing awareness of object permanence is to engage him in peekaboo games. Babies love these games because they are a fun and nonthreatening way to learn about how objects can "disappear" and "reappear" (but still exist in the meantime). They are also wonderful ways to be *Signing Smart* with children—engaging them in activities that heighten anticipation, focus conceptual and language learning energy, promote development, and

facilitate intimacy. A simple game of peekaboo can inspire lots of learning!

In *Signing Smart*'s variation of this family favorite, choose baby-safe objects from your Chosen Signs (e.g., **BALL, DUCK,** even **FINGER-FOODS**) that you can fit in your fists. **HIDE** an object in one hand, and ask your child, "**WHERE** is it?" or "**WHAT**'s in **DADDY**'s hand?" If she chooses the correct hand or names the object, reveal the toy and talk about it with words and signs ("Wow, you found the **CRACKER**. Do you want to **EAT** it?" or "Look, it's a **BALL**! Should we **PLAY**?"). Don't forget to look for other "invitation" behaviors—body wiggles, glances, points, babbles, and so on, taking advantage of the short but developmentally rich interactions fostered by this *Signing Smart* activity.

DEVELOPMENTAL DETAILS:
SIGNING AND TALKING

Even as your child begins speaking, *Signing Smart* will continue to enhance and facilitate communication. Learning to talk is a long journey for all children—they understand more than they are able to say, and early words are often difficult for parents to understand, leading to frustration on both sides. Here *Signing Smart* can be a lifesaver—allowing parents to distinguish their child's similar-sounding words.

SIGNING SMART PARENT STRATEGY:

Use *Signing Smart* Body Leans to ask your child, "You're saying 'ba!' Do you want the **BALL** (Body Lean to the left) or the **BOTTLE** (Body Lean to the right)?" This technique invites children to continue to use signs past the point of early words, clarifying their spoken requests. In fact, many children in *Signing Smart* families *spontaneously* vocalize words and produce signs at the same time (e.g., they say "ba" while signing **BALL**), allowing parents to understand what their children are saying when they produce an ambiguous-sounding word.

Even as children begin speaking, *Signing Smart* will allow parents to more easily understand their child's growing vocabulary. During their favorite Hide-and-Seek Hands game, fifteen-month-old Rachel says "ba" while signing **BALL**, allowing her mother to know exactly what she is talking about.

What's in Mommy's Bag?

Possible signs: **PLAY, WHAT, MORE, HELP, WHERE, PHONE, KEYS, BOTTLE, FINGER-FOODS, TURN, DADDY, MOMMY**. Please see the *Signing Smart* Illustrated Dictionary on page 192.

Ever notice that the zipper on your purse or diaper bag is fascinating to your baby? And why is it that the toy **PHONE** is never as interesting as the real one that **DADDY** uses? We developed this activity with an understanding of young children in mind, but be sure you are comfortable with giving any of the suggested items to your child. While babies learn through exploration, there are of course limits to what is safe and desirable for them to explore.

So fill your purse or diaper bag with interesting, baby-safe objects—a cell phone, keys, sunglasses, snacks, a bottle, a pacifier, your wallet (no change or money), loose credit cards, and so on. Feel free to include some "purse" objects that you don't know *the* sign for, remembering that you can use *a* sign instead (e.g., **PLAY, WHAT, MORE, HELP, SILLY**, or **WHERE**).

As your child pulls objects from your bag,

take these as invitations and create *Signing Smart* Opportunities by commenting on the object and initiating interactions around them ("You have **MOMMY**'s **PHONE**. Are you **CALLING GRANDMA**? Can **MOMMY** have a **TURN**?"). Follow your child's lead, expanding your interaction around the objects that hold his interest and moving past those that seem less enticing.

TROUBLESHOOTING: UNDERSTANDING *SIGNING SMART* CONCEPTUAL SIGNS

Parents often ask us what the signs for **BOTTLE** and **PACIFIER** are. Especially in the context of this activity, these are two great signs to have at your fingertips. While there are no standard signs for these two English words, we recommend the use of *Signing Smart* Conceptual Signs. Conceptual Signs are based on ASL classifiers—particular hand-shape-movement combinations that depict/describe items that have no standard signs (such as "yogurt," "baby bottle," "pacifier," and "finger foods"). Building on our knowledge of ASL classifiers, *Signing Smart*

Signing Smart Conceptual Signs allow parents to refer to objects that don't have a standard ASL sign. Here, thirteen-month-old Eli's mom comments that he preferred his milk in a **BOTTLE** rather than a cup.

has developed Conceptual Signs, which are representations of objects or actions that are based on true classifier forms. And while true classifiers are rarely isolated productions like those included in the dictionary for **BABY-BOTTLE**, **PACIFIER**, **FINGER-FOODS**, and **EAT-WITH-SPOON**, an ASL-user would still understand the general aspects of such signs. For instance, with **BABY-BOTTLE**, an ASL user would know that you were talking about a fist-sized object tipped at the mouth; with **FINGER-FOODS**, she would know you were describing small objects that were being picked up between the thumb and index finger. By helping parents understand the richness of ASL's classifier system and by teaching them to use Conceptual Signs when standard signs don't exist, *Signing Smart* stays true to (and respectful of) ASL, while at the same time providing parents with ASL-based ways to sign these items of importance to their children.

Oat Box

Possible signs: **HIDE, MORE, EAT, LOOK-FOR, WHERE,** Highly Motivating Signs. Please see the *Signing Smart* Illustrated Dictionary on page 192.

Children learn through all their senses, but as a parent of a young child, you know better than anyone that one of the primary ways babies explore is with their mouths. And while some babies are more oral than others, all use their mouths to better understand their

The Oat Box is a great place to allow babies to safely explore using all their senses. Here, three-year-old Kylie signs directly on nine-month-old Maya, commenting that she sees her **EATING** the oats.

world. For many families, this means of exploring makes trips to the playground difficult, as parents spend the entire visit trying to keep rocks and sand out of their child's mouth. So let *Signing Smart* bring a baby-safe sandbox to you!

Fill a box with an inch or two of uncooked, plain oats and place it on a sheet. Sit your child in the oat box, talking about the oats on his hands, feet, and in his mouth. ("Are you **EATING** the oats? **WHAT** are you **PLAYING** with? **WHERE** are your toes?") Choose a few toys from your Highly Motivating list to partially or fully **HIDE** in the oats (depending on your child's age and developmental level). Encourage your child to **LOOK-FOR** the **KEYS, DUCK,** or **BALL.** After he finds the toys, ask if he wants **MORE** and comment that you're **HIDING** the toy again.

DEVELOPMENTAL DETAILS:
"MY ELEVEN-MONTH-OLD CAN SAY THE WORD 'MORE'; SHOULD I BOTHER TEACHING THE SIGN?"

Sometime between ten and fourteen months, your child will begin to *say* his first words, making you wonder if you should continue to *sign* these words. While you don't *need* to, there are a number of reasons why doing so is beneficial. *Signing Smart* focuses on giving your child every resource to communicate, and many families notice their child's first words are those which *parents* have been signing! This is because *Signing Smart* not only allows parents to highlight spoken words with signs but also teaches them how to integrate these "highlighted words" into contexts that facilitate learning.

But why continue signing a word your child can say? If your child has the word, she understands the concept behind it and can thereby more easily learn its sign. Learning the *sign* for a word she can *say* will help her more easily understand the role of signing in communication in general. This in turn will allow her to more easily learn signs for words she cannot yet say. In this way, learning signs for words she *can say* will allow her to sign more words that *she cannot yet say* more quickly.

In addition, while your child has only a few words, you will easily identify her spoken word as "more." But when she has a good handful of similar-sounding words (and she will), you may not know whether she is say-

ing "more," "muffin," or "mama." In this situation, continuing to use the sign will be a life-saver. Your child may spontaneously pair words and signs, or you can *ask* her to "show Mommy," thereby allowing the sign to clarify her speech. In this way, you will be able to correctly respond to her spoken utterances, fostering the development of *both* signs and words (alone and in sentences) more quickly.

Gift Wrap Surprises

Possible signs: **WHAT, MORE, HELP, WHERE, IN, OUT, TURN, TOWEL**, Chosen Signs. Please see the *Signing Smart* Illustrated Dictionary on page 192.

As you know, children love to take things out of containers! In helping you to work with this developmental imperative, we designed this activity to satisfy your child's desire in a new way. Take an empty, wide, cardboard tube and cut it to various lengths (or cut the bottom out of a round oatmeal container). Gather scarves or small towels that you can shove into the tube, and choose a small selection of Highly Motivating objects. Remember, you don't have to be limited to only those toys whose sign you know—if you don't know *the* sign for an object, substitute *a* sign, using *Signing Smart* strategies such as Conceptual Grouping or using more General Signs.

Fill the tube, alternating towel-toy-towel-toy, or wrap the toys in the scarves or towels. You can also place a single toy in the center and stuff both ends with small towels. Encourage your child to pull the items from the tube. If your child takes them out one at a time, you can talk about the individual items; if she takes out many at once, you can comment on the process of taking things **OUT**. Have fun discovering the treasure within while *Signing Smart* with your child: "**WHAT** did you find this time? Oh, look, it's your **KEYS**. Are you putting them back **IN**?"

SIGNING SMART LITERACY EXTENSION:

One way to extend this activity is to ground it in a meaningful story. But don't limit yourself to a book that matches exactly! Any story about opening gifts will provide the perfect springboard to engaging your child in Gift Wrap Surprises in new and exciting ways. For example, read a board book version of *The Nutcracker,* connecting the story to the activity: "Clara loved opening the gift and seeing the **DOLL**. I wonder **WHAT** is **HIDING** in your 'gifts'!" Or, "**MOMMY HID** a **DOLL** in one of these packages, too. **WHERE** do you think it is? Can you **LOOK-FOR** it?"

TROUBLESHOOTING:

**"HELP! MY CHILD IS NOT DOING THE
ACTIVITIES RIGHT!"**

Don't worry if your child does the activities differently than we suggest. That is the marvelous thing about children—no two are alike! If your child delights in simply pulling the towels out with nary a moment to notice the interesting objects inside, you know your comments will be more about the process than the objects (asking your child if he needs **HELP** getting the **TOWELS OUT** or if he wants to put **MORE IN**). We have said this many times, but it is worth repeating: The intention of *Signing Smart* is to *create interactions around what interests your child.*

What you engage over with your child is less important than *the interaction you create together.* So let your child lead the way, but don't hesitate to invite her into your play— see if she wants to join you in **LOOKING-FOR** the **KEYS** among the array of **TOWELS**; playfully shout **SURPRISE** as the keys fall out; grab a towel and play an ad hoc game of peekaboo, and after each rendition ask your child if she wants **MORE**.

Letting go of what an interaction *should* be and participating in the moment as it *is* will allow both of you to have more fun. In addition, your child will learn more, and both of you will further your signing experiences faster if you let go of trying to "get your child" to notice or care about the *car* when she is really focused on the *experience* of making a mess!

Silly Scarves

Possible signs: **OUT, IN, MORE, SURPRISE, PLAY, HAT, DANCE**. Please see the *Signing Smart* Illustrated Dictionary on page 192.

There is something about a tissue box or opened wipe container that serves as a magnet for young children. Reyna remembers a time when fourteen-month-old Natasha was a little too quiet playing on the floor. When Reyna looked up, she saw a proud Natasha surrounded by a mound of tissues—and an empty box! To save you the trouble of picking up countless tissues, try this family-friendly version: Save some empty tissue boxes or wipe containers and gather some colorful scarves, washcloths, or other material that can be shoved in and then pulled out of the boxes. You may also choose to use a variety of shape-sorter containers, leaving corners of scarves peeking out of any number of holes.

This activity is a wonderful opportunity for you to integrate many of your See A Lot / Do A Lot Signs into playtime and to extend your child's conceptual learning. For instance, ask your child, "Do you want to **PLAY**? **WHAT** is in there? **WHAT** can you do? Can you take them **OUT**? Do you need **HELP** to get them **IN**? Can you take **OUT** some **MORE**?"

Let the array of colorful scarves dictate what happens next: Will your child throw them in the air? Cover her face for peekaboo? Place it on her head like a **HAT**? Use them as part of an impromptu **DANCE**? Whatever she does, you have your next invitation to another *Signing Smart* Opportunity, and many more laughs and hugs!

DEVELOPMENTAL DETAILS:
TURNING "NO'S" INTO "YES'S"
THE *SIGNING SMART* WAY!

Parents of toddlers often find that they say "no" more frequently than they would like to. Let *Signing Smart* take that "no" and turn it into a manageable "yes"! The key is employing a little redirection. First, understand that your child's actions are developmentally appropriate but are being expressed in an inappropriate context. Next, create a suitable environment for the very same behaviors.

The above activity is a perfect example of a *Signing Smart* Opportunity that redirects your child's actions. You can turn "No yank-

Signing Smart allows you to turn "no's" into "yes's." Here, Michelle invites fifteen-month-old Jack to pull scarves **OUT** of the wipe container, giving him a developmentally appropriate yet manageable outlet for this type of exploration. Taking appropriate control of this interaction, he tells her he wants to put the scarves **IN**.

ing the tissues out" into "Great idea! You like taking those **OUT**! Let's **LOOK-FOR** your wipe container and pull the *scarves* **OUT** instead." Take advantage of this guide to create *Signing Smart* Opportunities while also turning potential "no's" into "yes's":

- *No* = overturning drinks on the high chair tray;
  Yes = Food Surprises (see page 60)

- *No* = eating sand at the playground;
  Yes = The Oat Box (see page 118)

- *No* = coloring on the walls;
  Yes = Soap Scientists (see page 84)

- *No* = climbing on the furniture and jumping off;
  Yes = The Bear Went Over the Mountain (see page 162)

Spoon Fun

Possible signs: **IN, OUT, WHAT, WHERE, HELP, TURN, SPOON.** Please see the *Signing Smart* Illustrated Dictionary on page 192.

Working from children's universal fascination with taking things out of containers, we created this simple **IN/OUT** activity that will move you beyond pointing-and-naming (e.g., "Do you have a **SPOON**?") to using signs for long-term learning (e.g., "I see you putting the spoon **IN**! Can I **HELP**?).

Fill a plastic container with a collection of similar objects (e.g., infant spoons or cylindrical blocks). Watch your child as she naturally begins removing the spoons from the bin. Do you notice her spontaneous glance up at you to "show off" her accomplishment? Take advantage of this *Signing Smart* Opportunity, asking her if she took the spoon **OUT** (Body Lean to the right) and needs **HELP** putting it back **IN** (Body Lean to the left). If your child tires of this (or you do), shift the focus and ask your child **WHAT** she is doing or comment on the fact that she is **EATING** the **SPOON** or ask for a **TURN** to put the **SPOON IN**, and so on.

Signing Smart facilitates both early communication and long-term learning, allowing your family to benefit from these techniques for years to come. Throughout this guide, we have included activity extenders to allow you and your child to take full advantage of all that *Signing Smart* has to offer. Each activity is designed so that you can revisit it again and again, creating new or extended interactions each time. For instance, in addition to the above suggestions, you can further highlight the conceptual aspect(s) of this activity by signing only the word(s) you want your child to focus his learning energy on—in this case **IN** and **OUT**, or **HELP**, or **TURN**. Add some *Signing Smart* Assorted Cues (e.g., Body Leans, tone of voice, demonstrations of the actions you describe), and you have turned a simple activity into a language-rich, conceptual-learning experience!

Signing Smart strategies allow you to use ASL signs for both early communication as well as long-term learning. Here, fourteen-month-old Hannah learns more about the concepts of **OUT** and **IN** through her mother's use of words, signs, and *Signing Smart* strategies such as Body Leans.

Cloth Hiding

Possible signs: **PLAY, WHAT, HELP, WHERE, TURN,** Highly Motivating Signs. Please see the *Signing Smart* Illustrated Dictionary on page 192.

Believe it or not, thin cloths (baby washcloths, cloth diapers, and especially silk scarves) make great playthings for young children. They're easy to manipulate, fun to shake, and offer a wonderful tactile experience for even the youngest of babies. What's more, they are the primary ingredient of some playful but stimulating developmental tasks made famous by psychologist Jean Piaget. This activity will not only take advantage of children's fascination with lightweight materials but will also allow you to play amateur child psychologist. Can you figure out which Piagetian Stage your child is in?

Choose two or three identical cloths and a toy your child particularly likes. Show your child the toy, talk about it, let her play with it, and then hide it under one of the cloths. For children under eight months, *leave a portion of the object sticking out* from under the cloth. Ask, "**WHERE** did Mommy **HIDE** your **DUCK**? Let's **LOOK-FOR** it!" Encourage her to pick up the cloth; comment on her suc-

cess! Try hiding the object completely; if your child seems confused (as if saying, "Where did it go?"), ask if she needs **HELP** and remove the cloth for her. As your child grows, make the activity more complex by hiding the toy under one cloth and then moving it *in plain view* so that it's underneath the next. Can your child find it under the correct cloth or does she look where you first hid it? Can your child find it even if you *hide it in your hand* as you transfer the object from under the first cloth to the second? Just think how much fun your child is having while you are discovering something new about her developing cognitive skills!

DEVELOPMENTAL DETAILS:
PIAGETIAN STAGES OF THE DEVELOPMENT OF OBJECT PERMANENCE

Stage 3: Four to eight months: Infant reaches to get an object that's partially hidden, but doesn't search for a completely hidden object.
Stage 4: Eight to twelve months: Baby looks for a completely hidden object, but if you re-hide the object under a second cloth (even in the child's full view), she will still look under the first cloth.

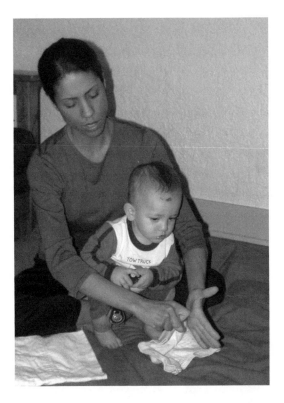

This simple hide-and-find game allows parents to become amateur psychologists, discovering at what stage of object permanence is their child currently. Here, thirteen-month-old Eli shows his mom that he knows where the **KEYS** went by finding them under the second cloth.

Stage 5: Twelve to eighteen months: Toddler will find an object that's fully hidden, even if it is rehidden, as long as he can watch you move it. If you move it secretly (in your fist so your child can't see it changing locations), he will only look under the first cloth and then move on to another activity.

Stage 6: Eighteen to twenty-four months: Toddler will continue looking for a hidden object (whether or not she saw it being moved) as if she's sure it *must* be somewhere!

What's in the Bag?

Possible signs: **PLAY, WHAT, TURN, OUT, IN, MORE,** Highly Motivating Signs, etc. Please see the *Signing Smart* Illustrated Dictionary on page 192.

Your child's early experience is one of constant discovery, so we developed this simple activity to nurture your child's drive for unearthing the wonders of his world while facilitating your use of *Signing Smart* strategies and techniques. Have your child go "shopping" around the house with you to **LOOK-FOR** different kinds of bags (gift bags, paper lunch sacks, or empty purses) as well as different Highly Motivating objects to put in them. Once you have toys in several sacks, create Heightened Anticipation (and facilitate early memory skills) by peeking inside one with an excited expression and asking, "**WHAT**'s in there? **SURPRISE**! Can Sara take it **OUT**?" Choose items that make noise to capture your child's attention (and to invite you to do Language Clustering!). You're also likely to find that your child wants to play with the bags themselves—a wonderful opportunity to talk about the different textures, colors, and qualities. "You like to **PLAY** with the paper bag. It crinkles. Do you want **MORE** bags?"

TROUBLESHOOTING:

"I THINK MY CHILD HAS ABOUT TWELVE SIGNS, BUT I HAVEN'T SEEN HALF OF THEM IN WHAT SEEMS LIKE WEEKS. WAS I JUST IMAGINING SHE HAD ALL THOSE SIGNS?"

The short answer is no, you aren't imagining that she has those signs. Our research with families in our *Signing Smart* play classes indicates that young signers, especially those under twelve months of age, tend to favor a subset of their signs for a period of time. Then this focus changes, and you will likely see a different subset of signs used frequently for a number of days to weeks. As your child grows, you will see many more of the signs in her vocabulary across a much shorter span of time.

DEVELOPMENTAL DETAILS:

"MY CHILD USED TO HAVE A HOST OF DIFFERENT TOY SIGNS, BUT NOW HE WILL ONLY SIGN 'BALL'. WHAT'S GOING ON?"

This is an example of a common developmental phenomenon called *U-shaped Development* —when children seem relatively advanced (having many signs) and then seem to regress (dropping to a single sign) and then (*weeks to months later*) seem to end up back where they started (with lots of signs again). This happens because children are in the process of organizing the information around them into manageable "chunks" or "units" known as categories. Previously, your child had merely memorized a list of names for different objects. And while this works for a time, needing to memorize the individual name for every item actually slows your child's vocabulary development. The solution? Category formation! So when your child drops signs in favor of a single one it is actually an advancement! He has learned to group a variety of individual ideas or concepts into a single category (in this case, possibly **FUN-TOY**) that he uses a single sign (**BALL**) to convey.

SIGNING SMART PARENT STRATEGY:

Determine the category your child has formed and use your *Signing Smart* tools to visually distinguish two of the different concepts your child has lumped with a single sign. For example, say, "Mommy sees you signing **BALL** [sign **BALL** as you do a Body Lean to the left]. But I see you pointing to your **KEYS** [sign **KEYS** as you do a Body Lean to the right]. I think you really want to **PLAY** with your **KEYS**." Patience is important during this frustrating time. Reminding yourself that your child is actually advancing in his development can sometimes help.

Reading and Playing with Your Child

Signing Smart makes it easy to combine story time with playtime, increasing both the fun and learning that reading affords. Tips to make reading together more enjoyable:

- "Reading" a book may last no longer than fifteen to thirty seconds. You may get several of these short interactions in a row, but interest in any one book is likely to be fleeting.

- Mouthing books, turning pages, and switching between books in a stack are actually ways your child is *participating* in the reading experience!

If you incorporate some of the *Signing Smart* Reading Strategies we specifically developed for use with young children, you will make the most of these short but rich reading interactions (see page 96 for Reading Strategies around bedtime):

- Stack the deck in your favor by sitting down with several books that highlight your *Signing Smart* Chosen Signs, especially those with the same character or action on every page.

- Use conceptually related props (e.g., a stuffed bear for a bear book, a ball for a story in which that object appears even once).

  * Use the props to hold your child's attention and to extend the amount of time you are able to spend on each book.

  * Our research demonstrates that conceptually related props facilitate Grounded Learning, making a two-dimensional picture "come alive." So make your stuffed tiger bounce; swoosh your rubber duck as if it's swimming; lay your doll down for a nap; or simply let your child play with the ball that appears but once, drawing animated attention to it when it does. No doubt you will find that these antics will hold the attention of even the most active child.

  * As your child gets older, encourage him to act out the actions in the book—either by himself or with the conceptually related props you both gather. This creates an incredibly rich "learning through play" experience.

- Remember that you do not have to read the

text word-for-word! This is especially true when turning reading time into playtime.

* Motivate your child to participate by asking engaging questions with General Signs such as **WHAT**, **WHERE**, **LOOK-FOR**, and **HIDE**.

* Be aware of your child's gaze, what he points to, and any rough attempts at signing. These are all ways that your child signals his interests—take advantage of each as a *Signing Smart* Opportunity!

Signing Smart makes reading more engaging and interactive for even very young children. Here, Lilly's grandmother combines Language Clustering with signing **EAT** directly on the book, clearly captivating seven-month-old Lilly.

* Include more than pointing and labeling ("There's the **BALL**. Here are some **KEYS**.") by connecting the book with your child's interests and everyday experiences. For example, "Here are some **KEYS**. **MOMMY** has **KEYS** too. You love to make my **KEYS** jingle!" or "That monkey is **JUMPING** on the **BED**. Do you think she will **FALL-OFF**? **OUCH** (Conceptual Grouping: **PAIN**), she needs some **HELP**!"

• Draw on your *Signing Smart* Adaptation Strategies to bring signs into your reading experience—remember to sign on the book, above the book, or on your child.

Signing Smart for Tired Parents

No one knows better than we do how busy the lives of young families are. Some days you feel lucky to take a shower, much less have time to sit and engage your child around topics of interest to her. At such moments—when you are tired and distracted—signing can feel like a burden. It is with this reality in mind that we offer you ways to be *Signing Smart* without your needing to get off the couch! Rather than decide you are too exhausted to take advantage of this book, have a look at the activities below. They will not only allow you to create *Signing Smart* Opportunities while relaxing on the sofa, but they will also allow you to *create moments of Heightened Anticipation,* where children are riveted and thereby primed to learn (see page 164 for more activities). So take a seat and put your feet up. *Signing Smart* is easy, even when you're tired, as long as you have the right tools:

- *Jack-in-the-Box:* Turn this simple game into a *Signing Smart* Opportunity by stopping midstream and asking your child **WHAT** will happen. When the clown pops up, talk about how **SILLY** the clown with the **HAT** is (signing directly on the clown), ask your child if he wants **MORE MUSIC**, and so on.

- *"I'm Hiding":* With young children, you can **HIDE** in plain sight and they will still have fun **LOOKING-FOR** you. So put a **BLANKIE** or pillow over your head and **SURPRISE** your child time and again with this stationary version of hide-and-seek.

- *Water Paints:* Grab a paintbrush or two and build anticipation as you "paint" or tickle your child (with or without **WATER**). Pause mid-design and ask if he wants **MORE**. As he gets older, have *him* paint *you;* preschoolers will love to try and guess the letter or shape you "paint" on their bellies or backs.

- *Straw Blowing:* Build off your child's delight in the above activity by bringing out a straw and blowing on various parts of your child's body. Build Heightened Anticipation by drawing in a noisy breath and making eye contact with a big smile, asking if she wants **MORE**.

- *Bounce and STOP:* With your child on your lap, begin to rhythmically bounce him on your knees. Then stop, signing **STOP** in his line of sight. Ask if he wants **MORE**. Allow him to control the session by inviting him to **STOP** you. Create Heightened An-

You can still be *Signing Smart*, even if you're tired or busy. Here, Michelle does nothing more than stop the Jack-in-the-Box music midstream and ask "**WHAT** will happen?" engaging the children in a moment of Heightened Anticipation. All are riveted and participate in their own way: nineteen-month-old Sophie signs **WHAT**, wondering what will happen; seventeen-month-old Roan shows with actions he knows how to find out; two-year-old Nicholas is starting to sign **HAT**, letting them all know the cat with the **HAT** will pop up.

ticipation by varying the number of bounces between each **STOP**.

- *Tickle Games:* Bring out a Highly Motivating animal (e.g., **BEAR**) and tickle your child with it. Pull it back and ask if he wants **MORE**. Or use your **KISS** hand and kiss your child's hands, feet, belly, and so on. Ask if she wants **MORE BEAR KISSES**. Don't forget that you can also do this activity while chanting children's rhymes. So, for example, have fun repeating "This Little Pig" on your child's hands or feet, asking if she wants **MORE** after each tickling.

CHAPTER 7:

Active Play

I S YOUR TODDLER always on the move? Does your infant give the heartiest giggles when he's swung through the air? Or are you looking for ways to interest your "sit-and-play" child in some *Signing Smart* active play? All children learn through exploration—and moving their bodies and discovering their world in this way is one important avenue for understanding how things work. We can take advantage of this universal way of learning by combining Grounded Learning techniques with gross motor play. Grounded Learning is when parents create a foundation for abstract concepts (such as running versus jumping) by allowing children to experience these concepts directly. This direct experience allows children to better understand and learn the concept/word/sign. Knowing the importance of this kind of play, *Signing Smart* has developed a host of simple but no less rich and engaging activities that combine physical exploration with both fun and learning.

TROUBLESHOOTING:

STRATEGIES FOR GROSS MOTOR PLAY

Because of the nature of gross motor activities, you will find your *Signing Smart* Attention-Getters and Adaptation Strategies particularly useful. We developed these strategies to not only help you bring signs into your child's world but also to keep the learning cycle intact. That is, when you sign in your child's line of sight, or directly on his body, he is able to hear the word, see/feel the sign, and continue to move/play with the object of interest. Our research has demonstrated that such techniques will considerably shorten the time frame for signing back and will help expand your child's vocabulary faster.

ATTENTION-GETTERS:

- *Bring the object to you:* Whether you're playing with vehicles or balls, roll the toy toward you or lift it up to catch your child's gaze before you sign.

- *Use Language Clustering:* From "honk honk" to "choo choo" to "bouncy bouncy," your use of fun and conceptually related noises are sure to capture your child's attention and aid learning all at once.

- *Use a sensory aspect of the object:* Does the car beep at the press of a button? Does the ball play music when it rolls? Can you use a beam of light to draw your child's gaze to you? These are ways you can use a toy itself to capture your child's attention while he's on the move.

- *Vary proximity:* As you and your child move about, get close to him to catch his gaze, then sign. Alternatively, if you have been running right beside him, playfully move away—the change in your proximity will lead him to look for you.

ADAPTATION STRATEGIES:

- *Sign on an object of interest:* This technique is great in combination with bringing an object to you. For example, catch your child's gaze by bringing the toy he is look at to you; then sign **BALL** around the ball, **MUSIC** above your instrument, or **TRAIN** on the smokestack.

- *Change the angle of your sign:* Whether your child is crawling next to you or running beside you, tip your hands down while you sign. This allows your child to see your sign "head-on" instead of just seeing the underside of your hands.

- *Use Signing Smart Baby-Talk:* Repeat a single sign throughout an entire sentence (e.g., repeatedly sign **TRAIN** while saying, "There goes your train. Choo Choo. Can you catch the train?"). This gives your child multiple opportunities to see your sign as he's racing after his toy.

Toddler Field Trips

Possible signs: **TREE, PLAY, OUT, FLOWER, WIND, BIRD, WHERE, WHAT, LOOK-FOR**. Please see the *Signing Smart* Illustrated Dictionary on page 192.

Sometimes young children just want to be held—whether they're tired, upset, experiencing after-nap crankies, or just in need of some carrying. While you will sometimes tote your tot around while tidying up, making phone calls, or trying to fit in other one-handed chores, allow the following suggestions to turn some of these "carry me" moments into *Signing Smart* "field trips."

House Tours: Tour the inside of your house looking for interesting "discoveries," especially in places less accessible to your child on her own. For example, notice items on a high bookshelf, the mantle, or on the wall. Use General Signs ("**WHAT** do you see? Do you want to look at the candle some **MORE**?") or strategically place Highly Motivating items for your child to discover ("**WHAT** do you see? Is there a **BEAR** up there?").

Mailbox Venture: Don't forget your child has a world to discover between your front door and the mailbox (be it at the bottom of the elevator or stairs, at the edge of the lawn, or a short walk away). So, however cranky she is, let *her* be your guide and structure your interactions around what *she* notices. Is she looking at the **TREES** blowing in the **WIND**, does she wiggle when she sees the **FLOWERS**? Does she stop and become alert to the sound of the **BIRDS**? Spend a few extra moments interacting about what holds her interest. When you get to the mailbox, draw on *Signing Smart* Interaction Strategies and ask, "**WHAT**'s in there? **HELP** me look!" or "Can you take it **OUT**? Ready to go **HOME**?"

On all such field trips, draw on some *Signing Smart* Adaptation Strategies by signing with one hand (e.g., sign **WHAT** or **WIND** with one hand) or by signing on your *child* as you tote him around. For example, sign **BEAR** on your *child's* chest, or plant the sign **HELP** on your *child's hand or knee* rather than on you own (occupied) hand.

DEVELOPMENTAL DETAILS:
WHEN YOUR CHILD SEEMS TO
STOP SIGNING

Parents sometimes report that their child has suddenly "stopped signing," or has "lost all his signs." When we hear stories such as these, our first question is whether the child is working on another fundamental developmental task, such as learning to crawl or walk. In such cases, it is exceedingly common for children to focus all their energy on that aspect of development, seeming to "regress" in other areas (such as signing). What parents find is that, once their child accomplishes her new feat, her signing picks right back up, often ahead of where she left off, *if the parents continue to use signs* (because she continues to absorb them). Other reasons children "stop signing" include illness or change in routine (e.g., starting child care, having visitors, or traveling).

Encourage your child through her phase, continuing to use signs yourself without "forcing" her to demonstrate her own sign knowledge. For example, if your child is learning to walk and is cranky and needs her **BLANKIE**, get it for her, even if she doesn't ask or "refuses" to sign what she happily would have signed only days before. As you give it to her, say, "Your special **BLANKIE** would sure help right now. I know you can ask for it yourself. You will when you're ready." In doing so, you remind her of the power of her signs while also supporting her need for her security object. Don't forget to continue to sign in various contexts yourself, even if your child is not signing back. She is continuing to learn the signs and *will* start signing again, once she's gotten more comfortable with walking.

Baby Amusement Parks

As adults, we can forget that what is mundane or routine for us is magical for our children. Babies are excited by experiences that bring what fascinates them to life. So open your mind, grab your house keys, and let *Signing Smart* unlock a world of wonder for you and your child. The suggested trips listed below are simple, can be made on short notice or with little preparation, and are inexpensive or free. Bring along this book to consult the *Signing Smart* Illustrated Dictionary on page 192, or check out our Web site at www.signingsmart.com for our convenient-to-carry Diaper Bag Dictionaries.

Your own neighborhood: Pack up the stroller, the baby sling, or your baby backpack and head into the bright **SUN**shine. Walk slowly and listen: Do you hear the **BIRDS**? Did a **BUG** go buzzing by? Are there **FLOWERS** to discover? Walk to the closest bus stop and watch the **CARS** or **BUSES** go by. Take a ride around the block on the **BUS**—no matter how many times you've done this, your child is sure to be captivated!

A trip to the airport: Usually you are harried and frantic when traveling by plane or picking someone up at the arrivals area. But don't miss the wonderful action-packed adventures that await you and your child at even the smallest of airports. Watch the **AIRPLANES** take off and land; ride the rental-car **BUSES** around and back again. Watch the people going by—how many **BABIES** can you see? People with **HATS**? How many purple **COATS**? The possibilities are endless!

The local pet-supply store, pet shop, or Humane Society: Children are endlessly fascinated by animals, and going to pet-supply stores or the like will allow your infant or toddler to see (and sometimes touch) real **FROGS**, **RABBITS**, **DOGS**, **FISH**, or **BIRDS** up close and personal. Kylie loves these trips so much—at almost four years old she still enjoys going to the "petting zoo"!

The local park or pond: What better way for your child to see the **DUCKS** and maybe **HELP** them **EAT**? If there are more geese than ducks to be found (as is true in Denver), draw on your Conceptual Grouping and Language Clustering strategies and sign **DUCK** or **BIRD** while talking about the "honk, honk" geese.

TROUBLESHOOTING:
REACHING THE SIGN CLUSTER AND THE LANGUAGE EXPLOSION

Sometimes parents think that once their child produces even one sign, he or she will begin "signing up a storm." However, our longitudinal research has demonstrated that there are three developmental milestones in any given child's *Signing Smart* journey. The first is the appearance of the first sign.

From there, a child will *slowly and gradually* add signs until she reaches her Sign Cluster (usually between five and ten signs). For some children, this second milestone will be reached in a matter of days; for others, in a matter of months. Chronological age plays a part; however, *a family's use of Signing Smart strategies will greatly influence the time it takes a child to reach her Cluster,* with some children reaching it as young as six months (as Maya did, with nine signs at that age). With the Sign Cluster usually comes the ability to combine signs into "minisentences."

The third milestone is the Language Explosion, which happens on average between eleven and thirteen months in *Signing Smart* families. Once a child reaches her Explosion, she will initiate signing more often, will sign

Children are fascinated by what we consider "mundane." Taking your child to exciting places, such as the local pet-supply store, allows her to interact with and experience animals and the world in completely new ways. Here, eleven-month-old Kylie is riveted by the **FISH** she sees swimming around in the tanks in front of her.

more consistently, will learn new signs very rapidly, and may quickly show a burst in spoken vocabulary as well. For more on these milestones and the anticipated time frame for signing back, see page 14.

Catching Cars

Possible signs: **MORE, WHAT, WHERE, OUT, SURPRISE,** vehicle signs. Please see the *Signing Smart* Illustrated Dictionary on page 192.

Whether you're motivating your baby to crawl or providing a fun way for your toddler to get his energy out, take advantage of the *Signing Smart* Opportunities afforded by this simple but engaging activity. Gather a collection of baby-safe vehicles that easily roll a good distance. Invite your child into play by using an Attention-Getter such as Language Clustering (e.g., "**WHAT** does **DADDY** have? A **BUS**, beep beep! **DADDY**'s going to roll the **BUS** to Emily."). Use the bus as a motivator to encourage your baby to crawl by slowly releasing the toy, letting it roll just out of your child's reach. For toddlers, push the vehicle as far as it will go. Keep the action going by releasing a new vehicle shortly after your child catches her prize. Be on the lookout for her invitations to create *Signing Smart* Opportunities: Does she look at you excitedly when she catches her bus ("You got it! You caught the **BUS**! Should we catch the **TRAIN** or the **CAR** next?")? Does she seem puzzled by how to get the out-of-reach toy ("Should **DADDY HELP**?

Here, can you get the **BUS** now?")? Does she clap her hands in an invitation to reinforce the sign **MORE** ("You'd like **MORE**? Yes, this is fun! Here comes **MORE**. Here's the **TRAIN**!")?

Variation: Take an empty oatmeal container or other enclosed tube and place a Highly Motivating toy inside. Capture your child's attention by shaking the container as you ask, "**WHAT** could be **INSIDE**?" Roll the container in front of your child. When he catches it, offer to **HELP** him open it, ask him to take the toy **OUT**, talk about the **SURPRISE** inside, and so on.

DEVELOPMENTAL DETAILS:
CLUES THAT YOUR CHILD IS UNDERSTANDING YOUR SIGNS

Even before your child produces his own signs, he will understand yours. Language comprehension of both signs and words always precedes production. So, in gathering evidence that your child understands your signs, consider the following:

- Notice whether your child watches your hands while you sign, or shifts his gaze

Catching Cars is a great activity to integrate Language Clustering, giving your child a way to "talk" about vehicles. Here, fifteen-month-old Rachel signs and talks about the "beep-beep" **CAR**.

from the toy he's interested in to your hands.

- Be alert for the *Signing Smart* Triple Look: When your child looks at your sign, at the object, and then at your sign again; or when she looks at the object, up to you for the sign, and then back down at the object/her hands.

- Notice whether your child looks away from his toy and then up to you expectantly, as if "asking" for sign information.

- On occasion, drop the spoken word and produce the sign alone: Does your child look around for, point at, or pick up the item you signed?

If you notice these behaviors, you have strong evidence that your child understands the role of signs in communication—be on the lookout for first sign attempts and begin adding to your Starter Signs!

Marching Band

Possible signs: **MORE, DANCE, STOP, SILLY, MUSIC**. Please see the *Signing Smart* Illustrated Dictionary on page 192.

Children love making and listening to music. And while much of their music making will be while sitting on the floor, part of *Signing Smart* is playfully altering the environments for learning and interaction! One way to build active play into music making is to form a mini Marching Band with your child. So grab an instrument for each of you, and either hold your baby or encourage your toddler to march on his own. Remember, the "instrument" can be as simple as a rattle to shake or a bowl and spoon to bang. Talk about the **MUSIC** you make, how you can **JUMP** or **DANCE** to the rhythm, and how **SILLY** you can be as you wiggle around!

An alternative is to turn listening to (and playing) music into a game of freeze dance. Turn on a CD or play your instruments while you **DANCE, JUMP**, march, or otherwise move around the room. Commenting on your activities using *Signing Smart* Baby-Talk (see page 31 for a description) gives your child multiple opportunities to see your signs as he moves about. Hit pause on the CD, stop playing your instrument, and ham it up as you encourage your child to **STOP** moving, modeling how you stop your *own* body. If your child seems to struggle with stopping on her own, pick her up while you **DANCE** and then **STOP** together. Using Grounded Learning techniques in this way allows her to experience these actions directly. Naturally, ask her if she wants to **DANCE** some **MORE**, and start the **MUSIC** again!

TROUBLESHOOTING:
TAKING ADVANTAGE OF GROUNDED LEARNING

One very powerful *Signing Smart* strategy is Grounded Learning—when we help children directly experience an abstract concept through our use of relevant toys or movement. These abstract concepts can be qualities of objects (e.g., cold versus hot—see Sense-ational Toys on page 112) or they can be actions that are not yet completely distinct in the experiences of a young child (the difference between jump, run, dance, skip, etc.). Because children have less control of their bodies than adults, holding them when we're engaged in different types of motion gives them a direct physical experience of that motion. They are then better able to connect the specific movement with the signs and/or words we are using. In this activity, we help "ground" children's understanding of dancing, jumping, running, walking, and so on by allowing them to feel what happens to their bodies.

There is an additional benefit to using Grounded Learning in teaching a concept like **STOP**. Playing Marching Band allows children to experience what will undoubtedly be a relatively frustrating concept overall (needing to stop) in a more enjoyable context. It is much harder for children to learn a concept like **STOP** when they are upset (let alone during a tantrum) than in a playlike context. When we use this activity to give children the kinesthetic feel for what it means to literally **STOP** moving, we facilitate an understanding of stopping in general, a necessary precursor to being able to **STOP** in other contexts. (For more on the benefits of using the sign **STOP** over "no," see page 157.)

Three in the Bed

Possible signs: **BED, FALL-OFF, MORE, HID-ING, SURPRISE, WHERE,** animal signs, or family signs. Please see the *Signing Smart* Illustrated Dictionary on page 192.

*S*igning *Smart* exposes your child to language-rich experiences in their many forms. Connecting songs, stories, and activities is a wonderful way to surround and engage your child in words, signs, and experiences. So bring out a story version of this song and invite your child to benefit from the many facets of *Signing Smart*! In this activity, we build off an old favorite, "There were Ten in the Bed," adapting it to a more infant-friendly "Three in the Bed" version. So clear off your bed, bring along your child and a stuffed friend or two, and set the stage for the song by talking about how the three of you are cuddling in **BED** and getting ready to **PLAY**. Act out the song using *Signing Smart* Grounded Learning techniques—when you sing about "rolling over," gather your child in your arms and roll back and forth. Then dip her over the side, or make a stuffed friend **FALL-OFF**. When you get to the end of the song, add additional Assorted Cues. For in-

stance, ham it up by closing your eyes, yawning, stretching, and so on as you pretend to go to **BED**. Does your child want **MORE**? Great, start all over again!

With siblings: Invite big sister to "**FALL-OFF**" the bed when it's her turn! Extend the learning with a game of peekaboo ("**WHERE**'s **SISTER**? Is she **HIDING**?") as she—**SURPRISE**!—pops up. Or, leave sister "asleep" on top and lift baby to peek over the bed, making her a more active participant in the game.

♫ SONG ♫

"There Were Three in the Bed"

There were three [or: two] in the **BED** and the little one said, "Roll over, roll over," So they all rolled over, and one **FELL-OFF**.

There was one in the **BED** and the little one said, "Good night! Sleep tight!" [Language Clustering: snoring sounds]

"MY CHILD SIGNS 'RABBIT' TO HER ELEPHANT AND HER BUNNY! IS SHE CONFUSED?"

Young children often use the "wrong" word/sign to label objects in their world. Take heart in knowing that your child's odd use of signs evidences her developing cognitive skills. When children call all animals with big ears **RABBITS**, or all vehicles **CARS**, they are *overgeneralizing* items into a different, larger category.

Children will use words and signs in funny ways. Here, nine-month-old Maya signs **RABBIT** to her stuffed elephants, a sign she also uses for the *Blue's Clues* dog. She has overgrouped these objects into a **THING-WITH-BIG-EARS** category.

SIGNING SMART PARENT STRATEGY:

First, determine the category your child has formed. Draw on your *Signing Smart* strategies and *acknowledge your child's sign attempt while also giving her corrective feedback.* For example, "Yes, she does have big ears like your **RABBIT** [Body Lean to the right]. But, this is an **ELEPHANT** [Body Lean to the left]—see his long trunk?" *Over time,* as your child sees and hears the correct signs/words *and categories* for his overgrouped items, he will gradually begin to differentiate them in his understanding and will produce various signs/words for the specific items/ideas. How soon this happens will depend in part on his age and level of experience with forming categories, and in part on your use of *Signing Smart* techniques to guide him.

Light Walk

Possible signs: **LIGHT, LIGHT-ON, LIGHT-OFF, WHERE, WHAT.** Please see the *Signing Smart* Illustrated Dictionary on page 192.

Children are endlessly fascinated with lights. So take advantage of your child's curiosity and explore your house in a whole new way! Cover a flashlight or two with colored plastic wrap or tissue paper (you may want to have several variations on hand); also having a baby-safe flashlight for your child gives her developmentally appropriate control over the experience. Take your child on a **LIGHT** walk by exploring your house with the flashlights as you provide an intermittent commentary.

You may choose to see what you and she naturally discover or you can **HIDE** specific treasures in unusual places. Notice the tops of cabinets, the undersides of chairs, and so on, using your General Signs when you do not know the specific one (e.g., **WHAT** is on top of the cabinet? How **SILLY**! Your stuffed caterpillar!). Examine things from your child's perspective—see how different the same object can look with the blue light versus the red one. Use *Signing Smart* Body Leans to set apart the two colors.

Variations: Have your child "catch" the **LIGHT** on the floor or wall. Then shine the light on your child (avoiding her eyes), commenting that the red **LIGHT** is on her foot or that the green **LIGHT** is on her belly, and so on.

For older children: Shine two different colored lights and ask her **WHERE** the *blue* **LIGHT** is; invite *her* to shine the *green* **LIGHT** on your foot, or to shine the **LIGHT** on the **BALL**.

SIGNING SMART FOR LONG-TERM LEARNING:
ASSORTED CUES: LIGHT AND DARK

As you know, children are constantly absorbing information; thus, the simplest of events to us is often ripe with potential learning for children! To help them understand new and increasingly abstract concepts, *Signing Smart* has developed a powerful strategy for encouraging long-term learning—using Assorted Cues. This means offering children multiple means to access and learn about ideas and experiences.

• Explain how an experience can be under-

Here, fourteen-month-old Justin signs **LIGHT** as he notices we have turned off the lights. Adding to this direct sensory understanding, his nanny explains in words and signs that when the **LIGHT's-OFF**, it gets **DARK**. Using *Signing Smart* Assorted Cues gives children of all ages multiple ways to understand and learn abstract concepts.

stood by breaking it into parts (e.g., with the **LIGHTS-OFF**, it's dark; with the **LIGHTS-ON**, it's bright).

• Add *Signing Smart* Body Leans to visually set apart two distinct concepts.

• Use tone of voice to highlight the two different concepts (e.g., use a high-pitched voice with **LIGHT**, a deep voice with **DARK**). The "ham-it-up" factor can also help engage your child and extend learning.

• Take advantage of *Signing Smart* Opposite-Handed Signing (e.g., emphasize the difference between **LIGHTS-OFF** and **LIGHTS-ON** by signing the first with your left hand and the second with your right); great in combination with Body Leans!

Zooming Balls

Possible signs: **BALL, TURN, IN, OUT, SUR-PRISE, SILLY, WET, WATER.** Please see the *Signing Smart* Illustrated Dictionary on page 192.

Children are fascinated both by balls and by objects that disappear and reappear, so take advantage of this interest by engaging in these *Signing Smart* "peekaboo" ball games. Collect a bunch of small baby-safe balls as well as several different lengths of tubing. You can use wide wrapping paper rolls, empty oatmeal containers (with the bottoms cut out), or you can roll and staple cardboard to make your own tubes. Use your imagination to find fun places to affix the tubes: tie them to the staircase handrail; lean them against the backyard steps; it will also work if you and your child each hold an end. Place the balls in the tube yourself, building Heightened Anticipation by saying, "**WHAT**'s going to happen? **WHERE** did the **BALLS** go? **SURPRISE**! They pop **OUT**!" (see page 164 for more). Encourage your child to chase after them as they roll out the other end. Then give your child a **TURN** to stuff the balls in the tube ("Are you putting the **BALLS IN**? I can't wait to see them come **OUT**!").

Talk about how far the **BALLS** go on the carpet compared to the wood floor; how **SILLY** it is when they bounce off the walls; how they **JUMP** down the stairs. Try and get the **BALLS** to land **IN** a laundry basket, on a **TOWEL, IN** a bag, and so on. If you are outdoors, see what kind of **WET** splashes they make landing in small buckets with different levels of **WATER** in them. Try using different kinds of balls (soft and hard, light and heavy, bumpy and smooth) to extend the interaction even more. The kinds of balls you use will affect how easy it is to hold them, how fast they come out of the tube, whether they bounce, float, and so on.

TROUBLESHOOTING:

"MY CHILD IS CONFUSED—SHE MAKES THE SAME SIGN FOR 'MORE' AND 'BALL.'"

Children commonly produce "the same sign" to refer to very different concepts. At *Signing Smart* we have identified this phenomenon as the production of *Overlapping Movement Patterns,* and it is a very common occurrence! Children make the same types of overlapping *sound* patterns with words, calling their ball and their bus "ba." Parents naturally recognize these productions as two distinct words when used in the appropriate contexts. So extend the same recognition to your child's Overlapping *Movement* Patterns as well. Is your child confused? If your child appropriately uses each sign in the correct context, the answer is an emphatic, "No." In such cases, your child really does have two signs—**MORE** *and* **BALL**. They just look identical because his motor skills aren't yet developed enough for him to make two distinguishable signs.

SIGNING SMART PARENT STRATEGY:

Use *Signing Smart* Body Leans to provide corrective feedback to your child and to separate out the two words (e.g., "Are you saying **BALL** [Body Lean to the right], or do you want **MORE** [Body Lean to the left]?"). *Over time,* he will better distinguish the two forms. Despite how different these signs look when adults produce them, the following sets of signs often look "exactly the same" on children's hands:

MORE / BALL / SHOES / CLAPPING / HELP / KEY

PLEASE / BEAR / BATH / MONKEY

BED / PHONE / HAT

EAT / WATER / DRINK / PACIFIER / MOMMY / FLOWER / BOTTLE

BUNNY / HORSE / COW / DADDY

LIGHT / FAN / BUBBLES / MILK / BIRD / DUCK

PIG / FROG

BIRD / DUCK / DRINK / FLOWER

Balls Galore

Possible signs: **BALL, TURN, MORE, SILLY, CLEAN-UP, IN, OUT.** Please see the *Signing Smart* Illustrated Dictionary on page 192.

Please see the *Signing Smart* Illustrated Dictionary on page 192.

Balls are the quintessential toy for young children: They are extremely versatile, come in a variety of textures, shapes, and sizes, and allow for a wide range of learning and play at every age. So grab a handful of balls and allow your child to safely explore not only cause and effect (e.g., "When you roll the ball, it moves toward me." "When I throw it, it flies forward.") but also properties such as gravity (e.g., "When I drop the ball, it hits the floor and bounces.").

Infant ball fun: Partially deflate a small beach ball and lay your infant stomach-down atop it. Rock her gently, pausing to see if she wants to **PLAY MORE** on the **BALL**. This will also work well on a larger exercise ball, where you can sit with your child and bounce up and down. Warn her when you are going to **STOP** bouncing (taking advantage of Grounded Learning to teach about stopping) and ask her if she wants **MORE**. Also try bringing out a basket of balls for your infant to take **OUT** or put **IN** one by one.

♪ **SONG** ♪

"Roll the Ball"
(TUNE: "ROW YOUR BOAT")

BALL, BALL, roll the **BALL,**
Roll the **BALL** to **BROTHER,**
Now it's little Cameron's **TURN,**
BROTHER will roll the **BALL** to you

Toddler games: You can set up some challenges for your toddler by bringing out a laundry basket or bucket and, depending on whether it is on its side or upright, encourage her to throw, kick, or roll a **BALL IN**. Facilitate her catching abilities by tossing a nubby ball or a partially deflated small beach ball. Use a broom to **CLEAN-UP** the **BALLS**, sweeping them **IN** the basket.

All children love to play with balls, and they are wonderful objects to use in helping children learn to take turns, a necessary reality for families with more than one child. Here, three-year-old Kylie tells ten-month-old Maya it is her turn with the **BALL**.

DEVELOPMENTAL DETAILS:
HELPING CHILDREN LEARN TO 'TAKE-TURNS'

While all parents want their child to share, this is a very difficult concept for children to learn, partly because it requires children to understand (and care) that something they enjoy is also enjoyable to someone else. This advanced conceptualization will take many,

many, experiences to master (most children do not truly share until after age three!). However, children can begin to understand what it means to **TAKE-TURNS** considerably earlier. This is because turn taking is more concrete to young children, both as a sign (it moves from the person who had the turn to the person getting the turn) and as an experience (when it's my turn I have it to myself and when it's your turn I don't have it at all).

SIGNING SMART
PARENT STRATEGY:

While it is fine to continue to talk about sharing, you will better ground this abstract concept for your child (and thereby make it easier for her to understand and learn) if you yourself talk and sign about **TAKING-TURNS**. You can help your child understand **TURN-TAKING** through activities such as "Roll the Ball" on the previous page.

Bubbles, Bubbles Everywhere

Possible signs: **BUBBLE, MORE, POP, JUMP, DANCE, WHERE, HELP, FALL**. Please see the *Signing Smart* Illustrated Dictionary on page 192.

Bubbles fascinate children of all ages and are the primary ingredient in many exciting games. But don't let their simplicity fool you. There are many possible *Signing Smart* Opportunities hiding in these bubble adventures. Invest in some high-quality bubble solution and a blower that yields many bubbles at once. These steps will ensure that the bubbles stay in the air as long as possible and will free your hands and mouth for signing, chatting, and singing.

♪ S O N G ♪

"There Are Bubbles in the Air"

(TUNE: "IF YOU'RE HAPPY AND YOU KNOW IT")

There are **BUBBLES** in the air, in the air [sing 2 times],
There are **BUBBLES** in the air, there are **BUBBLES** everywhere,
There are **BUBBLES** in the air, in the air

There are **BUBBLES** way up high . . . in the sky
There are **BUBBLES** way down low . . . on your toe

BUBBLE ACTIVITIES

Activity 1: Lead your child on a "bubble chase" by walking backward as you blow your bubbles, asking "**WHERE** are we going? Can you **POP** the **BUBBLES**? I bet you can reach the **BUBBLES** if you **JUMP**!" When your child reaches up to catch the bubbles, her movement will likely look remarkably similar to the sign **BUBBLES**. Reinforce this "accidental" movement as if she were intentionally signing, and you will see her begin signing **BUBBLES** "for real" sooner than you think. "I see your arm in the air. You're signing **BUBBLES**. That's right, **POP** those **BUBBLES**!"

Activity 2: Sing the accompanying song, encouraging your child to move to the lyrics:

When fifteen-month-old Isaam reaches up to pop the bubbles, it is the perfect time for Reyna and the parents in class to reinforce this natural movement that resembles the sign. "Yes, you *are* playing with **BUBBLES**!"

Invite him to **DANCE**, stretch (when there are bubbles way up high), and shrink (when there are bubbles way down low). Expect your child to ask for **MORE** of this engaging song and enjoyable activity!

Activity 3: High-quality bubbles often land on the floor without bursting—what a great invitation to stomp, run, **JUMP**, **DANCE**, and **FALL** to get those **BUBBLES** to **POP**! You may see your child clapping her hands together while playing with bubbles in these ways, especially if you cheer her on as she chases and pops them. Is she clapping or saying **MORE**? Reinforce the clap as the sign **MORE**: "Yes, you're catching the **BUBBLES**. Oh, do you want **MORE**? Okay, here are **MORE BUBBLES**." If you blow more bubbles when your child claps (and if you try and respond to her claps during other activities as if she were asking for **MORE**), in short order you will be rewarded by knowing for sure that she is "really" signing **MORE**!

Activity 4: With older toddlers and preschoolers, engage in a game of bubble catching. See whether your child can catch a **BUBBLE** on her finger, her elbow, or with her own bubble wand. Offer **HELP** and encouragement when necessary.

CHAPTER 8:

Pretend Play

ONE WONDERFUL ASPECT OF *Signing Smart* is that the tools we give you will be useful well beyond when your child speaks her first words (sometime between ten and fourteen months). Understanding two related myths about children's early words will give you a better sense of what *Signing Smart* beyond first words can bring to your family:

Myth of the First Five Words—Rapid Word Growth. Many parents believe that once a child "begins to speak" a handful of words, full-fledged talking will soon follow suit. While indeed the child is on the road to speaking more words more often, the reality is that the development of clearly articulated sentences and extensive vocabularies, even once words begin to appear, takes one to two years! We developed our *Signing Smart* strategies so that *while* speech is developing, your child can continue to extend and expand her vocabulary and her sentence production through *both* words *and* signs.

Myth of the First Five Words—Words Are Easily Understood. Once a child has a handful of words, many parents believe that communication will be facile and smooth. It is true

that parents may find this is the case for their child's *initial* words. For one thing, most of the time parents have a context or the actual object their child is speaking about to help them understand their child's words. For example, a word such as "-at" means hat if the child is holding her hat. In addition, a child's first words tend to refer to a select group of objects, making comprehension more manageable. However, parents will find that in a relatively short period of time, their child's vocabulary of similar-sounding words will increase, making the word "-at" quite hard to interpret—it could be any one of a number of possible items (e.g., hat, cat, bat, mat, that, or rat)! Add the complication that as children begin to talk more and more about abstract ideas and absent objects, parents have less and less ability to use context to help them decipher their child's speech.

The solution? *Facilitating both Early Communication and Long-Term Learning.* Parents who continue to use signs beyond the early word phase have children who continue to sign while they're speaking. These parents can also invite children to sign when words

Two-year-old Kylie still benefits from *Signing Smart*. Here, she is using words and signs to extend the animated adventure she and Mommy are having. They are pretending to be bunnies collecting **GRASS** for their basket.

are unclear. These practices give *parents* multiple cues to better understand their child's speech (e.g., when a child says "-at," and signs **CAT**, the parent knows exactly what their child is talking about). Continuing to sign past the early word phase will also give *your child* multiple resources to ask and converse about topics of interest to her. In addition, *Signing Smart* techniques allow parents to use signs to extend learning and deepen understanding of abstract concepts and ideas.

With this in mind, we developed these pretend play activities for the older infant, toddler, or even preschooler, but that does not mean you have to wait to give them a try, even with your younger baby. Just use *Signing Smart* strategies such as Grounded Learning to make the interaction more "accessible" for your infant. So put on your thinking cap, pull out your imaginary wand, and have fun exploring all the ways to use *Signing Smart* for long-term learning!

Acting like Animals

Possible signs: Animal signs, action signs, (e.g., **BUNNY, JUMP**). Please see the *Signing Smart* Illustrated Dictionary on page 192.

During pretend play, parents and children can use a variety of *Signing Smart* techniques to extend and deepen interactions. Here, two-year-old Malena and her mom roar like **LIONS**. Using Language Clustering in this way allows children to use both signs *and* words/sounds to extend their animated play.

Very young children ascribe human qualities to the creatures all around them. *Signing Smart* builds off their universal identification with animals and invites children to become animals themselves. The ability to "become" another creature is not one that develops quickly, and thus this is a wonderful activity to return to over time, watching your child's imagination develop at each new opportunity. Ask an older toddler to walk like an **ELEPHANT**, demonstrating the movement yourself by lumbering around on all fours. Or, prowl around, growling like **LIONS** (using Language Clustering). With a younger child, grounding the learning will be important—so have inflatable lions or stuffed elephants on hand. Invite him to make his **ELEPHANT** toy **JUMP** or his stuffed **LION** growl (he can either toss the elephant up in the air or jump himself while holding the toy; encourage him to move his lion's head up as if roaring to the sky). Children delight in these simple invitations to mimic animal behavior. Not only will they get your child's attention and allow him to participate with words/sounds/actions from a very young age, they'll also open the door to extended interactions and learning through play.

TROUBLESHOOTING:
STRATEGIES FOR INVITING INTERACTION

DEVELOPMENTAL DETAILS:
STOP VERSUS NO

Signing Smart gives you the tools to allow your child developmentally appropriate control that simultaneously facilitates her language skills. What better way to do both than to provide structured opportunities for her to be "right" and you to be "wrong"? So integrate playful "incorrect" information coupled with *Signing Smart* cues into your interaction: Break into a big smile, shake your head "no" while talking, or raise your eyebrows while tilting your head deeply.

For instance, while roaring like a lion, ask your child: "Am I being a **SPIDER** [with a smile and deep head tilt sideways]? [*pause*] I'm not a **SPIDER** [with headshake]! **WHAT** am I? Show Mommy with your hands [*pause*]." Add a Pregnant Pause by drawing in a noisy breath and by beginning to sign **LION** (but not finishing the sign). If your child is not yet ready to participate, add, "When you are ready, you will show Mommy how you say **LION** with your hands. For now, why don't we each roar like a **LION**."

Have you noticed yourself saying "no" more often than you would like? *Signing Smart* can help you use signs strategically to become a *partner* in your child's development, rather than a constant enforcer of rules. One way is through redirection. Instead of saying "no jumping off the couch," scoop your child up and announce that it is time to **DANCE** instead.

Another strategic use of signs is to use **STOP** as opposed to "no." We can help our child learn how to **STOP** an action through Grounded Learning (see page 142 for more), but how can a child learn "no"? **STOP** is also a sign that gives control back to your child. That is, even a young child will benefit from the appropriate outlet of aggression that **STOP** affords. Signing **STOP** allows him to assert his "space" with parents or intruding toddlers (or preschoolers) without pushing, hitting, or biting. In all these ways, *Signing Smart* allows you to be *Parenting Smart* by working *with* your child's developmental imperatives in ways that remain manageable.

Teddy Bears' Picnic

Possible signs: **BEAR, EAT, DRINK, MORE, BLANKIE, CUP**, food signs. Please see the *Signing Smart* Illustrated Dictionary on page 192.

Creating engaging contexts where children play a role will allow them to sign back sooner and more prolifically. Here, just-turned fifteen-month-old Hannah, with thirty-three signs and twenty-six words, signs **DRINK** along with Michelle.

For this activity, we draw on the much-loved "Teddy Bears' Picnic" to extend signing and playing into the realm of books, songs, and pretend play. So grab a cuddly friend, pull out a **BLANKIE**, and find a plastic teaCUP or two to set up your own rendition of this all-time favorite. Or sing along with a book version of the song (e.g., *Teddy Bears' Picnic* by Jimmy Kennedy) as you set up your picnic or even as you play. Using the book as a basis for acting out/signing the story not only grounds the pretence of the tale, but also allows your child to more fully experience the story and advances early literacy skills. So don't be surprised if your child eagerly signs **BEAR** or **DRINK** as he flips through the pages of the book. What a wonderful way to encourage play, interaction, and early "reading" in very young children!

Get down on the floor and allow yourself to fully participate in the adventure. Pour **WATER** into your cups, inviting your child to **DRINK** up. Feed yourselves and the bears some real **CRACKERS**. Remember, even pretend bears are real to young children. Thus your child may insist on giving them real **WATER**. If so, just switch gears and talk about how the **BEARS** are now **WET** from their **DRINKS**.

As children grow: Extend the literacy aspect of this activity into the preschool years by encouraging your child to make formal "invitations" for his guests or by having *him* "read" the story or sing the song to his fuzzy friends. Invite him to animate the characters, and you are sure to have fun with this activity for years to come.

DEVELOPMENTAL DETAILS:

"MY CHILD SIGNS 'BEAR' ONLY FOR HER SPECIAL BEAR: WHY?"

Children sometimes use signs (and words) more narrowly than we do as adults; the category label they have chosen is too specific. Think of your child's category-formation system as a collection of little "boxes" in her brain—each "box" has a label on it with a list of defining characteristics. Children sometimes have a box that is too small—an undergeneralization (e.g., having a box labeled "**CARS**" that only includes toy cars, or one labeled "**BEAR**" that only includes their special bear). Remember that such "mistakes" are really evidence of growth and development— your child is learning how to sort and categorize information.

SIGNING SMART PARENT STRATEGY:

Look at these "mistakes" as *Signing Smart* Opportunities and invitations. They are a chance to gain insight into your child's development and enhance your overall role as a source of knowledge and support in your child's life. How? Once you understand the label for the "box" your child has created, you can provide structured interactions and experiences so that he can come, *over time,* to label his "boxes" as we do. One way to do this is to be sure *you* are using the undergeneralized sign in a variety of contexts.

Feeding Time at the Zoo

Possible signs: **EAT, MORE, SILLY,** animal signs. Please see the *Signing Smart* Illustrated Dictionary on page 192.

Feel free to take creative liberties as to what you consider "zoo animals." Here, Michelle and two-year-old Nicholas talk and sign about the **APPLE** they are "feeding" the caterpillar.

Sometime around twelve to fifteen months, children enter a new world of make-believe and pretend play. And while their abilities will not be fully developed until the preschool years, there are many ways to encourage your child's budding imagination. One simple way is to invite your child along to your pretend zoo for feeding time. While you can go all out and "set up" different areas of your living room for different animals, the activity will work just as well if you grab a handful of animal bath mitts (that will allow the animal to "eat" the food) or other stuffed toys and begin playing. Wear the puppet on your nondominant hand to allow you to sign most easily. Do two-handed signs like **MORE** with the puppet still on your hand, and don't worry that the sign may look distorted.

Remember that the interaction you create with your child is more important than fancy props or elaborate setups. So "become" the puppet and make loud "munching noises" as you gobble down the **FOOD** your child will delight in offering. Move the *animal's* hands to sign **MORE, PLEASE, THANK YOU,** and so on. Sign **EAT** directly on the puppet, holding your child's interest and allowing him to see the sign at the same time. Have the two of you **LOOK-FOR MORE FOOD,** with you maintaining the tone of voice of a hungry beast. Taking on the persona of the animal is key to this kind of pretend play, grounding the experience for even the youngest of children. Give your child a **TURN** with the puppet, inviting him further into the fun. Show him how to bounce the animal up and down as if "talking," or encourage him to make the puppet "run" to find more **FOOD.**

Note: Whenever children see their parents "change" in some way (e.g., put on a mask, wear a hat, or speak in a strange voice), it can initially be disconcerting. If this happens, simply scale back this aspect of the game. Over time, your child is sure to love such *Signing Smart* activities.

DEVELOPMENTAL DETAILS:
"WHY DOES MY CHILD SIGN 'MILK' TO THE PUPPET, HER ANIMALS' HATS, AND EVEN THE DOG? DOES SHE REALLY KNOW WHAT SHE IS SAYING?"

We cannot say it enough: Children are fascinating but confusing creatures! There are a few reasons why your child may be making a movement that looks like **MILK** toward various items. She may be using this movement to say **THAT** (see page 103 for more) or as a general Attention-Getter. It is also possible your child has learned that moving her hands has meaning, but not yet learned that *specific* movements have *specific* meanings.

SIGNING SMART PARENT STRATEGY:

Use Body Leans to help your child understand that different items have different signs. For example, say, "I see you signing **MILK** [Body Lean to the left], but you're looking at Mommy's **DUCK** puppet [Body Lean to the right]." Notice here that the parent *chose not* to use the sign she was trying to *under*emphasize (e.g., **MILK**), thereby drawing *more* visual attention to her other sign, **DUCK**. While it will take your child time to restrict her use of **MILK** and expand her vocabulary of other signs, more important are the kinds of interactions you share where you show her you understand her *intent*.

The Bear Went Over the Mountain

Possible signs: **MORE, WHAT,** animal signs, vehicle signs, other Chosen Signs. Please see the *Signing Smart* Illustrated Dictionary on page 192.

A wonderful way to bring pretend play to the youngest of children is to ground the learning with conceptually related props. This is especially true when the play is tied to a song. Even simple props help engage children and create *Signing Smart* Opportunities as they provide children and their parents with something to talk *about* while singing. Don't be afraid to stop singing midverse in order to have a miniconversation within the song. For instance, after singing "The **TIGER** went over the mountain," pause and ask your child: "**WHERE** did the **TIGER** go?" or "**WHAT** do you think he saw? **AIRPLANES**? Yes! Maybe he did see **PLANES**!" Then pick up with the next line of song, adding the new item of interest directly into the lyrics. Or become airplanes yourselves, **FLYING** over the mountain. So gather up some pillows and make a mountain, invite your child to **LOOK-FOR** some fun friends to travel with (e.g., **BEARS, TIGERS, CARS,** and even **CRACKERS** work!), and explore the possibilities this

song affords. Get a book version of the song (e.g., *The Bear Went Over the Mountain* by John Prater) and see how engaged your child becomes by *reading* about what she has *acted out* in another context. Or use the book to "invite" your child into the activity itself.

SIGNING SMART FOR LONG-TERM LEARNING: ENCOURAGING SINGING ALONG

Even if your child has a sizable vocabulary in either signs or words, it will be easier for her to "sing" along with a song by signing, at least initially. The speed of songs is often too fast to allow children to plug in newly learned spoken words, whereas they can more easily produce signs. In this way, signing past the point when children are speaking allows them to more actively participate in various fast-paced forms of *spoken language* interchanges.

One way to specifically encourage children to plug signs/words into songs is with *Signing Smart* Pregnant Pauses. "Invite" your child to sing or sign by moving your own hand(s) to the starting position of a sign (e.g., holding the beginning position of the sign **TIGER**) and *pause for a moment*. Draw in a

Regardless of your child's age, conceptually related props will ground his learning and extend the interaction. Here, toddlers, preschoolers, and parents enjoy making the **TIGER** go over the mountain.

"noisy breath" to help get your child's attention, build Heightened Anticipation, and help you to remember to wait. This technique also lets your child know you are waiting *for her.* If she does not choose to participate at this particular moment, continue to sing and sign the song. Give your child many invitations to sing, letting her know that it is something the two of you can do together (turning singing from a passive experience into a *Signing Smart* Opportunity) and that she has an important role to play, regardless of her vocabulary size. Signs, points, words, and actions are all communicative elements in such interactions, so give each one an enthusiastic response.

♪ SONG ♪

"The Bear Went Over the Mountain"

The **BEAR** [or other toy] went over the mountain, [sing three times],
To see **WHAT** he could see,
But all that he could see, [sing two times],
Was a lot of **FLYING AIRPLANES**, [or other items of interest] [sing three times],
Was all that he could see

Asleep and Awake

Possible signs: **BED, WAKE-UP, MORE, SUR-PRISE, DADDY, WHAT, BLANKIE,** animal signs. Please see the *Signing Smart* Illustrated Dictionary on page 192.

Rather than get into a war with your toddler's need to exert control over her environment, let *Signing Smart* provide appropriate outlets for these developmental imperatives in playful contexts both you and your child can enjoy! One way to do this is to let your child play at "controlling" when *you* go to **BED** and **WAKE-UP**. Bring a pillow and **BLANKIE** over to a chosen spot in your family room. Exaggerate how tired you are, telling your child you are getting ready for **BED**. See what your child does: Is she interested but confused, wondering whether she is "allowed" to **WAKE-UP DADDY**? Peek out noticeably, inviting your child with nonverbal cues to come over with a tickle or a hug to **WAKE** you up. If necessary, pop up and shout "**SURPRISE! DADDY** is **AWAKE!**" Then flop over again, announcing you are going back to sleep (Conceptual Grouping: **BED**). Continue in this fashion until your child realizes the powerful role she is in—to **WAKE-UP DADDY** and put him to **BED**!

This is a wonderful activity for creating moments of Heightened Anticipation. For instance, after you **WAKE-UP**, make eye contact with your child, and ask her, "**WHAT** is **DADDY** doing?" Begin forming the sign **BED**. See whether your child either finishes the sign or shows with actions that she is engaged and participating (e.g., pushing you down onto the pillow, pulling the covers over your head, or breaking into a big smile). It is in such moments of complete engagement that children are most primed to learn, so be sure to take advantage of your child's attention. Get creative in what can be playfully woken up—consider using a stuffed **BEAR**, a puppet, or Maya's favorite—the family **DOG**!

TROUBLESHOOTING:

HELPING CHILDREN LEARN A SIGN: CREATING HEIGHTENED ANTICIPATION

Our research demonstrates that there are particular contexts in which children are most primed to learn. Rather than tell parents to sign all the time, we have developed strategies and methods from our findings that give you the tools to recognize, capitalize on, and create *Signing Smart* Opportunities. We de-

Creating moments of Heightened Anticipation will not only engage your child, but it will also focus her learning energy on the signs and words you integrate into these moments. Here, twenty-month-old Anna and her mom converse about what will happen when she opens the lid—**SURPRISE**! A snake will pop out!

veloped each of the activities in this guide with an understanding of children in mind; each one gives parents new tools and greater understanding of how to *enrich what they are already doing* to capture attention and bring words and signs to moments when children are most receptive to learning them.

One way to capture children's interest and attention is by creating moments of *Heightened Anticipation,* the moment just before something exciting happens, when your child's attention or interest is at its peak (e.g., just before you "wake up" and shout **SURPRISE!**). In these moments, your child is relaxed and engaged, and her attention is locked on the object or action of interest. It is at this time when she is most receptive to learning new ideas, words, or concepts. Part of *Signing Smart* is recognizing or creating

such moments for everyone's benefit. (See page 131 for more Heightened Anticipation activities.)

Magic Mirror

Possible signs: **WHERE, HIDE, SURPRISE, CHANGE,** clothing signs, family signs. Please see the *Signing Smart* Illustrated Dictionary on page 192.

Signing Smart gives you many tools to engage and stimulate young children from early infancy to well past toddlerhood. Here, two-year-old Malena and her dad become animated buzzing **BUGS**.

Mirrors are magic to young children. From their earliest days, children will sit transfixed by the "other baby" inside it. Alter the mirror image with some silly accessories and you have the makings for a heap of fun! So gather some hats, scarves, glasses, and other props of various sizes and styles, park your child in front of a full-length mirror, and let *Signing Smart* help you take advantage of your child's wonder when he sees both of you **CHANGE** before his very eyes. Put on a **HAT** or **HIDE** behind your **GLASSES.** If your new appearance seems to unsettle your child, scale back somewhat; if not, ham it up. Comment on how **SILLY DADDY** looks and pop out from behind your **GLASSES** with a hearty "**SURPRISE!**" Then give your child a **TURN** to dress up. Place a huge **HAT** atop his head and ask **WHERE** Malcolm is, moving the sign under the hat brim, in his line of sight. Point out his new look in the mirror and see if he recognizes the image as himself; e.g., see if he grabs his own

hat brim rather than reaching out to touch the hat he sees in the mirror (on the "other baby"). This is a late developmental accomplishment that does not occur until sometime between sixteen and twenty months.

Variation: Take advantage of nonscary masks as well, allowing you and your child to become insects or animals, adding Language Clustering to extend the interaction. Remember that young children do not care if everything looks exactly right, only that it is an experience for the two of you to share.

As Children Grow: Dress up like particular people—**DADDY** with a hat and tie, or even stuck-in-the-hole Winnie-the-Pooh (Conceptual Grouping: **BEAR**), who can be accurately represented by simply pulling a shirt over your child's head, mimicking Pooh's stuck head peeking out of **RABBIT**'s hole. Then engage your child in wonderful storytelling about the time Pooh **BEAR** ate so much **FOOD** he got trapped at **RABBIT**'s.

SIGNING SMART LITERACY EXTENSION:

Bring over a book like *Froggy Gets Dressed* by Jonathan London. Let this activity motivate your child's interest in the book, or let the book stimulate her interest in the activity. Even books like *Winnie-the-Pooh* by A. A. Milne can spark interactions.

DEVELOPMENTAL DETAILS:
"MY CHILD SIGNS 'HAT' TO HER BOTTLE LID—WHAT'S GOING ON?"

Young children often overgeneralize words/concepts; their initial understanding of what makes up a category/idea may be too broad. Your child may think that all items that go atop others are "hats." Think of this as an amazing window into her thinking!

SIGNING SMART PARENT STRATEGY:

Remember, *Signing Smart* encourages you and your child to work together to better understand each other. So don't let your child's words confuse or frustrate you—let the knowledge you are gaining from this guide help you to better understand how she currently forms categories. Give her credit and congratulate her clever thinking, responding to her communicative *intent* but still providing correct information. Draw on strategies such as *Signing Smart* Body Leans and Opposite-Handed signing to allow your child to *see* the two concepts you are distinguishing. For instance, you might say, "It does go right on top, just like its own little **HAT** [sign with your left hand; Body Lean to left]! This is the *lid* to your **BOTTLE** [sign with your right hand; Body Lean to the right]."

Grandma's Trunk

Possible signs: **SILLY, DOLL,** clothing signs. Please see the *Signing Smart* Illustrated Dictionary on page 192.

Even very young children enjoy walking in someone else's shoes once in a while. Here, fifteen-month-old Rachel smiles as she tells her mom she is wearing Michelle's too big **SHOES.**

As you undoubtedly know, children thrive on the familiar, which gives them a sense of control over their experiences as they can anticipate what will happen next. Children also learn a great deal in such contexts because their understanding of the routine frees up their energy and attention for learning. However, learning also happens when we *break* expectation in ways that remain manageable to our children, thereby piquing their attention. Thus we offer you Grandma's Trunk. We take the familiar routine of getting dressed and break expectation by including a number of novel interactions, taking advantage of the playful ways you can facilitate learning.

Put a variety of large and small clothes, **COATS, HATS, SHOES,** gloves, mittens, slippers, and more into a bin. Dress your child in the funny clothes (have a mirror on hand to show your child how **SILLY** he looks in the big **HAT, COAT, SHOES,** etc.). Help your child dress a **DOLL** using the big clothing. Try to put some of the smallest clothing on yourself—ham it up as you try to squeeze your hand through a sleeve, place a tiny **HAT** on your head, and so on. Remember, you do not need to know *the* sign to use *a* sign. So sign **SHOES** when talking about your slippers (Conceptual Grouping); ask **WHAT** your child thinks of your tiny T-shirt (General Sign), or **WHERE** he is **HIDING** the gloves. Extend (or preface) the activity by bringing out a book about dressing up, such as *Caillou Dresses Up* by Francine Allen.

Regardless of your props, grounding stories in activities that engage children in manageable yet new or expectation-breaking experiences makes them more eager to read; reading stories about activities they are then invited to enact makes children eager to play! To take advantage of the break in your child's expectation, go to town with the "funny factor"—add strange voices, quick movements, and a playful tone. Of course, gauge your level of intensity according to your child's comfort level, knowing that over time, even shy or hesitant children are likely to be squealing in delight along with you.

DEVELOPMENTAL DETAILS:
"I THINK MY CHILD HAS BEGUN SIGNING 'MORE,' BUT IT LOOKS JUST LIKE SHE'S CLAPPING. HOW CAN I TELL THE DIFFERENCE?"

Children will create their own version of almost any sign they see, but they do so in predictable ways. What you describe—clapping hands—is a very common child-version of **MORE**. How can you know whether your child is "really" signing **MORE**?

SIGNING SMART PARENT STRATEGY:

One factor that helps you distinguish clapping from **MORE** is your child's gaze. If she is looking directly at you (and often not with the huge smile that accompanies a clap); directly at something in her world (such as the bowl of food you're serving from); or directly at her hands, you have a good indication that she's asking for **MORE**. However, even if you think your child is "only" clapping, now is the time to create a *Signing Smart* Opportunity. You as the parent can *create* meaning from the movements and respond to your child as if she is saying **MORE** intentionally, thus allowing her to see the cause and effect of her hand motions ("When I clap, Mommy gives me more; if I want more, all I have to do is clap!"). Doing so will actually facilitate signing back with a variety of signs, sooner.

Signing Smart Storytelling

If your child is more interested in throwing a book than looking at it, have no fear—*Signing Smart* strategies and techniques are developed with just this reality in mind. Even very active children can be easily engaged in the dynamics of *Signing Smart* storytelling. Some ideas to choose from:

Signing Smart Storytelling: Puzzles:

Let go of "doing" the puzzle; instead, animate the pieces, tell stories, or act out actions. Don't forget to let *your child* control the pieces as well.

- Choose puzzles that depict actual nursery rhymes and turn the puzzle pieces into impromptu "puppets" to tell any number of tales, even those that go beyond the specific rhyme.

- Choose Hide-and-Find puzzles and use sound effects, play peekaboo with the "characters," or engage your child with storytelling: "**WHERE** is the **COW HIDING**? Let's pretend we're farmers going to **LOOK-FOR** him. Moo! **COW, WHERE** are you? Here he is! **COW**, why were you **HIDING**? **WHAT** were you scared of? [Bring in another puzzle piece.] The big **DOG**? Oh, I'll **HELP** [shoo the dog away]."

Signing Smart Storytelling: Puppets:

Wear the puppet on your nondominant hand to allow you to sign in the most natural way possible. Tell familiar tales or ones that you invent.

- Very young children regale in the retellings of even mundane events, especially those that have *them* as main characters. So create simple tales about familiar routines or events (e.g., a story about Nyoman's favorite rice dinner, Marissa's morning, or Ryan's trip to the zoo).

- Don't forget, you can even turn a peekaboo or tickle game with puppets into a story. Try, "I'm **LOOKING-FOR** a belly to tickle. **WHERE** is a belly? Oh, I got Sam's belly. Now **WHAT** should I do? I'm going to **EAT** Sam up! Mummm, mumm."

Other Signing Smart Storytelling Props:

- Felt pieces and felt board

- Magnets and a magnet board, a cookie tray, a washing machine side, or a fridge door

- Velcro pieces and Velcro-hook board

- Dolls and stuffed animals

Signing Smart does not need to end when children begin talking. Here, twenty-five-month-old Malena, who knows over six hundred words and signs, and her dad use *Signing Smart* Storytelling techniques to make "Little Miss Muffet" come alive. When Dad talks to Malena about Miss Muffet being **SCARED**, she can tell him *why:* because of the **SPIDER**!

• Baby-safe plastic figures or wooden block people

Signing Smart Storytelling: Singing Stories:

• *There Was an Old Lady Who Swallowed a Fly:* Feed a **GRANDMA DOLL** various items from the song (adapt them to reflect your Chosen Signs). Pause in between verses to talk about how **SILLY** it is that she **EATS** the **SPIDER**, the **CRACKERS**, or even the **CARS**, and ask whether your child wants to **EAT** them also. You may never finish the song, but you sure will have a great time together!

• *Little Cabin in the Woods:* Bring out your toy **RABBIT** and pretend she is being chased by the hunter as you sing; go ring your own doorbell and have the **RABBIT SURPRISE** you and ask for **HELP**. Again, the song is secondary to the active involvement of your child (and you) in the story.

More Singing Stories are listed in Appendix 3, page 216.

Imaginary Friend's Tea Party

Possible signs: **DRINK, EAT, MORE, PLEASE, CUP, THANK-YOU, SPOON.** Please see the *Signing Smart* Illustrated Dictionary on page 192.

One wonderful aspect of *Signing Smart* is its adaptability to benefit both older and younger children. Here, Reyna grounds the Imaginary Friend's Tea Party for nine-month-old Nadia by giving her real utensils and using a real doll.

Signing *Smart* allows children to benefit from ASL's iconic (picturelike) quality and its conceptual foundation for both early communication and long-term learning. For this activity, we use ASL signs to ground experiences and to serve as a bridge to pure pretend play for older toddlers. In this way, *Signing Smart* allows parents to integrate spoken language, signs, lively gestures, and imaginary play. This facilitates not just linguistic and cognitive development, but also literacy skills in very young children.

Pull out a **BLANKIE** and ask an imaginary friend to **PLEASE** come to your party. The idea here is to *not* have any props other than the signs themselves. So use your *hands* and *exaggerate* the signs to create images of you **DRINKING**. Use *Signing Smart* Baby-Talk and talk about the **CUP** you will *mime* pouring **MILK** into. Use Language Clustering, signs, and mime to ground the interaction in reality for your child—making munching noises as you **EAT** your pretend **CRACKERS**,

asking for **MORE** pretend **FINGER-FOODS**, slurping your pretend **DRINK** as you stir it with your pretend **SPOON**.

Younger Child Version: Ground the interaction by having a **DOLL** or stuffed **BEAR** present; give your child a real **SPOON** or **CUP**. These objects will help make your imaginary play concrete enough to thrill even the youngest of babies. But, rather than use the utensils to feed the doll yourself, continue to *use only the signs, your embellished gestures, and Language Clustering.* These techniques will allow your child to "see" and "experience" the tea party while stretching her developing imagination.

"MY CHILD SEEMS TO BE USING WORDS AND SIGNS TOGETHER. IS SHE CONFUSED?"

By continuing *Signing Smart* past the point of early words, you have given your child an incredible gift—the means to use all available resources to communicate as extensively and comprehensively as possible from as early an age as possible. One way children do this is to combine signs and/or words into minisentences: Two-sign sentences, e.g., **MORE MILK**; sign and word sentences, e.g. "more" **MILK**; gesture and sign/word sentences, e.g., headshake "no" **MORE**/"more". In this way, *Signing Smart* allows children the opportunity to *combine modalities* so that they can express more complex thoughts sooner than if they had to wait to learn to *say* them with words alone. See page 179 for more on sign combinations.

Facilitate this development by consciously using multiple signs in a single sentence and by going beyond "pointing and labeling"—a familiar strategy you have seen throughout this guide. Ask your child **WHAT** she wants to **EAT**, if she wants **MORE MILK** or **WATER** to **DRINK**, comment on the **WARM DUCK**, or ask if she needs **HELP** with the **TRAIN**. From these kinds of examples, she will learn more quickly how to use signs and words to "converse" in increasingly complex ways.

CHAPTER 9:

The Magic of *Signing Smart*— Encouraging Little Minds and Strengthening Young Families

IGNING SMART INVOLVES MORE than teaching parents a number of signs to "toss" at their children. On the contrary, as we have emphasized throughout this guide, *Signing Smart* is about opening young minds and strengthening young families by allowing parents to become partners in their child's development through new understanding, additional tools, and enriched interactions. It is about simultaneously facilitating early communication, fostering intimacy, and promoting long-term learning. While this may seem like a tall order, with *Signing Smart* in hand you have all the tools you need to experience the magic of interaction, understanding, and communication in its many forms—from your child's earliest days, throughout early childhood, and beyond.

Signing Smart Beyond Early Communication Means:

1. Building solid parent-child interactions

2. Providing tools to parents and children:
   - To understand the transition from signs to words
   - To facilitate spoken language development
   - To ease times of emotional intensity
   - To aid concept development
   - To increase intimacy in the preschool years

3. Laying a foundation of emotional rewards that last a lifetime

BUILDING SOLID PARENT-CHILD INTERACTIONS

One primary goal of *Signing Smart* is to facilitate parent-child interactions. Even more important than the number of signs your child has, how often she uses them, or how fast she acquires them, is the *relationship* the two of you are building around communication. As a result of the many *Signing Smart* strategies and techniques you have learned, your child knows that you are looking to her for meaning, she knows she has an important role to play in the interchange, and she knows you are eager to respond to her attempts and requests.

Signing Smart is a family affair, inviting each of you to become a partner in the fun. In this way, no matter what your child's number of signs or words is, everyone benefits. Here, Mom and Dad read and learn along with thirteen-month-old Eli, using *Signing Smart* Adaptation Strategies to talk about the big **COW** on the page.

Importantly, you are helping her to better understand her world through the use of signed highlights, *Signing Smart* strategies, and the enriching interactions you engage in together. That is *priceless,* no matter how many signs your child uses herself. It is this *foundation* that all future communication will be built upon, and its importance cannot be overstated. Remember also that if your child *already has one sign* (we prefer this vantage point to saying she *only* has one sign), you have given her a magical key to unlock the world of interaction. A single sign will allow you to marvel at the things she notices, enjoys, desires, thinks about, and *is able to share with you.* Imagine what it will be like when your child is using dozens (even hundreds) of signs and/or words!

As you have seen in each of the activities we developed for this guide, *Signing Smart* helps to create positive interactions in which you and your child are partners and playmates. While the primary focus of this book has been on encouraging communication and learning, don't overlook the *Parenting Smart* strategies that are natural components of these techniques (e.g., turning "no's" into "yes's," page 122; helping children understand how to stop, page 157, and so on). Such strategies are the foundation for positive interactions that you will build on as your toddler reaches the "terrible twos," and as your preschooler asserts her independence and initiative more and more.

TO UNDERSTAND THE TRANSITION FROM SIGNS TO WORDS

Many families drawn to baby sign language are well aware of its benefits during the months before children start saying their first words. But *Signing Smart* is more than something that holds you over until your child starts to talk. Rather, it is a powerful bridge you and your child build and then walk across together. The bridge will take both of you from preverbal communication, through early words, all the way to when your child is talking in full discourse.

In fact, once children are off and running with signs, many *Signing Smart* parents discover that spoken words are soon to follow. Our research with thousands of families in *Signing Smart* programs indicates that there are several different anticipated patterns of transition from signs to words as the primary mode of communicating: Complementary Acquisition, Dual Acquisition, and Facilitated Acquisition. Naturally, it takes many months for children to fully transition to speech alone, but fairly early on parents can often tell which pattern their child is following. For many

> ### *Signing Smart:* Transitioning from Signs to Words
>
> 1. Complementary Acquisition
> 2. Dual Acquisition
> 3. Facilitated Acquisition

Signing Smart children, there is one clear pattern that they adopt and continue to follow. However, some children use one pattern for particular words/signs and another pattern for other vocabulary. Some children will display one pattern early on in development and then "switch" to another as they get older. Each approach is completely normal, so enjoy your child's developing talking skills, no matter which route she chooses.

Note: Your child will replace a majority of his signs as his spoken words take over. However, when *parents* continue *Signing Smart* or invite their child to sign in particular situations, their *child* will be able to draw upon his signing skills in these contexts, to everyone's benefit.

COMPLEMENTARY ACQUISITION

Signing Smart children who follow the Complementary Acquisition pattern tend to sign some words while speaking others; during this time they may have two sets of vocabulary. With this pattern, signs expand on what a child can communicate about and complement the child's spoken vocabulary. Complementary Acquisition occurs because the child focuses her *spoken* language learning energy on words that she doesn't know the sign for. You will likely find that her two vocabularies remain separate for a good while.

Some parents wonder why their child "won't" or "can't" say simple words like **MORE**, **BALL**, or **WHAT** (which they will sign) and yet can say more complex things like "alligator" or "starving." The reason is that the child *can* in fact say **MORE**; she is just doing so with her hands. Don't worry, she *will* be able to *speak* all the words in due time. For now, realize that instead of devoting "needless energy" to *speak* words she can sign, she is learning to speak words that relate to new and interesting experiences. One *Signing Smart* child was talking in full sentences and continued to sign the word **WHAT**. The first time we ever heard her say the word "what" was when she was twenty months old and she asked, "Mommy, what is that over there?" One day, she simply plugged "what" into a very sophisticated sentence! Meanwhile, over the months of using the sign **WHAT**, she had gained many other new words and grammatical skills that were advantageous to her.

The benefit of this pattern is that these *Signing Smart* children often have much larger vocabularies than is typical early on—one signed and one spoken. Don't worry about how long it takes to replace the signs with words; rather, keep noticing your child's overall language advancements.

DUAL ACQUISITION

Signing Smart children who follow the Dual Acquisition pattern frequently vocalize while producing signs. Both early on and as their spoken vocabulary grows, these vocalizations are rough melodic approximations of words and would be difficult to understand without signs for support. Therefore, children who follow this pattern use signs to augment and clarify their ever-expanding spoken vocabularies. Naturally, over time, these children's words become more clear, and they gradually drop many of their signs as speech takes over as their primary means of communicating.

The advantage of this pattern is that parents get invaluable clues to their child's spoken utterances, resulting in much less frustration on both sides. For this reason, after your child has begun to speak while signing, and after he starts dropping signs as his speech matures, continue to draw on signs and *Signing Smart* strategies yourself. By continuing to expand your child's signed vocabulary and by continuing to model the value of signing while also speaking, you encourage your child to maintain his use of signs to clarify his speech. What a wonderful way to reduce the frustration that results from being misunderstood.

FACILITATED ACQUISITION

Signing Smart children who follow the Facilitated Acquisition pattern tend to learn a sign and then quickly replace it with the word (within weeks), often from very early on. With this pattern, the child uses signing primarily as a means of facilitating spoken language development; signs alone are used for a short transitional period. Facilitated Acquisition happens because *Signing Smart* strategies help children access words, signs, and concepts in contexts most amenable to learning. A child's brief use of individual signs can make parents wonder if there is a point to continuing to sign. However, while the *child* may use a sign for only a short period, she will benefit from her *parent's* continued use of signs and *Signing Smart* strategies as a stepping stone into the world of words and ideas—even if the child signs minimally. In fact, what many families find is that once their child is less frantic to talk (as a parallel, when children get frantic to crawl or walk or achieve any developmental milestone, this is *all* they will want to do), he will again begin to draw on signs and *Signing Smart* strategies in contexts most useful to him.

The advantage to this type of acquisition pattern is that the parents get very quick proof from their child that *Signing Smart* strategies allow signs to be used as a bridge to words. Because we often hear the most "concern" about this pattern of acquisition (e.g.,

"My child does not seem to be signing much and seems very interested in talking. Should I bother to continue to sign with her?"), we offer these additional *Signing Smart* Parent Strategies. Naturally, all of these strategies and techniques are also beneficial for children who follow the two other patterns of transition from signs to words; however, they might not come into play until somewhat later in those families' *Signing Smart* journey.

- As your child's words come in, use two- to four-sign combinations yourself to give your child more "advanced" tools for signing. Children eager to talk can use word and sign combinations to go further with communication than early words alone allow.

- "Skip ahead" to using signs for words that are hard to pronounce. Children who are avid talkers will still falter at difficult to pronounce words. Here *Signing Smart* strategies and "advanced" signs can be your family's best friend.

- Move forward with *Signing Smart* for learning and conceptual development, letting go of how much your child is or is not signing.

- Encourage your child to sign and speak as much as possible (but do not force it).

To Facilitate Spoken Language Development

SIGNED AND SPOKEN "SENTENCES"

Signing Smart facilitates spoken language development and cognition. One of the most obvious ways many families see this demonstrated is through the early appearance of children's signed and spoken "sentences." In fact, *Signing Smart* children start combining signs together (or combining signs and words together) *six months to a year earlier* than nonsigning children combine words!

Specifically, nonsigners generally begin producing simple spoken two-word "sentences" (e.g., "bye-bye Dada") at eighteen to twenty-four months of age. In striking contrast, our research with children in *Signing Smart* programs indicates that a majority begin producing similar *signed* sentences at eleven to fourteen months of age (with some combining signs at as early as six months old!). In addition, many *Signing Smart* children produce sentences with three or more signs/words from a very young age, a good number even before twelve months of age. Compare this to nonsigning children, who are generally upward of two years old before they are able to do this with words alone.

What this means is that while nonsigning eighteen- to twenty-four-month-old children are just beginning to say sentences such as

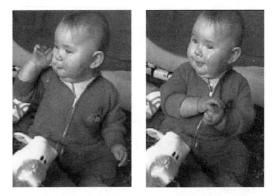

Signing Smart children begin combining signs into sentences months (sometimes years!) before nonsigners do with words. Here, six-month-old Maya is transfixed, watching Scott shovel snow off the deck. When he walks out of view, she "calls" him back, signing **MORE DADDY**.

"bye-bye Dada," most *Signing Smart* children of the same age have already had extensive experience producing sentences. These months of precocious sentence use allow *Signing Smart* children to develop longer utterances and to converse about more abstract ideas in both signs and words by the time (or before) nonsigners first *start* using sentences!

Examples of what *Signing Smart* children talk about:

- A baby at ten months signs, "**DOG WATER FINISH**," also saying "gone, gone, gone" after noticing her dog's overturned water bowl.

- A fourteen-month-old signs/says, "**SQUIRREL** 'outside' **TREE EAT HUNGRY EAT** 'yep' " to tell Mom about the squirrel in the tree who is eating because he is hungry.

- A sixteen-month-old signs/says, "'I want' **MORE** 'fish' **CRACKERS**" to request another handful of goldfish crackers.

- A toddler at eighteen months is playing with her doll and says "baby" and "juice" while signing, "**BABY DOLL THIRSTY JUICE.**" She then puts her sippy cup to the doll's mouth.

- An eighteen-month-old hears a baby crying at a restaurant and says "baby" while using Language Clustering (making "crying noises") and signing, "**HEAR BABY CRY, SAD, WHERE?**" simultaneously looking around for the infant.

As you can imagine, the depth of two-way conversation that can ensue after these kinds of comments (versus simpler sentences such as "bye-bye Dada") allows *Signing Smart* children to engage their parents in enriched interactions, and advance beyond nonsigners in both word and concept development, even after words come in.

Why do we see such a difference in sentence-production ability between nonsigners and *Signing Smart* children? Children whose families use *Signing Smart* techniques have a great deal of early experience using symbolic language, an important prerequisite to ad-

The *Signing Smart* Advantage with Signed and Spoken "Sentences"

For children:

1. Allows children extensive experience with symbolic language from a very young age

2. Provides children with large and broad vocabularies from early on

3. Allows children to take advantage of all possible resources, including combining signs *with* early words

For parents:

1. Gives parents the tools to recognize children's early sentences

2. Gives parents the tools to expand the number of contexts within which children use sentences

3. Provides parents with strategies to directly facilitate their children's sentence use

vancing beyond the one-word (or one-sign) stage of development. This advancement is built off a number of things. First, children's vocabularies must be sufficiently large. Our research indicates that in signs this critical number of vocabulary items is surprisingly small: seven to fifteen signs (around when children hit their Sign Cluster). In *spoken words*, on the other hand, children generally begin using sentences when their vocabulary reaches about fifty words (when children hit what is known as the Vocabulary Burst).

As we have described previously, *Signing Smart* not only gives children a large vocabulary from early on but also broadens the *variety* of signs and/or words children use from a very young age. This breadth of vocabulary is another important precursor to producing simple, and then more complex, sentences. Third, *Signing Smart* gives children the ability to combine signs *with* early words. This serves to extend the resources *Signing Smart* children have to draw from for communication, and it allows them to converse as extensively as possible, from as young an age as possible.

Signing Smart also gives *parents* the tools to more quickly recognize and respond to their child's early sentences, thereby increasing the number and frequency of such communications. In addition, *Signing Smart* techniques provide parents with tools to expand the number of contexts within which children can use these more advanced sentences.

In contrast, nonsigning children must wait for all the necessary sound patterns to mature in order to produce basic single words. They then must wait for their vocabulary to grow large and broad enough, and for them to acquire all the necessary experience with symbolic language before they can begin

> ## *Signing Smart* Strategies to Facilitate Signed and Spoken "Sentences"
>
> Key 1—Create *Signing Smart* Opportunities
> - Take advantage of *Signing Smart* Opportunities as contexts that encourage *both* of you to use signed sentences
> - Respond to sentence attempts and extend interactions
>
> Key 3—Recognize early sentences
> - Know what types of combinations to look for
> - Understand how signs or hand shapes blend when combined in "sentences"
> - Know how quickly a signed sentence can be produced—they can be easy to miss
>
> Key 4—Facilitate both early communication and long-term learning
> - Recognize that signed sentences are often a combination of See A Lot / Do A Lot and Highly Motivating Signs
> - Continue to include both in your set of Chosen Signs
> - Use sign combinations yourself

to combine words. Having to wait months longer than *Signing Smart* children to reach these milestones means that nonsigners' speech is often not as complex as *Signing Smart* children's signed and spoken communication.

Signing Smart children's ability to communicate in sentences at very young ages is not limited to their combination of *signs* or *signs with words*. Rather, our research indicates that they also begin to produce relatively advanced *spoken-only* sentences at a relatively young age—at thirteen to sixteen months. One reason this speech ability occurs months earlier in *Signing Smart* children is because children's signed sentences empower them to express complex thoughts from a very young age. This ability to engage their caregivers and participate meaningfully in sophisticated interchanges, in combination with the interactions that *Signing Smart* facilitates (e.g., those that build on children's interests; incorporate signs and words when children are most primed to learn; and go beyond basic naming), further develop these children's *spoken language* abilities. In this way, *Signing Smart* allows parents to give children both the *motivation and the means* to incorporate spoken words into their sentences months ahead of what is generally seen in nonsigning children.

Strategies to Facilitate Signed and Spoken Sentences

As is the case with encouraging children to sign back initially, the more parents recognize and respond to their child's first *sentence* attempts as intentional and meaningful ("I see you asking for **MORE CRACKERS**! Here you go."), the quicker and more prolifically they will see their child communicate in signed and signed/spoken sentences. Don't forget to take advantage of the *Signing Smart* Opportunity your child has initiated with his sentence—deepen and extend the interaction. If your child signs **BIRD EAT**, go beyond simply acknowledging his statement that the bird is eating. Ask him **WHAT** the **BIRD** is **EATING**, or **WHERE** he thinks the **BIRD** got the **FOOD**, or if the **BIRD** needs a **DRINK**, or if the **MOMMY BIRD** will **LOOK-FOR FOOD** for her **BABY**, and so on.

Just as with children's early productions of individual signs, parents often miss their child's early signed *sentences,* compromising their ability to most effectively support and further their child's use of multiple signs/words. Knowing how to identify early signed sentences as such can be the difference between extended interactions and missed opportunities.

First, be prepared to see any and all of the following:

- Two-sign sentences, e.g., **MORE MILK**

- Sign/word sentences, e.g., **BIG** "bebe" (big baby) or "mo" **MILK** (more milk)

- Gesture and sign/word sentences, e.g., head shake **MORE**/"mo" (no more)

- Simultaneous sign and word sentences, e.g., signing **PLEASE** *while saying* "up" (please pick me up)

Second, be aware that the signs children use in sentences, especially early on, may be "blended" in several ways. In sign-only sentences, there may be very quick transitions or little separation between the signs. In addition, the hand shape used in the signed sentence might mix together the hand shapes found in two individual signs. For example, if your child says **DRINK MILK**, he may open and close his fist *while* tipping it back and forth, in a blended production of both **DRINK** and **MILK**. Therefore, signs combined into a sentence might look different than the same signs used in isolation.

Third, be aware of how fast these sentences can happen. They are often over in a flash, and therefore can be easily missed. Because of these characteristics of early sentences, a parent's role in *Signing Smart* is to hone the eyes to be better equipped to notice them. In knowing what to look for and how to respond, you are more likely to recognize and facilitate this important milestone from the time of your child's earliest sentences.

Another *Signing Smart* strategy for encouraging signed sentences is to be sure *you* are using signs that lend themselves to combination, including **MORE, FINISH, PLEASE, HELP, WHAT, WHERE, COLD, HOT, LOOK-FOR, HIDE**, and so on. You'll notice that these "sentence initiating" signs are mainly from the See A Lot / Do A Lot category. The "sentence completion" signs tend to be Highly Motivating Signs, which speaks to the importance of keeping a balance of these two kinds of signs. In addition, when families continue to use signs for both early communication and *long-term learning*—even if their child has a sizable spoken vocabulary—children continue to benefit cognitively, linguistically, and emotionally. That is, when parents use signs for both purposes, children are exposed to, and therefore are more readily able to produce, See A Lot / Do A Lot Signs *in conjunction with* Highly Motivating Signs in sentence form: **MORE FLOWERS, COLD DUCK, WHERE CRACKER**, and so on. In addition, part of using signs to extend long-term learning is to use sign combinations *yourself*. For example, ask your child if he wants a **CRACKER** to **EAT** or if she wants **MORE DRINK**, talk about the **WET CAR** or the **HOT VEGGIES**, ask if he needs **HELP** with the **TRAIN**, and so on.

WHEN CHILDREN TALK IN INCREASINGLY COMPLEX SENTENCES

When children build a sizable spoken vocabulary, and especially after they begin speaking in sentences, many parents ask how long they should continue to sign with their child. As we have emphasized throughout this guide, the usefulness of *Signing Smart* does not diminish as these spoken milestones are reached. While children will likely need and use *signs* less as they begin to speak more, *Signing Smart strategies* will continue to be useful for *clarification* and *expansion* of spoken language utterances. Why?

Children's intonation patterns are weak compared to adults, and thus their pronunciation of words is often compromised until well after the age of three or four. For this reason, even when your child has a full and complex vocabulary, and even when he talks in complete sentences, you will still struggle to understand him at times. This is especially true because as young children grow, what they talk about is less and less grounded in the immediate context. In addition, children make connections between objects and events that seem strange to us. Thus, your child may talk about anything under the sun at any given time, making connections that will leave you clueless at times. Sometimes you may not understand his out-of-context utterances at all, and sometimes you may understand his words but not their *meaning*.

When families continue *Signing Smart* on a less regular (or even infrequent) basis, signs will help clarify their child's speech. That is, if *you* continue drawing on the *Signing Smart* techniques, even after your child is talking in full sentences, *both you and your child* will continue to benefit. For example, Michelle and Kylie (who has the vocabulary of a five-year-old but intonation patterns more in line with her chronologic age of three years) continue to draw on both signs and *Signing Smart* strategies to clarify ideas or correct misunderstandings. Michelle recalls:

A few weeks ago, we were at a store that had a neon-lit display wall full of interesting objects. Kylie was transfixed and asked me to tell her about the "signy wall." Confused, I asked her if she meant the wall with the display signs (Conceptually Grouping with the sign POSTER). No, she wanted to know about the "signy wall." "SIGNING wall?" I asked with the sign, hoping to clarify the concept she was trying to talk about. "No mommy, signy! The signy wall" she corrected, spontaneously adding the sign LIGHT. Bingo! Shiny! She was asking about the shiny wall! In an instant, the mystery was solved, the interaction was successful, and our frustration was alleviated, all by merely drawing on familiar tools and Signing Smart strategies in a useful context.

Even with large vocabularies, children's intonation patterns can make it difficult to always understand what they are saying. Here, seventeen-month-old Hayden's long-winded but difficult to decipher request for a **BOOK** is made crystal clear with the addition of a single sign.

So, whether your child spontaneously pairs her signs and words or whether she plugs in signs only when asked, "Show me with your hands," *Signing Smart* gives parents the tools to help them understand that "fu" means **FISH** in one situation, **FOOD** in another, and **PHONE** in yet a third. Even if your child produces only a single sign for a whole sentence (or an entire paragraph), you are given an entry into your child's spoken attempt. Knowing your child is talking about a **FISH**, for instance, gives you a context in which to decode the rest of her utterance. This will alleviate her frustration at not being quickly understood despite multiple earnest attempts, and allow the conversation to deepen and extend, further fostering intimacy, language development, and concept development.

Signing Smart techniques also allow you to focus your child's attention on the idea or word you want him to *say aloud*. When reading a book, for example, engage your child in verbal discussion by asking a question, waiting for a response, and then guiding her thinking. For instance, when reading *The Very Hungry Caterpillar*, by Eric Carle, ask your child **WHAT** happens to the caterpillar when he eats too much food. If your child does not chime in right away, begin to form the sign for **SICK** and then *wait*—this invites your child to answer the question in words, but gives him a clue as to the answer you are looking for.

Having entry into children's emotional struggles through signs is one way *Signing Smart* will benefit your family for years to come. It is so much nicer to have your two-year-old tell you she is **SCARED**, as opposed to having to guess why she is upset.

PROVIDING TOOLS TO PARENTS AND CHILDREN: TO EASE TIMES OF EMOTIONAL INTENSITY

Children often lose their ability to communicate when frustration or fear mounts, or when coming out of a full-fledged tantrum. These are prime moments to be *Signing Smart*: Invite your child to sign instead of trying to get her to talk about it. You may be surprised at what your child can communicate with signs when words won't come.

One of the most useful signs in times of negative emotional intensity is the sign **STOP**. It is incredibly physical for your child (he can intensely make his hands connect), and in this way helps him release some of his pent-up frustration and anger in an allowable physical manner (as opposed to hitting, shoving, biting, etc.). In contexts with other children, **STOP** helps him give voice to what it is he wants the other child to do ("stop bothering me / hitting me / getting in my space," etc.).

If your child has a bad dream and seems hesitant to talk about it, draw on your *Signing Smart* strategies: Ask him if he can "show you with his hands." Even just a sign or two will help you to alleviate his fear about the **SPIDER** in his dream. You can also use the sign **STOP** in such instances, giving your child the power to literally **STOP** his own bad dreams.

> ## *Signing Smart* for Concept Development
>
> 1. Clarifying children's misperceptions of new ideas
>
> 2. Conceptual Grouping
>   - Identifying specific items with a larger category marker
>   - Highlighting salient qualities of items/situations
>   - Using single-sign identifiers of larger categories of meaning (e.g., "things that are dangerous," "things that are safe to explore," etc.)

To Aid Concept Development

Because *Signing Smart* techniques allow children to pull concepts and ideas out of the stream of grammar and language in which they are embedded, they are the perfect tools to help parents emphasize contrasts or similarities for their children. This is true from the earliest days of *Signing Smart* well into your child's preschool years. Throughout this book, we have highlighted numerous ways to use *Signing Smart* techniques to encourage your child's cognitive development. For example, you can use the *Signing Smart* strategies of Assorted Cues (e.g., tone of voice, Opposite-Handed Signing, physical actions,

etc.) and *Signing Smart* Body Leans to talk about opposites or otherwise highlight and emphasize particular ideas in relation to each other. (For more on how to use *Signing Smart* to facilitate ongoing cognitive development, please see the *Signing Smart for Long-Term Learning: Intermediate Handbook* available on our Web site at www.signingsmart.com.)

CLARIFYING MISPERCEPTIONS OF NEW IDEAS

Recall Ross's story from the introduction. While reading about a hare, his mother used *Signing Smart* strategies to show him that this word did not refer to the hair on his head, but rather to the **BUNNY** in the book. In a similar way, parents can use *Signing Smart* techniques to "make visual" the phonetic distinctions between words that may be easily "misheard." From rhyming words like "duck" and "stuck" (that Max from the introduction had trouble with) to somewhat odd confusions like "telephone" and "elephant," when you pair words with their respective signs, you help clarify the *conceptual* difference (with the signs) as well as *phonetic* distinction (by emphasizing the way the words are pronounced). This practice gives your child multiple avenues to understand the differences between the words and ideas, and to more easily learn them.

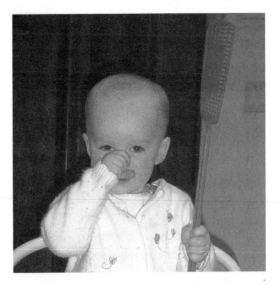

Signing Smart Conceptual Grouping allows parents to support children's concept development. Here, twenty-month-old Anna shows she has learned well, signing **BUG** while talking in full sentences about the flies she is catching.

CONCEPTUAL GROUPING

Identifying Specific Items with a Larger Category Marker

You can use *Signing Smart* to aid concept development by taking advantage of Conceptual Grouping. This is more than a *Signing Smart* strategy to extend your own signing vocabulary and your ability to sign in a variety of situations. It is also a wonderful tool to help children understand the way objects and actions in their world are related to one another. For example, talking about dragonflies while signing **BUG**, or about the ocean when signing **WATER**, gives children a conceptual handle on new, abstract, or complex information without overloading them with a great deal of additional spoken explanation. The task of learning is simplified because you are helping your child know that new ideas are related to concepts he already understands. In this way, using Conceptual Grouping helps your child understand how new ideas fit into larger (familiar) categories.

Highlighting Salient Qualities of Items/Situations

There are other ways to use Conceptual Grouping to facilitate your child's cognitive development. For example, you can pull out an important aspect of what you're discussing by emphasizing it with a single sign. So, when you see your child headed to your newly watered lawn for some fun rolling in the grass, try signing **WET**—while saying something like, "Oh my goodness! Are you headed for the grass? It looks like so much fun. But what do you think will happen if you sit in that grass?" This draws your child's attention, from the very beginning to the important message that the grass is **WET**, without your having to say the word! In fact, *not* saying the word **WET**, but rather asking *your child* what would happen if he sat on the watered lawn, allows *him* to tell *you* (in words or signs) that the grass is too **WET** for sitting on. Involving him in this way allows him to become an active participant in the necessary limit-setting that will ensue (e.g., *he* tells *you* the grass is wet and you *agree* and then ask what the two of you can do as an alternative activity, as opposed to having to impose some top-down "discipline" by simply telling him he can't play in the wet grass).

You can use this same strategy when talking to your child about the mug of steaming coffee you're drinking. For instance, sign **HOT** while saying, "Yes, Mommy's drinking her coffee. It looks yummy, doesn't it? Do you think it is safe to touch?" When your child shakes his head no, continue signing **HOT** as you ask him, "Why not? Why do you think it's not safe to touch?" Again, the sign gives your child a clear message as to the salient aspect of the situation so that *he* can now converse with *you* about the coffee being hot. In addition, you have fostered his thinking skills

by engaging him in a discussion about the abstract topic of "things that are unsafe because they are hot and might hurt you." In these ways *Signing Smart* not only helps your child learn the qualities of items but also invites your child into conversations and abstract discussions about safety and limit-setting. When you engage children in limit-setting and "discipline" in these positive ways, you foster the parent-child partnership and allow your child developmentally appropriate control—all with *Signing Smart* interactions that are fun and stimulate learning.

Using Single-Sign Identifiers of Larger Categories of Meaning

You can also take Conceptual Grouping a step further, to help your child learn categories such as "things that are dangerous in some way" or "things that are safe to play with." To do so, use a sign like **HURT** whenever you talk about things that can cause your child pain—from thorns on a rose bush, to the hot oven, to an ungated staircase. So, for example, when your child reaches for the captivating flower in front of her, you might sign **HURT** as you say, "Oh! Ouch! That rose has thorns!" You might also sign **HURT** as you call to your child, "Brianna, the stove is hot! Be careful!" or sign **HURT** while saying, "Look out! Those are stairs!" If you predictably follow up the signed/spoken explanation with actions (e.g., reaching for your child's hand to prevent her from pricking herself on a thorn, physically removing her from proximity to the oven, or carrying her down the unsafe stairs), your child will come to know to stay away from new items or situations that you label with **HURT**—even if she doesn't necessarily know the specific danger that is lurking.

Notice that you *could* also sign **HOT** while talking to your child about the stove. However, choosing to use a broader sign like **HURT** to denote a group of items that are dangerous in some way will make the "stay away" message instantly clear to your child, regardless of the specific danger or the *words* you spontaneously use to get her attention. Therefore, you *could* also choose to respond to the coffee example described above by signing **HURT** when talking about how it is hot, to help categorize the situation as one that could cause pain.

Remember, there is no "right way" to take advantage of these Signing Smart strategies. It simply depends on the emphasis *you as a parent* are seeking to make, the concept you are looking to highlight, and the interaction in which you are hoping to engage your child.

To use Conceptual Grouping to *support* your child's explorations, you can use a sign like **PLAY** when talking about items or experiences that share the quality of "things that are safe to play with and explore." So, when your child glances your way the second before he reaches for the plastic fruit on your neighbor's table, you can let him know his actions are safe and acceptable by signing **PLAY** as you say something like, "Those are really interesting fruits, aren't they? What will you do with them?" Creating such a "safe to explore" category will then allow you to help your child quickly identify behaviors he can continue and to encourage his drive to explore his world from across the room, even with nary a word spoken.

Tools for Parents and Children: To Increase Intimacy in the Preschool Years

- For intimacy (e.g., **I-LOVE-YOU** through the window as you drop your child off at preschool)

- To have your own "special" language between you and your child

- For privacy (e.g., to tell your child to stop an unwanted activity, to wait a moment, to go to the bathroom, and so on, without *you* embarrassing *him*)

- To allow your *child* to ask for help, to let you know she has to go to the bathroom, and so on, without *her* embarrassing *herself*

- To silently remind your child to say please, thank you, and so on

- To allow your child to communicate while her mouth is full

- To communicate silently (during worship, at a wedding, and so on)

- To interact in very loud settings (across the table in a noisy restaurant, at an amusement park, and so on)

- To communicate secretly under the water

- To communicate with your child while you are on the phone or otherwise unable to respond verbally

- When a new baby comes along, giving the big brother a role in sharing *Signing Smart* with his baby sibling

For all these reasons (and more), parents and children will not "outgrow" Signing Smart strategies and techniques for years to come!

The bond created by being able to communicate the gift of love lasts a lifetime. Shortly before he undergoes life-threatening surgery for cancer, Grandpa and nineteen-month-old Isabel take a moment to say **I-LOVE-YOU**.

LAYING A FOUNDATION OF EMOTIONAL REWARDS TO LAST A LIFETIME

When all is said and done, we know that nothing matters more to you than your child—his safety, his heath, his happiness, and his well-being. In the end, this love, more than any other motivator, is the most important reason for *Signing Smart* with your child. It was our desire to give our own children the

world that led us to create this program. We know you will find, as have countless families, that nothing is more powerful than the bond that is formed between parent or caregiver and child when each understands the other more fully. Nothing is more empowering to *children* than to know they will be listened to, and understood; to know that they can ask about, learn about, and—in *appropriate* ways—control their world. There is no greater relief and joy to *parents* than knowing what it is that their child wants, needs, finds fascinating, or wonders about.

In this way, this book is its own labor of love—a gift from our families to yours, to allow you and your child to experience the intimacy, richness, and wonder that *Signing Smart* can bring. We hope that its pages can help make the transition from infancy to toddlerhood to the preschool years smoother, more enjoyable, and more magical. Whether you use the information in this book for months or years, there is no doubt that with your child as your guide, and *Signing Smart* along for the ride, you are embarking on the most rewarding and amazing journey of your life!

THE *SIGNING SMART* ILLUSTRATED DICTIONARY

ALPHABETICAL LISTING OF THE 130 CONCEPTS REPRESENTED IN THE *SIGNING SMART* DICTIONARY:

AIRPLANE	CEREAL	FALL-OFF (see JUMP)
ALL-DONE (see FINISH)	CHAIR (see SIT)	FAN
BABY	CHANGE	FINGER-FOOD*
BALL	CLEAN	FINISH
BATH	CLEAN-UP (see CLEAN)	FISH
BEAR	COAT	FLOWER
BED	COLD	FLY (see AIRPLANE)
BIRD	COOK (see CLEAN)	FOOD (see EAT)
BLANKIE	COW	FROG
BOAT	CRACKER	FRUIT
BOOK	CUP	GENTLE
BOTTLE*	DADDY (see MOMMY)	GLASSES
BROTHER	DANCE	GO-BY-BOAT (see BOAT)
BRUSH-TEETH	DOG	GO-BY-TRAIN (see TRAIN)
BUBBLES	DOLL	GOOD (see THANK-YOU)
BUG	DRINK	GO-OUT (see OUTSIDE)
BUNNY	DRIVE (see CAR)	GRANDMA (see MOMMY)
BUS	DUCK	GRANDPA (see MOMMY)
BUTTERFLY	EAT	HAT
CALL (see PHONE)	EAT-WITH-SPOON*	HELP
CAR	(see CEREAL)	HIDE
CAT	ELEPHANT	HOME

*Denotes a *Signing Smart* Conceptual Sign (see page 116 for more information)

HORSE

HOT

HURT (see PAIN)

I-LOVE-YOU

IN

INSIDE (see IN)

JACKET (see COAT)

JUMP

KEY

KISS

LIGHT

LIGHT-OFF (see LIGHT)

LIGHT-ON (see LIGHT)

LION

LOOK-FOR

MEDICINE

MILK

MOMMY

MONKEY

MORE

MUSIC

NICE (see CLEAN)

OUT

OUTSIDE

PACIFIER*

PAIN

PET (see GENTLE)

PHONE

PIG

PLAY

PLEASE

POP (see BUBBLES)

RABBIT (see BUNNY)

RAIN

SEARCH (see LOOK-FOR)

SHEEP

SHOES

SICK

SILLY

SISTER (see BROTHER)

SIT

SOCKS

SOFT (see WET)

SPIDER

SPOON* (see CEREAL)

STAND (see JUMP)

STOP

SUN

SURPRISE

TAKE-TURNS (see TURN)

THANK-YOU

TIGER

TOOTHBRUSH

 (see BRUSH-TEETH)

TOWEL

TRAIN

TREE

TURN

VEGETABLE/VEGGIE

WAKE-UP (see SURPRISE)

WARM

WATER

WET

WHAT

WHERE

WIND

THEMATIC LISTING OF DICTIONARY CONCEPTS

ANIMALS

BEAR

BIRD

BUG

BUNNY/RABBIT

BUTTERFLY

CAT

COW

DOG

DUCK

ELEPHANT

FISH

FROG

HORSE

LION

MONKEY

PIG

SHEEP

*Denotes a *Signing Smart* Conceptual Sign (see page 116 for more information)

SPIDER

TIGER

BATH

BATH

BOAT

BUBBLES/POP

DUCK

TOWEL

WATER

WET

BED

BEAR

BED

BLANKIE

BOOK

BOTTLE*

BRUSH-TEETH/
    TOOTHBRUSH

MILK

PACIFIER*

WAKE-UP

**BEHAVIOR/HEALTH &
    SAFETY**

CLEAN

CLEAN-UP

COLD

FALL-OFF

FINISH/ALL-DONE

GENTLE/PET

GOOD

HELP

HOT

HURT/PAIN

I-LOVE-YOU

JUMP

KISS

LOOK-FOR/SEARCH

MEDICINE

MORE

NICE

PLAY

PLEASE

SICK

STAND

STOP

TAKE-TURNS/TURN

THANK-YOU

WARM

WHAT

WHERE

DIAPER/DRESSING

CHANGE

CLEAN

COAT/JACKET

GLASSES

HAT

SHOES

SOCKS

FAMILY

BABY

BROTHER

DADDY

GRANDMA

GRANDPA

MOMMY

SISTER

FOOD

BOTTLE*

CEREAL

COOK

CRACKER

CUP

DRINK

EAT/FOOD

EAT-WITH-SPOON*

FINGER-FOOD*

FRUIT

MILK

SPOON*

VEGETABLE/VEGGIE

GENERAL SIGNS

BALL

DRINK

EAT/FOOD

FINISH/ALL-DONE

GENTLE

HELP

HIDE

IN/INSIDE

JUMP/STAND/FALL-OFF

LIGHT/LIGHT-ON/
    LIGHT-OFF

*Denotes a *Signing Smart* Conceptual Sign (see page 116 for more information)

LOOK-FOR/SEARCH
MORE
MUSIC
OUT
PLAY
PLEASE
SILLY
STOP

OUTSIDE
BIRD
BUG
BUTTERFLY
COAT/JACKET
COLD
DUCK
FLOWER
GO-OUT/OUTSIDE
HOME
HOT

IN/INSIDE
RAIN
SHOES
SUN
TREE
WARM
WET
WIND

TOYS/PLAY
BABY
BALL
BUBBLES/POP
BEAR
BOOK
CAR
DANCE
DOLL
FAN
HIDE

IN/INSIDE
JUMP
KEY
LIGHT/LIGHT-ON/
   LIGHT-OFF
LOOK-FOR/SEARCH
MUSIC
OUT
PHONE
PLAY
SILLY

VEHICLES
AIRPLANE
BOAT
BUS
CAR
TRAIN

**AIRPLANE /
FLY**

A: Bounce
"airplane"
hand forward
and backward
repeatedly
F: "Fly" hand
forward

BEAR

Scratch chest
repeatedly

BABY

Cradle and
rock imaginary
baby

BED

Tap side of
head several
times, as if
laying head on
pillow

BALL

Bounce curved
hands toward
each other, like
the shape of a
ball

BIRD

Open and
close "beak"
hand several
times

BATH

Scrub hands
on upper chest

BLANKIE

Snuggle
imaginary
security
blanket against
your cheek

BOAT/GO-BY-BOAT
B: Bounce "boat" hands on "waves" repeatedly
G-B-B: Move "boat" hands forward

BRUSH-TEETH/TOOTHBRUSH
Make brushing motion in front of teeth/lips several times

BOOK
Open and close "book" hands repeatedly

BUBBLES/POP
B: Repeatedly create "bubbles" with alternating hands
P: Firmly pop "bubbles" with alternating hands

BOTTLE*
Bounce "bottle" hand in front of lips repeatedly

BUG
With thumb on nose, bend two fingers repeatedly

BROTHER/SISTER
B: With thumb touching *temple*, drop hand to end atop other hand
S: From *chin* to hand

BUNNY/RABBIT
Twitch fingers of "bunny ear" hand up and down repeatedly

*Denotes a *Signing Smart* Conceptual Sign (see page 116 for more information)

BUS
Move back hand toward shoulder, as if showing the length of a bus

CEREAL/ EAT-WITH- SPOON* /SPOON*
C/E-W-S: Repeatedly move "spoon" hand from "bowl" hand to mouth
S: Use "spoon" hand only

BUTTERFLY
Keeping arms stationary, flutter hands like wings beating

CHANGE
Rotate hands so bottom fist ends up on top of other fist

CAR/DRIVE
C: "Steer" your car
D: Stationary "steering" hands go forward

CLEAN/ CLEAN-UP/ NICE/COOK
C/N: Wipe hand once
C-U: Repeat CLEAN
COOK: Flip hand repeatedly

CAT
Repeatedly pinch and trace "cat's whiskers" outward

COAT/ JACKET
Outline lapels of "jacket" with your thumbs

*Denotes a *Signing Smart* Conceptual Sign (see page 116 for more information)

COLD
Move fists as if shivering

DANCE
Swing "legs" hand side to side repeatedly, as if swaying to the music

COW
Twist wrist of "horn" hand back and forth

DOG
Slap leg, then bring fingers to a snap, as if calling a dog to you

CRACKER
Tap elbow with fist repeatedly, as if grinding wheat

DOLL
Scrape hooked finger down nose repeatedly

CUP
Tap "cup" hand on other palm repeatedly

DRINK
Tip "cup" hand to mouth

DUCK
Using two
fingers and
thumb, open
and close
"duck's bill"
hand
repeatedly

**FINGER-
FOOD***
With
alternating
hands,
repeatedly
"pick up"
imaginary
small items

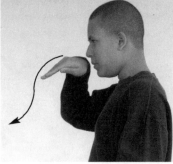

EAT/FOOD
E: Bring
imaginary
food to mouth
F: Tap hand to
mouth
repeatedly

**FINISH/ALL-
DONE**
Flip hands
over, as if
dropping
something
you're done
with

ELEPHANT
Trace shape of
trunk down
from nose

FISH
Flutter "fish"
hand forward,
like a fish
swimming

FAN
Repeatedly
trace the way
fan blades
circle

FLOWER
Touch "flower"
hand to each
side of nose,
as if smelling a
flower

*Denotes a *Signing Smart* Conceptual Sign (see page 116 for more information)

FROG
With hand under chin, repeatedly straighten and rebend fingers, like frog legs jumping

HAT
Repeatedly tap hand to side of head

FRUIT
Repeatedly tip "F" hand forward and back

HELP
Bottom palm "helps" lift other hand

GENTLE/PET
Stroke back of hand repeatedly with fingertips

HIDE
"Hide" thumb under other hand

GLASSES
Pull hands back, outlining frame of imaginary glasses, ending with fingers touching thumbs

HOME
Tap corner of mouth, then upper cheek

HORSE
Twitch fingers of "horse ear" hand several times

JUMP/STAND /FALL-OFF
J: Repeatedly jump and bend "legs" hand
S: "Legs" hand stands on palm
F-O: "Legs" hand falls off palm, ending pointing up

HOT
Sharply twist hand away from mouth, as if turning away hot food

KEY
Twist "key" hand in palm repeatedly, as if turning a key in a lock

I-LOVE-YOU
Gently shake hand left and right

KISS
Move "kiss" hand from side of mouth to touch other fingertips

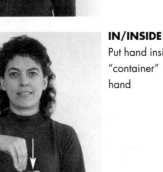

IN/INSIDE
Put hand inside "container" hand

LIGHT/ LIGHT-ON/ LIGHT-OFF
L: Repeatedly close and open fingers, like light rays shining
ON: Open hand once
OFF: Close hand once

LION
With claw hand, outline "lion's mane" above your head

MOMMY/ DADDY/ GRANDMA/ GRANDPA
M: Tap *chin*
D: Tap *brow*
GM/GP: Arc down and away in two bounces from M or D starting point

LOOK-FOR /SEARCH
L-F: Move hand in circles in front of face
S: Tighter circles

MONKEY
Repeatedly scratch sides

MEDICINE
Rock finger on other palm, as if crushing a pill

MORE
Tap fingertips repeatedly, as if adding two things together

MILK
Repeatedly open and close fist, as if milking a cow

MUSIC
Swing hand over forearm repeatedly, as if conducting

OUT

"Grasp" imaginary item and pull out of "container" hand

PHONE/CALL

P: Repeatedly tap "phone" hand to cheek
C: Move "phone" hand outward from cheek

OUTSIDE/ GO-OUT

O: Close fingertips to thumb while moving hand away from you; repeat
G-O: Do movement once

PIG

Straighten and rebend hand at knuckles several times, like slop dripping

PACIFIER*

Repeatedly tap sides of mouth with fingers

PLAY

Twist hands at wrist several times, like "hang loose"

PAIN/HURT

Repeatedly bounce hands toward each other in front of hurt area

PLEASE

Repeatedly rub upper chest in small circles, as if asking earnestly

*Denotes a *Signing Smart* Conceptual Sign (see page 116 for more information)

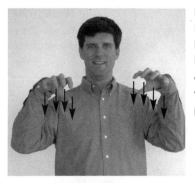

RAIN
Repeatedly bounce claw hands downward at wrists, like rain pouring down

SILLY
Repeatedly scrape thumb across nose

SHEEP
"Shear" forearm repeatedly

SIT/CHAIR
S: "Legs" hand "sits" on other hand
C: Tap "legs" hand on other hand repeatedly

SHOES
Tap fists together several times, like clicking your heels

SOCKS
Scrape edge of fingers up and down several times, as if generating static electricity

SICK
Tap middle fingers to head and stomach

SPIDER
With arms stationary, wiggle fingers, like a spider's legs moving

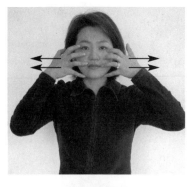

STOP
Sharply drop hand into other palm

TIGER
Outline "tiger's stripes" in front of your cheeks

SUN
Move hand in circle; open fingers so "rays" shine down on your face

TOWEL
Move fists back and forth repeatedly, as if drying back with a towel

SURPRISE/ WAKE-UP
S: Spring fingers of each hand open to an "L" shape
W-U: Open fingers more gradually to an "L" shape

TRAIN/GO-BY-TRAIN
T: Slide top fingers back and forth repeatedly over bottom fingers
G-B-T: Zip top hand off

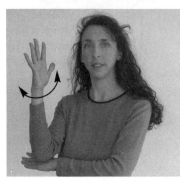

THANK-YOU/GOOD
T-U: Drop hand from chin
G: Drop hand into other palm at midchest

TREE
Twist wrist of "tree" arm several times, like a tree moving in the wind

TURN/TAKE-TURNS
T: Flip wrist from direction of "turn giver" to "turn receiver" (pictured: **MY-TURN**)
T-T: Twist wrist repeatedly

VEGETABLE/VEGGIE
Twist "V" hand so middle finger touches face; repeat same movement

WARM
Open hand while moving it away from mouth, like steam rising

WATER
Tap index finger of "W" hand to chin repeatedly

WET/SOFT
W: Close fingers to thumb and drop hands sharply
S: Repeat movement gently

WHAT
Shake hands back and forth in natural questioning gesture

WHERE
Move finger in a pendulum motion, as if asking if it's here or there

WIND
Sway hands side to side repeatedly, like wind blowing

LIKELY CHILD VERSIONS OF EACH SIGN

AIRPLANE = straight arm extended at angle up to sky; index finger bouncing next to face; splayed fingers with arm making jabbing movements

ALL-DONE = see FINISH; *see page xxiii for child photo*

APPLE = poking cheek with index finger or fist; twisting index finger or fist into cheek; *see page 160 for child photo*

BABY = putting hands on chest and moving whole body side-to-side; clasping hands together and moving them side to side; *see page 49 for child photo*

BALL = vague bouncing motion (likely to be one-handed); often much larger movements than the adult version; *see pages xx, 24, 115, and 151 for child photos*

BATH = flat hand(s) scrubbing on chest; flat hand(s) slapping upper chest; pulling at shirt; *see page 74 for child photo*

BEAR = quick scratching of the chest, with one or two hands, without crossing the arms; done on upper chest, belly, or even legs (if sitting); *see page 99 for child photo*

BED = flat palm beside cheek, much like the adult version; may be one- or two-handed; may be done with repeated tapping (similar to **HAT**); *see pages xxi, 5, 42, 87, and 89 for child photos*

BIRD = a whole hand opening and closing in front of the face without touching it; opening/closing of the hand beside shoulder; palm or fist planted on mouth or twisting in front of mouth; often looks the same as a child's sign for **DUCK**; *see page 36 for child photo*

BLANKIE = fist to chest; rubbing of neck with palm or fist

BOAT = less precise but similar to adult sign; often without the bounce

BOOK = hands flipping upward, not necessarily touching each other; hands splayed side by side and stationary; clapping motion; *see page 184 for child photo*

BOTTLE* = sucking thumb (for non-thumb-suckers); tapping fist to mouth; may mimic a child's sign for **DRINK**

BROTHER = open hand, fist, or index finger moving down from forehead; may or may not "crash" into other hand; *see page 76 for child photo*

BRUSH-TEETH = index finger touching lips several times; sucking on index finger; swiping index finger back and forth in front of mouth without touching lips

BUBBLES = opening/closing of the hand(s) in a way similar to **LIGHT**, but not necessarily over head; *see pages 84 and 153 for child photos*

BUG = flapping or waving motion in front of or next to face; touching index finger or fist to nose; *see page 187 for child photo*

BUNNY = hand touching side of head, grabbing hair, or brushing side of head; fist on ear; *see page 145 for child photo*

BUS = flat hands, one palm hitting the back of the other; flat hands shaking next to each other

BUTTERFLY = hands not crossed and perhaps facing the wrong direction with fingers flapping; hugging chest and twisting body; *see page xxii for child photo*

CAR = fists or loose hands swinging back and forth in front of chest, moving at the same time (as opposed to alternating); often involves whole arm movements; *see page 141 for child photo*

CAT = brushing whole hand against cheek or mouth; jabbing fist into cheek; *see page 71 for child photo*

CEREAL = repeated slapping of the "spoon" hand into the "bowl" hand; may be done with index fingers or splayed fingers

CHAIR = see **SIT**

CHANGE = loose hands flipping around each other; loose hands twisting beside each shoulder in a much larger movement than the adult form; two hands "waving" to each other; fists touching, moving in a jerky motion

CLEAN = done much like the adult sign but with a bigger movement; likely to look the same as the sign **CLEAN-UP**; *see page 54 for child photo*

*Signing Smart Conceptual Sign. See page 116 for more information.

CLEAN-UP = done much like the adult sign but with bigger movements; *see page 54 for child photo*

COAT = sliding one or two hands down chest; patting body with palms near shoulder and then near waist

COLD = much like the adult sign but often with less "control" of the small movement

COOK = vertical clapping, often without the flipping motion

COW = hand, index finger, or thumb touching head, forehead, or temple (very similar to **HORSE**); often done close in on the face

CRACKER = tapping hand or fist on elbow or close to the wrist; clapping of hands

CUP = tapping of one hand into the palm of the other; may not have a curved "cup" hand

DADDY = index finger or hand tapping forehead; child may touch/tap head with thumb, pinky, index finger, or several fingertips; may also be done to the side of face; or with the front or back of the hand; *see pages xxiv and 179 for child photos*

DANCE = waving of one hand over the other,

or single hand waving in space; may look like a child's version of **MUSIC**; often done while bouncing up and down

DOG = slapping of hand on torso rather than thigh, with one or multiple repetitions

DOLL = straight index finger, whole hand, or fist swiping nose; flip of the wrist in space in front of the nose without touching it

DREAM = index finger to head, pulled outward; *see page 5 for child photo*

DRINK = a very loose hand twisting by mouth or beside shoulder; fist brushing mouth several times; *see pages 23 and 158 for child photos*

DUCK = opening/closing of the whole hand in front of the face (not touching the face) or beside the shoulder; grabbing of mouth with hand; palm or fist planted on mouth or twisting in front of mouth; often looks the same as a child's sign for **BIRD**; *see pages 25 and 36 for child photos*

EAT = one finger in mouth; "slapping" mouth and chin with fist or open hand; sucking on fingers; *see pages 61, 118, and 224 for child photos*

EAT-WITH-SPOON* = See CEREAL

*Signing Smart Conceptual Sign. See page 116 for more information.

ELEPHANT = wrist flapping next to head or beside shoulder; index finger or palm to nose; *see page 39 for child photo*

FALL-OFF = index finger or tips of open hand moving off palm of other hand

FAN = whole hand opening/closing or forearm flapping back and forth; hands in the air with wrists flipping back and forth; often looks similar to **LIGHT**

FINGER-FOOD* = pinching or grabbing in the air with whole hands; pointing down and bouncing with both hands

FINISH = flapping hands up and down or a variation of a wave; *see pages xxiii and 9 for child photos*

FISH = loose hand flapping to side or in front of body; palm and arm extended as a stiff unit moving side to side; *see page 139 for child photo*

FLOWER = tapping the nose with index finger or whole hand rather than controlled movement; twist of the wrist planted on chin; twisting/swiping hand on nose; *see page 1 for child photo*

FLY = See AIRPLANE

FOOD = See EAT; *see pages 61 and 118 for child photos*

FROG = grabbing or poking at neck; brushing hand on chin

FRUIT = index finger swiveling on cheek; brushing movement similar to a child's version of **CAT**; tapping or twisting of the splayed fingers on the side of face; may be done at side of head or near ear

GENTLE = tapping, slapping, or rubbing back of one hand with the fingers of the other hand; *see page 95 for child photo*

GLASSES = opening and closing hand(s) or fingers near eyes; wiping or tapping side of face with index finger or hand; stationary index finger to side of head

GO-BY-BOAT = See BOAT

GO-BY-TRAIN = See TRAIN

GOOD = grabbing of mouth and dropping hand down, often without being "caught" in other hand

GO-OUT = See OUTSIDE

GRANDMA = index finger, thumb, or palm

---

*Signing Smart Conceptual Sign. See page 116 for more information.

brushing chin or side of face, similar to **MOMMY**; may or may not "bounce" outward

GRANDPA = index finger, thumb, or palm brushing forehead or temple, similar to **DADDY**; may or may not "bounce" outward

GRASS = tapping loose hand at bottom of chin, palm up or palm down; rubbing of chin; *see page 155 for child photo*

HAT = tapping palm on head; grabbing head with hand; *see page 132 for child photo*

HELP = brushing of one hand over the other; fist to palm; clapping motion, with or without a lift; *see page 3 for child photo*

HIDE/HIDING = pounding of curved hand atop other fist

HOME = index finger or fist tapping mouth then cheek or tapping/twisting at cheek only

HORSE = hand, index finger, or thumb touching head (similar to **BUNNY** or **COW**, although often higher on the head)

HURT = touching of the index fingertips; holding tips apart with no movement at all; or big movements of the arms, much like the sign **BALL**; *see page 3 for child photo*

I-LOVE-YOU = whole hand or index finger waving back and forth by shoulder; thumb, index finger, and middle finger (or index finger and thumb only) splayed and waving; *see page 190 for child photo*

IN/INSIDE = much like the adult version but with less controlled movements; *see page 123 for child photo*

JACKET = see COAT

JUMP = whole hand clapping/slapping against other hand or against object (e.g., book where character jumps); fingertips of one hand moving up and down from palm of other hand

KEYS = index finger or thumb to palm; brushing of one hand over the other; fist or open hand twisting in palm of opposite hand

KISS = hand or fist bumping object/item to be kissed with kissing noises; bumping of mouth with hand or fist

LIGHT/LIGHT-ON/LIGHT-OFF = opening and closing of fist (one- or two-handed), often at or above shoulder level; often looks similar to **FAN**; *see pages 9, 10, 91, 93, and 147 for child photos*

LION = rubbing, tapping, or grabbing of head/hair; *see page 156 for child photo*

LOOK-FOR = hand waving back and forth in front of face

MEDICINE = rubbing of one palm on top of the other; thumb to palm; index finger to palm, often without separating out the other fingers; *see page 4 for child photo*

MILK = large opening and closing movement of the hand, most likely at shoulder level or in the direction of breast or bottle; *see page 4 for child photo*

MOMMY = index finger or hand tapping chin; child may touch/tap chin with thumb, pinky, index finger, or several fingertips; may also be done to the side of face; may be done with the front or back of the hand; *see page 83 for child photo*

MONKEY = poking side with one or two hands; grabbing of the chest; often looks like the child's version of **BEAR** or **BATH**

MORE = clapping or fists colliding; grasping of hands in front of the body or bringing together of fingertips loosely; tapping index to palm; *see pages 3, 10, 38, 179, and 225 for child photos*

MUSIC = one or both hands making a "conducting" type of motion (e.g., flipping or waving) without being aligned in correct orientation

NICE = done much like the adult sign but with a bigger movement

OUT = jerking out loose hand from on or next to loose "container" hand

OUTSIDE = jerking of hand from shoulder to extended arm without hand change; open and close of hand beside shoulder without arm extending out

PACIFIER* = tapping of mouth with loose open hand

PAIN = see **HURT**; *see page 3 for child photo*

PET = see **GENTLE**; *see page 95 for child photo*

PHONE = back of entire hand at side of face; palm, fist, or index finger at side of face; may be stationary or tapping; may look similar to **BED**

PIG = loose hand tapping underside of chin; grabbing of the neck; brushing of the lower chin; *see pages 53 and 113 for child photos*

PLAY = shaking of loose wrists or fists

*Signing Smart Conceptual Sign. See page 116 for more information.

PLEASE = swiping or dragging of the hand across chest; repeated patting movement as opposed to a circular movement; hand may be in a fist or open; *see page 19 for child photo*

POP = see BUBBLES; *see pages 84 and 153 for child photos*

PUMPKIN = pounding of one fist atop the other; *see page 4 for child photo*

RABBIT = see BUNNY; *see page 145 for child photo*

RAIN = fingers lax and wrists bobbing up and down in front of chest, one- or two-handed

SCARED = slapping loose hands to chest, planting hands on shirt; big jerky arm movements; *see page 185 for child photo*

SEARCH = see LOOK-FOR

SHEEP = loose hand brushing other arm; tapping hand on back of opposite wrist

SHOES = clapping; fists colliding with palms touching each other; often will mimic a child's sign for MORE; *see page 168 for child photo*

SICK = a whole hand to the head; index finger to head; *see page xix for child photo*

SILLY = fist tapping or brushing nose; large swiping movements across face; index finger to nose

SISTER = open hand, fist, or index finger moving down from chin; may or may not "crash" into other hand

SIT = one hand slamming onto top of other

SOCKS = tapping or swiping of index fingers; loose open hands; or fists

SPIDER = hands atop one another (not necessarily crossed) with random-looking finger movements; clutching of one hand, wrist, or arm by the other with no other movement; *see page 171 for child photo*

SPOON* = exaggerated movement with the whole hand

STAND = tips of fingers on palm of other hand

STOP = similar to, but less precise than, the adult version; hands may be bent rather than rigid; contact may be palm to palm rather than side of pinky to palm; some form of two hands colliding, not necessarily in the correct orientation

SUN = splaying of the fingers without the ini-

---

*Signing Smart Conceptual Sign. See page 116 for more information.

tial circle; may mimic a child's version of **LIGHT**

SURPRISE = opening of whole hand or index finger and thumb beside temple or in front of the body; may be done as a stationary hand beside face, without the opening; *see page 165 for child photo*

TAKE-TURNS = whole hand flipping between two people; arm bending and straightening at the elbow; *see page 51 for child photo*

THANK-YOU = repeated tapping on mouth (can sometimes look like **EAT**) or like child is blowing a kiss

TIGER = swiping of hand(s) on cheek(s)

TOOTHBRUSH = see **BRUSH-TEETH**

TOWEL = much like the adult version but with bigger movements; may look like child's version of **CAR** or **PLAY**

TRAIN = whole hand rubbing or resting on top of other hand; index finger rubbing or resting on top of other index finger

TREE = one-handed vertical arm, waving or twisting back and forth

TURN = see **TAKE-TURNS**; *see page 51 for child photo*

VEGETABLE/VEGGIE = index finger swiveling on cheek; cheek-tapping movement similar to a child's version of **CAT**; tapping or twisting of the fist on the side of face; may be done at side of head or near ear

WAKE-UP = see **SURPRISE**; *see page 165 for child photo*

WARM = open hand moving upward in front of chin or mouth; *see page 113 for child photo*

WATER = whole hand or index finger tapping mouth or chin

WET = opening and closing of the hands without the dropping movement; dropping down of the hands without the open/close movement; *see page 83 for child photo*

WHAT = looks like the natural gesture, either one- or two-handed; *see page 132 for child photo*

WHERE = index finger or splayed fingers flipping back and forth in front of body; *see page 67 for child photo*

WIND = swiping or twisting of hand(s) or arm(s) back and forth in front of body

ADDITIONAL RESOURCES FOR PARENTS AND
BABY SIGN LANGUAGE INSTRUCTORS

BOOKS TO READ WITH YOUR CHILD:

Books with the same animal, object, or idea on each page:

Bingo by Rosemary Wells

Bouncing Bunnies, Playful Puppies, Chirping Chicks, and *Cuddly Kittens* by Emma Books Ltd.

Find the Puppy, Duck, Piglet, Bird, Kitten, Teddy books by Stephen Cartwright

Five Little Monkeys Jumped on the Bed or *Five Little Monkeys Sitting in a Tree* by Eileen Christelow

Freight Train by Donald Crews

Good Dog, Carl series by Alexandra Day

Little Rabbit books by Alan Baker

Moonbear books by Frank Asch

One Duck Stuck by Phyllis Root

That's Not My Puppy (*Train,* and so on) by Fiona Watt

Lucky Ladybug, Butterfly's Surprise, and *Cricket's Song* by Muff Singer

Books with many pictures on the page to discuss/describe:

Good Night, Gorilla by Peggy Rathman

Goodnight Moon by Margaret Wise Brown

I Spy series by Jean Marzollo

Ten Little Ladybugs by Melanie Gerth

Short stories that will hold young children's attention:

Brown Bear by Bill Martin, Jr.

Crocodile Beat by Gail Jorgensen

Can't Catch Me by Nancy I. Sanders

Do You Want to be My Friend? by Eric Carle

Good Night, Baby by Elizabeth Hathon

Guess How Much I Love You by Sam McBratney

I Went Walking by Sue Williams

Jamberry by Bruce Degen

Little Miss Spider stories by David Kirk

The Napping House by Audrey Wood

Sheep in a Jeep by Nancy E. Shaw

Time for Bed by Mem Fox

The Very Hungry Caterpillar by Eric Carle

We're Going on a Bear Hunt by Michael Rosen

What Shall We Do With the Boo-Hoo Baby? by Cressida Cowell and Ingrid Godon

Books you can use with some of the activities in this guide:

The Bear Went Over the Mountain by John Prater

Caillou Dresses Up by Francine Allen

Corduroy by Don Freeman

Duck Is Dirty by Satoshi Kitamura

Five Little Ducks by Raffi

Froggy Gets Dressed by Jonathan London

Itsy-Bitsy Spider by Iza Trapani

The Nutcracker by E. T. A. Hoffmann

Roll Over!: A Counting Song by Merle Peek

The Teddy Bears' Picnic by Jimmy Kennedy

We're Going on a Bear Hunt by Bill Rosen

Winnie-the-Pooh by A. A. Milne

Books that incorporate baby sign language:

See www.signingsmart.com for suggested infant and toddler books that incorporate signs.

Be aware that some baby sign language books state that they are ASL-based but instead use invented gestures. Figuring out which are made-up signs and which are ASL can be confusing to parents and children alike. We suggest investigating before you buy.

Singing Stories to act out or extend storytelling:

"5 Green and Speckled Frogs"

"5 Little Monkeys Jumping on the Bed"

"5 Little Monkeys Swinging in a Tree"

"Baa, Baa Black Sheep"

"Itsy-Bitsy Spider"

"Little Cabin in the Woods"

"Oh Where, Oh Where Has My Little Dog Gone?"

"There Was an Old Lady Who Swallowed a Fly"

FOR CHILDREN:

The Treasure Chest: Toys and Signs Children's Video: Children of all ages will be delighted by this magical journey of discovery. Join us as we lead you and your child to a treasure trove of toys, play, songs, and signs. The compelling visual images provide endless opportunities for families to connect with their little ones. Designed to engage and inspire your children again and again. See *Signing Smart* strategies in action in the parent strategy section at the end of the video. Visit www.signingsmart.com for more details.

Signing Smart Diaper Bag Dictionary Series: Baby Sign Language Flashcards: Infants, toddlers, and preschoolers will enjoy learning ASL signs from the adorable and engaging toddlers pictured on these cards; adult photos and descriptions for Mom and Dad are on the backs! The sets come on convenient-to-carry rings, so flip through the cards in the car, at a restaurant, or anywhere—without the worry of losing any! See www.signingsmart.com for a list of sets in the series.

Other children's products: Signing Smart is constantly developing new products and materials. Be sure to check out our Web site at www.signingsmart.com for the most current items available.

FOR PARENTS:

Signing Smart for Early Communication: Beginner Handbook and *Signing Smart for Long-Term Learning: Intermediate Handbook:* The perfect way to extend what this guide has to offer. The books are organized thematically and contain not only a great many additional "family-friendly" signs but also additional *Signing Smart* strategies to help make signing accessible, fun, and successful from day one into the preschool years. See www.signingsmart.com for more details.

Basic or Complete Starter Kits: For those who are just beginning to sign with their child as well as for those well on their way. These kits make the perfect baby shower, new baby, or first-birthday gift. The kits give families tools and resources available nowhere else. They provide parents with wonderful resources to integrate signing into family life, and they engage and motivate children to communicate and interact in whole new ways. See www.signingsmart.com for more details.

Signing Smart Holiday Handbook: This nonreligious handbook is a must-have for the holiday season. Includes over seventy-five seasonal signs along with a host of *Signing*

Smart strategies and relevant developmental information to make the holidays a time of wonder, fun, and learning for the whole family. See www.signingsmart.com for more details.

Signing Smart Diaper Bag Dictionary Series: These baby sign language flashcards are on a convenient-to-carry ring with adult photos and descriptions on one side, and toddler photos on the other side (to see what signs look like on little hands). The rings allow you to customize your set to bring along the most useful signs or to leave the most important ones with a sitter or child care provider. All cards feature ASL signs, and each set includes its own *Signing Smart* strategies card. See www.signingsmart.com for a list of sets in the series.

Dancing with Words: Signing for Hearing Children's Literacy by Marilyn Daniels. This book reports Dr. Daniels's research on the benefits of signing with preschoolers. For parents looking for still more.

Signs for Me: Basic Sign Vocabulary for Children, Parents, and Teachers by Ben Bahan and Joe Dannis. Line drawings of great ASL vocabulary.

Other parent products: Signing Smart is constantly developing new products and materials. Be sure to check out our website at www.signingsmart.com for the most current items available.

FOR BABY SIGN LANGUAGE
INSTRUCTORS:

Signing Smart Beginner, Intermediate, and Holiday Play Class Curricula: For instructors looking for engaging play class activities for hearing babies and toddlers. Different from the at-home activities in this book, the almost three hundred activities in these curricula were specifically designed for a play class environment. Step-by-step guide to running comprehensive programming that integrates these and many other *Signing Smart* strategies, techniques, and developmental details; ten-, ten-, and four-week programming.

Signing Smart Workshop-in-a-Box for a Parent Audience (Beginner and Advanced); a Child Care Audience; and a Preschool Teacher Audience: Four entirely different curricula that contain all you need to run one-of-a-kind adult-only workshops. Each contains activities and information to use in either a single-session workshop or in a miniseries format. All include detailed and comprehensive program descriptions, and where appropriate, they also include instructor DVDs of *Signing Smart* families, reproducible handouts, and overheads/PowerPoint presentations.

Other instructor products: Signing Smart is constantly developing new curricula and programs. Be sure to check out our Web site at www.signingsmart.com for the most current items available.

FREQUENTLY ASKED QUESTIONS BY TOPIC

Children signing back

"How do I motivate my child to sign back to me?" (Motivating Your Child to Sign, page 80)

"How can I help my child to sign back more?" (page 80)

"I think my child has about twelve signs, but I haven't seen half of them in what seems like weeks. Was I just imagining she had all those signs?" (page 128)

"How do I get my child to initiate signing more?" (Strategies for Inviting Interaction, page 157)

"How do I know if my child even understands the signs I have been using?" (Clues that your child is understanding your signs, page 140)

"When will my child sign back?" (*Signing Smart* Milestones, page 14)

For more information related to this topic, see pages 7 and 19.

Helping your child participate in the activities

"How can I encourage my child to participate more in the activities?" (page 76)

"My child is not doing the activities right! What can I do?" (page 121)

"Why does my child want the same game again and again? I find it boring . . ." (page 75)

Signing and reading

"Should I stick to books that have lots of signs I know?" (Reading favorite books with very young children, page 96)

"My child won't sit still for reading; what should I do?" (*Signing Smart* Storytelling, page 170)

Signing and singing

"I would love to do more singing and signing, but I know so few songs. What should I do?" (page 108)

For more information related to this topic, see page 48.

Signing and talking; when children "stop signing"

"My child has started talking. Should I bother continuing to sign with him?" (Signing and Talking, page 114)

"My eleven-month-old can say the word 'more'; should I bother teaching the sign?" (page 118)

"My child seems to be using words and signs together. Is she confused?" (page 173)

"My child isn't signing anymore. How can I encourage her to sign, or should I just stop signing too?" (When your child seems to stop signing, page 136)

For more information related to this topic, see Transition from signs to words, page 176 and Facilitating spoken language development, page 179.

Signing with full hands

"How do I sign when my hands are full?" (Adaptation Strategies for full hands, page 88)

For more information related to this topic, see pages 33, 46, 56, and 76.

Taking activities beyond pointing and naming

"I feel like I'm just labeling toys. How can I be more creative with my signs?" (Going beyond basic labeling, page 26)

"How can I extend interactions with signs?" (page 79)

For more information related to this topic, see page 20.

When children seem to use signs the "wrong" way

"My child has only one sign: **FAN**! What should I do?" (page 105)

"My child signs **RABBIT** to her elephant and her bunny! Is she confused?" (page 145)

"My child is confused—she makes the same sign for **MORE** and **BALL**." (page 148)

"My child will only sign **MORE** while eating, never anywhere else. What's wrong?" (page 63)

"My child seems to be confused and will sign **DUCK** and **LIGHT** the same way. What should I do?" (page 64)

"Whenever I sing this song, my child opens and closes both his hands by his ears. Could he be signing **LIGHT** even though his sign looks nothing like mine?" (page 93)

"All I have to do is put my son down on his back and he immediately signs **MORE**, even when I haven't tickled him yet. Does he really know what **MORE** means?" (page 94)

"My child signs **BED** when I *know* he is not tired. I put him in anyway, and he cries and cries! Should I just ignore his sign?" (page 98)

"My child signs the same sign for almost everything!" (page 103)

"My child used to have a host of different food signs, but now he will only sign **EAT**. What's going on?" (page 129)

"My child signs **BEAR** only for her special bear. Why?" (page 159)

"My child signs **HAT** to her bottle lid—what is going on?" (page 167)

"I think my child has begun signing **MORE**, but it looks just like she's clapping. How can I tell the difference?" (page 169)

For more information related to this topic, see page 36.

When will signing get easier?

"My child still only uses a few signs—when will signing be as magical as my friends say it is?" (Reaching the Sign Cluster and the Language Explosion, page 138)

"I try and sign before, during, and after every activity but I have found it impossible. I'm ready to give up! What should I do?" (page 83)

For more information related to this topic, see the Sign Cluster and the Language Explosion, pages 14–15.

When you don't know the sign for the object you're talking about

"What do I do when I don't know a sign?" (Using *a* sign even if you don't know *the* sign, page 70)

For more information related to this topic, see *Signing Smart* Opportunities, page 20; Diaper and Dressing, page 46; Bedtime, page 86.

1. D. Slobin, N. Hoiting, M. Kuntze, R. Lindert, A. Weinberg, J. Pyers, M. Anthony, Y. Biederman, H. Thumann, "A Cognitive/Functional Perspective on the Acquisition of 'Classifiers,' " in *Perspectives on Classifier Constructions in Sign Languages,* ed. K. Emmorey (Lawrence Erlbaum, 2003).

2. R. Lindert, "Hearing Families with Deaf Children: Linguistic and Communicative Aspects of American Sign Language Development" (Ph.D. diss., University of California, Berkeley, 2001).

3. L. Acredolo, S. Goodwyn, and C. A. Brown, "Impact of Symbolic Gesturing on Early Language Development," *Journal of Nonverbal Behavior* 24 (2000): 81–103.

4. L. P. Acredolo, and S. W. Goodwyn, "The Long-Term Impact of Symbolic Gesturing During Infancy on IQ at age 8" (paper presented at the meetings of the International Society for Infant Studies, Brighton, UK, 2000).

5. M. Daniels, *Dancing with Words: Signing for Hearing Children's Literacy* (Bergin and Garvey, 2001).

6. A longitudinal study looks at one group over a period of time. Michelle investigated the same children over a two-year period.

7. M. E. Anthony, "The Role of American Sign Language and 'Conceptual Wholes' in Facilitating Language, Cognition, and Literacy." (Ph.D. diss., University of California, Berkeley, 2002).

8. M. H. Goldstein, and M. J. West, "Consistent Responses of Human Mothers to Prelinguistic Infants: The Effect on Prelinguistic Repertoire Size," *Journal of Comparative Psychology,* 113 (1999): 52–58.

9. Deaf is spelled with a capital D to signify cultural Deafness: membership in the Deaf community, which uses American Sign Language (ASL) as its natural language; "deaf" with a small "d" simply refers to hearing loss.

Adaptation Strategies, 28
AIRPLANE/FLY sign, 196, 208
airports, trips to, 138
Allen, Francine, 169
anticipation, heightened, 132–133, 164–165
Assorted Cues, 146–147, 186
attachment, increased, 5
Attention-Getters
   list of, 28
   nonverbal, 30
   sensory, 30–31

babbling, responding to, 22–23
Baby Amusement Parks, 138–139
BABY sign, 196, 208
Baby-Talk, 31–32, 172
BALL sign, 11, 196, 208
Balls Galore, 150–151
"Bath, Bath, Take a Bath" (song), 76–77
BATH sign, 19, 196, 208
bathtime activities
   Bathing the Doll, 78–79
   overview, 74–85
   Pop and Drop, 80–81
   Soap Scientists, 84–85
   songs, 76–77, 82–83
BEAR sign, 13, 196, 208
"Bear Went Over the Mountain" (song), 163
Bear Went over the Mountain, The (Prater), 162–163, 217
"Bears Are Sleeping" (song), 98–99
BED sign, 12, 42, 196, 208
bedtime activities
   Bears (and Children) Are Sleeping, 98–99
   books for, 96–97
   Brush, Brush, Brush Your Teeth, 92–93
   Good Night Walk, 88
   overview, 86–99

songs, 86–87, 98–99
   Tickle to Touching, 94–95
   Turn Off the Lights, 90–91
BIRD sign, 36, 196, 208
BLANKIE sign, 196, 208
BOAT/GO-BY-BOAT sign, 197, 208
Body Leans, 115, 149, 186
BOOK sign, 197, 208–209
BOTTLE sign, 197, 209
Bounce and STOP, 132–133
BROTHER/SISTER sign, 197, 209
"Brush, Brush, Brush Your Teeth" (song), 92–93
BRUSH-TEETH/TOOTHBRUSH sign, 197, 209
Bubbles, Bubbles Everywhere, 152–153
BUBBLES/POP sign, 197, 209
BUG sign, 197, 209
BUNNY/RABBIT sign, 197, 209
BUS sign, 198, 209
BUTTERFLY sign, 198, 209

Caillou Dresses Up (Allen), 169, 217
Car Wash, 110–111
CAR/DRIVE sign, 13, 198, 209
CAT sign, 13, 35, 198, 209
Catching Cars, 140–141
category formation, 129
CEREAL/EAT-WITH-SPOON sign, 198, 209
CHANGE sign, 198, 209
"Change the Diaper" (song), 48
CLEAN/CLEAN-UP/NICE/COOK sign, 35, 198, 209–210
Cloth Hiding, 126–127
COAT/JACKET sign, 198, 210
COLD sign, 199, 210
communication. See also signs (listed by name)
   through complex sentences, 183–185
   and conceptual grouping, 58,

70–71, 186, 187
conversation initiators, 2–3
   crossing the threshold to, xvii
   early, 19–20, 41–42, 154–155
   and easing times of emotional intensity, 174, 185–186
   going beyond basic labeling, 26–27
   increasing intimacy through, 5, 19, 174, 189–191
   and language clustering, 29–30, 53, 135, 156, 166–167, 172
   and the language explosion, 14–15, 139
Complementary Acquisition pattern, 176–177
conceptual
   development, aiding, 186–187
   grouping, 58, 70–71, 186, 187
Corduroy (Freeman), 98, 217
COW sign, 199, 210
CRACKER sign, 199, 210
CUP sign, 199, 210

DADDY/GRANDMA/GRANDPA/MOMMY sign, 203, 213
DANCE sign, 199, 210
diaper activities, 46–55
Dog Hunt, 73
DOG sign, 13, 30, 199, 210
DOLL sign, 199, 210
Down syndrome, 3, 33, 102
dressing activities
   Find the Frog, 52–53
   and helping children with turn-taking, 50–51
   I Want to Be Just like Mommy and Daddy, 54–55
   overview, 46–55
   songs, 54–55
DRINK sign, 12, 199, 210
Dual Acquisition pattern, 176, 177
Dual Labeling, 72, 103, 112–113

Duck is Dirty (Kitamura), 78, 217
DUCK sign, 25, 200, 210

early communication, 19–20,
    41–42, 154–155. *See also* com-
    munication
EAT/FOOD sign, 12, 29, 200, 210
ELEPHANT sign, 39, 200, 211
emotional intensity, easing times of,
    174, 185–186
empowerment, 5

facilitated
    acquisition pattern, 176, 178–180
    memory, 2–3
    speech, 2
FAN sign, 13, 200, 211
feedback, corrective, 145
Feeding Time at the Zoo, 160–161
Find the Frog, 52–53
FINGER-FOOD sign, 200, 211
FINISH-ALL-DONE sign, 12, 200,
    211
FISH sign, 200, 211
FLOWER sign, 200, 211
Food Surprises, 60–61
"For Kylie" (song), 86
"For Maya" (song), 87
Freeman, Don, 98
FROG sign, 201, 211
Froggy Gets Dressed (London), 167
FRUIT sign, 201, 211
"Fruits and Veggies" (song), 59
frustration, *xvi–xvii*, 4–5

GENTLE/PAT sign, 201, 211
Gift Wrap Surprises, 120–121
GLASSES sign, 201, 211
Good Night Walk, 88
Goodnight Moon (Brown), 96, 97,
    216
Grandma's Trunk, 168–169
Grounded Learning, 130, 143–144

Hand-over-Hand Signing, 32–33
HAT sign, 201, 212
Heightened Anticipation, 132–133,
    164–165
HELP sign, 11, 34, 201, 212
HIDE sign, 201, 212
Hide-and-Find puzzles, 170
Hide-and-Seek Hands, 114–115

Hiding Tower, 106–107
High Chair Pull-up Toys, 64–65
Highly Motivating Signs, 8–11, 183
HOME sign, 201, 212
HORSE sign, 202, 212
HOT sign, 202
Humane Society, 138

I Like to Eat, 58–59
I Want to Be Just like Mommy and
    Daddy, 54–55
I'm Hiding, 132
I-LOVE-YOU sign, 202, 212
ideas, misperceptions of new,
    clarifying, 186–187
Imaginary Friend's Tea Party,
    172–173
intimacy, increasing, 5, 19, 174,
    189–191
items/situations, highlighting
    salient qualities of, 187–188
"Itsy-Bitsy Spider" (song), 108–109

Jack-in-the-Box, 132, 133
JUMP/STAND/FALL-OFF sign, 202,
    212

Kennedy, Jimmy, 158
KEY sign, 13, 202, 212
KISS sign, 202, 212
kitchen activities, 73. *See also* meal-
    time activities

labeling, going beyond basic, 26–27
Language Clustering, 135,
    166–167, 172
    and Acting Like Animals, 156
    and dressing activities, 53
    overview, 29–30
    story time and, 131
Language Explosion, 14–15, 139
laundry, activities related to, 72
learning
    grounded, 130, 143–144
    long-term, 19–20, 41–42,
        154–155, 172, 183
Light Walk, 146–147
LIGHT/LIGHT-ON/LIGHT-OFF
    sign, 9–11, 90–91, 202, 212
limit-setting, 188–189
LION sign, 203, 213
Little Cabin in the Woods, 171

London, Jonathan, 167
Long-Term Learning, 19–20, 41–42,
    154–155, 172, 183
LOOK-FOR/SEARCH sign, 203,
    213
lullabies, 86–87. *See also* bedtime
    activities

Mailbox Venture, 136
Marching Band, 143
mealtime activities
    Food Surprises, 60–61
    High Chair Pull-up Toys, 64–65
    I Like to Eat, 58–59
    Mini-Me Cooking, 68–59
    overview, 56–73
    Pots and Pans Band, 70–71
    Silly Puppet, 62–63
    songs, 59
    WHERE Game, 66–67
MEDICINE sign, 203, 213
memory, facilitated, 2–3
MILK sign, 12, 203, 213
Mini-Me Cooking, 68–69
MOMMY/DADDY/GRANDMA/
    GRANDPA sign, 203, 213
MONKEY sign, 203, 213
MORE sign, 11, 203, 213
motivation
    Highly Motivating Signs, 8–11,
        183
    motivating your child to sign,
        56–57
movements, responding to natural,
    22–23
MUSIC sign, 11, 203, 213
Myth of the First Five Words, 154

National Institutes of Health, 5–6
NO sign, 157
Nutcracker, The (Hoffman), 120,
    217

Oat Box, 118–119
object permanence, development
    of, 126–127
OUT sign, 204, 213
OUTSIDE/GO-OUT sign, 204, 213
overgeneralization, 94
Overlapping Movement Patterns,
    37, 39–40, 148–149

PACIFIER sign, 204, 213
PAIN/HURT sign, 204, 213
peekaboo games
    Dual Labeling PeekaBoo, 72
    Hide-and-Seek Hands, 114–115
    storytelling and, 170
Pennsylvania State University, 6
pet shops, 138, 139
PHONE/CALL sign, 204, 213
Piagetian stages, 126–127
PIG sign, 204, 213
play
    Acting Like Animals, 156–157
    active, 106–107, 134–153
    Asleep and Awake, 164–165
    Baby Amusement Parks, 138–139
    Balls Galore, 150–151
    Bear Went Over the Mountain,
       162–163
    Bubbles, Bubbles Everywhere,
       152–153
    Car Wash, 110–111
    Catching Cars, 140–141
    Cloth Hiding, 126–127
    combining story time with,
       130–131
    Feeding Time at the Zoo, 160–161
    floor-time, 102–133
    Gift Wrap Surprises, 120–121
    Grandma's Trunk, 168–169
    Hide-and-Seek Hands, 114–115
    Hiding Tower, 106–107
    Imaginary Friend's Tea Party,
       172–173
    Light Walk, 146–147
    Magic Mirror, 166–167
    Marching Band, 142–143
    Oat Box, 118–119
    pretend, 154–173
    Sense-ational Toys, 112–113
    Silly Scarves, 122–123
    Spoon Fun, 124–125
    Streamer Fun, 104–105
    Teddy Bears' Picnic, 158–159
    Three in the Bed, 144–145
    Toddler Field Trips, 136–137
    What's in the Bag?, 128–129
    What's in Mommy's Bag?,
       116–117
    Zooming Balls, 148–149
PLAY sign, 204, 213
PLEASE sign, 19, 204, 214
Pop and Drop, 80–81
Pots and Pans Band, 70–71
Pregnant Pauses, 162
proximity, varying, 30

puppets, 62–63, 170

RAIN sign, 205, 214
Rapid Word Growth, 154
repetition, desire for, 75
"Roll the Ball" (song), 150
rooms, straightening, 72

safety issues, 188–189
See A Lot/Do A Lot signs, 7–9, 11,
    19, 183
self-esteem, 5
Sense-ational Toys, 112–113
sentences, increasingly complex,
    183–185
SHEEP sign, 205, 214
SHOES sign, 205, 214
"Shoes, Shoes, Put On Your Shoes"
    (song), 55
SICK sign, 205, 214
sign(s). *See also* signs (listed by
    name)
    changing the angle of, 35
    cluster, 14–15, 139, 180
    on an object of interest, 34–35
    recognizing your child's versions
       of, 19, 36–37
    starter, 6–13, 41–43
    two-handed, making, into one-
       handed signs, 34
    on your child's body, 33
    in your child's line of sight, 33
Sign Language Acquisition Lab
    (University of California), *xvii*
Signing Smart Adaptation Strategies,
    28
Signing Smart Attention-Getters
    list of, 28
    nonverbal, 30
    sensory, 30–31
Signing Smart Baby-Talk, 31–32,
    172
Signing Smart Opportunities,
    17–18, 20–28
Signing Smart Starter Signs. *See also*
    signs (listed by name)
    overview, 6–13
    when to add, 41–43
Signing Smart success, four keys to,
    17–29, 43
signs (listed by name). *See also*
    signs
    AIRPLANE/FLY sign, 196, 208
    BABY sign, 196, 208

BALL sign, 11, 196, 208
BATH sign, 19, 196, 208
BEAR sign, 13, 196, 208
BED sign, 12, 42, 196, 208
BIRD sign, 36, 196, 208
BLANKIE sign, 196, 208
BOAT/GO-BY-BOAT sign, 197,
    208
BOOK sign, 197, 208–209
BOTTLE sign, 197, 209
BROTHER/SISTER sign, 197, 209
BRUSH-TEETH/TOOTHBRUSH
    sign, 197, 209
BUBBLES/POP sign, 197, 209
BUG sign, 197, 209
BUNNY/RABBIT sign, 197, 209
BUS sign, 198, 209
BUTTERFLY sign, 198, 209
CAR/DRIVE sign, 13, 198, 209
CAT sign, 13, 35, 198, 209
CEREAL/EAT-WITH-SPOON
    sign, 198, 209
CHANGE sign, 198, 209
CLEAN/CLEAN-UP/NICE/COOK
    sign, 35, 198, 209–210
COAT/JACKET sign, 198, 210
COLD sign, 199, 210
COW sign, 199, 210
CRACKER sign, 199, 210
CUP sign, 199, 210
DADDY/GRANDMA/
    GRANDPA/MOMMY sign, 203,
    213
DANCE sign, 199, 210
DOG sign, 13, 30, 199, 210
DOLL sign, 199, 210
DRINK sign, 12, 199, 210
DUCK sign, 25, 200, 210
EAT/FOOD sign, 12, 29, 200, 210
ELEPHANT sign, 39, 200, 211
FAN sign, 13, 200, 211
FINGER-FOOD sign, 200, 211
FINISH-ALL-DONE sign, 12, 200,
    211
FISH sign, 200, 211
FLOWER sign, 200, 211
FROG sign, 201, 211
FRUIT sign, 201, 211
GENTLE/PAT sign, 201, 211
GLASSES sign, 201, 211
HAT sign, 201, 212
HELP sign, 11, 34, 201, 212
HIDE sign, 201, 212
HOME sign, 201, 212
HORSE sign, 202, 212
HOT sign, 202

I-LOVE-YOU sign, 202, 212
JUMP/STAND/FALL-OFF sign, 202, 212
KEY sign, 13, 202, 212
KISS sign, 202, 212
LIGHT/LIGHT-ON/LIGHT-OFF sign, 9–11, 90–91, 202, 212
LION sign, 203, 213
LOOK-FOR/SEARCH sign, 203, 213
MEDICINE sign, 203, 213
MILK sign, 12, 203, 213
MOMMY/DADDY/GRANDMA/ GRANDPA sign, 203, 213
MONKEY sign, 203, 213
MORE sign, 11, 203, 213
MUSIC sign, 11, 203, 213
NO sign, 157
OUT sign, 204, 213
OUTSIDE/GO-OUT sign, 204, 213
PACIFIER sign, 204, 213
PAIN/HURT sign, 204, 213
PHONE/CALL sign, 204, 213
PIG sign, 204, 213
PLAY sign, 204, 213
PLEASE sign, 19, 204, 214
RAIN sign, 205, 214
SHEEP sign, 205, 214
SHOES sign, 205, 214
SICK sign, 205, 214
SILLY sign, 205, 214
SIT/CHAIR sign, 205, 214
SOCKS sign, 205, 214
SPIDER sign, 205, 214
STOP sign, 157, 185–186, 206, 214
SUN sign, 206, 214
SURPRISE/WAKE-UP sign, 206, 215
THANK-YOU/GOOD sign, 206, 215
TIGER sign, 206, 215
TOWEL sign, 206, 215
TRAIN/GO-BY-TRAIN sign, 206, 215
TREE sign, 206, 215
TURN/TAKE-TURNS sign, 207, 215
VEGETABLE/VEGGIE sign, 207, 215
WARM sign, 207, 215
WATER sign, 207, 215
WET/SOFT sign, 207, 215
WHAT sign, 11, 207, 215
WHERE sign, 12, 66–67, 207, 215

WIND sign, 207, 215
Silly Puppet, 62–63
Silly Scarves, 122–123
SILLY sign, 205, 214
single-sign identifiers, 188–189
SIT/CHAIR sign, 205, 214
Soap Scientists, 84–85
Sock Tickle Monster, 72
Sock Toss, 72
SOCKS sign, 205, 214
song(s)
  "Bath, Bath, Take a Bath," 76–77
  "Bear Went Over the Mountain," 163
  "Brush, Brush, Brush Your Teeth," 92–93
  "Change the Diaper," 48
  "Fruits and Veggies", 59
  "Itsy-Bitsy Spider," 108–109
  "Roll the Ball," 150
  "Shoes, Shoes, Put On Your Shoes," 55
  "There Are Bubbles in the Air," 152
  "There Were Three in the Bed," 144
  "This Is the Way," 49
  "Three Little Ducks," 82–83
speech, facilitated, 2
SPIDER sign, 205, 214
Spoon Fun, 124–125
STOP sign, 157, 185–186, 206, 214
story time
  combining, with play time, 130–131
  recommended books, 216–217
  singing stories, 171
  storytelling ideas for, 170–171
Straw Blowing, 132
Streamer Fun, 104–105
SUN sign, 206, 214
SURPRISE/WAKE-UP sign, 206, 215

Teddy Bears' Picnic (Kennedy), 158, 217
Tent Hideaway, 72
THANK-YOU/GOOD sign, 206, 215
There Was an Old Lady Who Swallowed a Fly, 171
"There Were Three in the Bed" (song), 144
"There Are Bubbles in the Air" (song), 152

"This Is the Way" (song), 49"
"Three Little Ducks" (song), 82–83
Tickle Games, 133
TIGER sign, 206, 215
Toddler Field Trips, 136–137
TOWEL sign, 206, 215
TRAIN/GO-BY-TRAIN sign, 206, 215
TREE sign, 206, 215
Triple Look, 141
TURN/TAKE-TURNS sign, 207, 215
turn-taking, helping children with, 50–51

University of California, *xxii*
U-shaped Development, 129

VEGETABLE/VEGGIE sign, 207, 215
Very Hungry Caterpillar, The (Carle), *xxii*, 217
vocabulary, expanded, 4, 181
Vocabulary Burst, 181

WARM sign, 207, 215
Water Paints, 132
WATER sign, 207, 215
We're Going on a Bear Hunt (Rosen), 217
WET/SOFT sign, 207, 215
WHAT sign, 11, 207, 215
What's in the Bag?, 128–129
What's in Mommy's Bag?, 116–117
WHERE Game, 66–67
WHERE sign, 12, 66–67, 207, 215
Wide-Eyed Learning, LLC, 1
WIND sign, 207, 215
Winnie-the-Pooh (Milne), 167, 217

Zooming Balls, 148–149

MICHELLE ANTHONY, M.A., PH.D.

Having graduated with honors from Brown University in 1991 with a B.A. in Educational Studies, Dr. Anthony went on to get her master's in Child Studies and her K-3 Teacher's Certificate from Tufts University. Dr. Anthony has been signing for more than twelve years and received her certification in ASL and Deaf Studies from Northeastern University. After teaching young children in the classroom for five years, she returned to school to study Developmental Psychology at the University of California, Berkeley. She spent three years doing research in the Sign Language Acquisition Lab as well as the Child Language Lab at the Institute of Human Development at UC Berkeley. Her dissertation examined how ASL enhances language development, cognition, and literacy.

Dr. Anthony has also worked as a learning specialist with elementary and middle-school students and has taught classes at the University of Colorado at Denver School of Education and at Saint Mary's College School of Education. Dr. Anthony is a preferred provider of both Developmental Pathways

Michelle, three-year-old Kylie, and ten-month-old Maya all comment on being ready to finish taking pictures so they can get something to **EAT**.

and Denver Options, teaching developmentally delayed children and their parents how to use signs to enhance communication and learning. She is the mother to two signing children.

REYNA LINDERT, M.A., PH.D.

Dr. Lindert is a certified parent educator with broad experience working with young children and their families. She graduated with distinction with a B.S. in Human Development and Family Studies from Cornell University. She then earned her M.A. and Ph.D. in Developmental Psychology from the University of California, Berkeley. She spent five years doing research in the Language and Cognition, the Sign Language Acquisition, and the Child Language labs at the Institute of Human Development at UC Berkeley. Her dissertation examined the ways in which ASL can enhance communication and foster extended parent-child interactions about child-friendly themes. Dr. Lindert has been signing for more than sixteen years, and her ASL certificate comes from Vista Community College, a nationally renowned institution for sign language instruction. She has worked extensively in the Deaf community, including as a student teacher in a class of toddlers at the California School for the Deaf.

Complementing her work with *Signing Smart,* Dr. Lindert also runs interactive *Parenting Smart* workshops for families with preschoolers in Portland, Oregon. She is the mother of two signing children.

Drs. Michelle Anthony and Reyna Lindert co-developed the *Signing Smart* program. Their work with *Signing Smart* includes conducting ongoing research about hearing children's linguistic, cognitive, and emotional development. Drs. Anthony and Lindert also create curricula and train instructors in the United States and abroad to run *Signing Smart* play classes and workshops. In addition, they are continually developing materials and products for parents and young children. To find out more about *Signing Smart* programs, products, and materials, please see www.signingsmart.com.

Reyna and five-year-old Natasha ask thirteen-month-old Nadia if she wants **MORE** water. She happily signs **MORE** in agreement.